D1279293

The Natural History of

SEALS

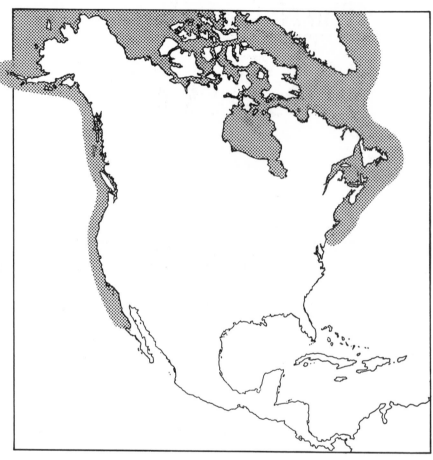

Distribution of phocid seals around the shores of North America. For individual species distributions, see species accounts on pages 77–97.

The Natural History of

SEALS

W. NIGEL BONNER

Facts On File
New York • Oxford • Sydney

First published in the United States of America by Facts On File, Inc.

Facts On File, Inc.
460 Park Avenue South
New York NY 10016
USA

Library of Congress Cataloging-in-Publication Data

Bonner, W. Nigel (William Nigel)
    The natural history of seals / Nigel Bonner,
    p.   cm.
    Includes bibliographical references.
    Summary: Describes the natural history of this popular animal, focusing on its behavior, relationship to man, and prospects for survival.
    ISBN 0–8160–2336–0
    1. Seals (Animals) [1. Seals (Animals).] I. Title.
    QL737.P6B678   1990
    599.74'8–dc20

    89–37620
    CIP
    AC

Facts On File books are available at special discounts when purchased in bulk quantities for businesses, associations, institutions or sales promotions. Please contact the Special Sales Department of our New York office at 212/683–2244 (dial 800/322–8755 except in NY, AK or HI)

10 9 8 7 6 5 4 3 2 1

Printed in Great Britain

Contents

List of colour plates   vi
List of figures   vii
List of tables   x
Acknowledgements   xi
Series editor's foreword   xiii
Preface   xv
1. What is a seal?   1
2. Feeding and diving   21
3. Reproduction and growth   40
4. Breeding patterns and social organisation   52
5. The diversity, classification, and origin of seals   77
6. Interactions with Man: 1. Seals as prey   105
7. Interactions with Man: 2. Seals as competitors   126
8. Interactions with Man: 3. Indirect effects   145
9. Conservation and seals   163
References   181
Index   192

Colour plates

1   Leopard seal and crabeater seals; Coronation Island, South Orkney Islands.
2   Hawaiian monk Seal.
3   Weddell seal.
4   Ross seal, showing the characteristic streaky marks at the side of the neck.
5   Old male crabeater seal.
6   A young southern elephant seal.
7   Northern elephant seals mating.
8   A herd of northern elephant seals on San Miguel Island, California.
9   A dominant bull northern elephant seal amongst his cows on Año Nuevo Island, California.
10 Two southern elephant seals fighting, South Georgia.
11 A hunter drives a southern elephant seal bull to the shore in South Georgia.
12 A newly weaned southern elephant seal pup.
13 Male spotted seal.
14 A female northern elephant seal and her newly-born pup.
15 A ringed seal pup in its lair in the fast ice off Nome, Alaska.
16 A leopard seal on Bird Island, South Georgia.
17 Male ribbon seal.
18 A young male harp seal in the breeding habitat on sea ice.
19 A yearling harbour seal on a sand-bank in the Wash, East Anglia.
20 The 'roman nose' of the grey seal is characteristic of the species.

Figures

1.1   The pinnipeds, or seal-like mammals. (a) A true seal;   2
(b) a walrus; (c) a fur seal

1.2   Variety in mammalian orders. Two artiodactyls, the   2
hippopotamus and the fallow deer; two rodents, the
wood-mouse and the capybara

1.3   The skeleton of a typical mammal, the dog, and that of   5
the seal

1.4   Limb skeletons of dog and seal   6

1.5   The hind flippers of a seal in the power and recovery   8
strokes

1.6   The surface volume relationship. As the volume of a   11
body increases the ratio of surface to volume becomes
less, hence larger bodies have less relative surface area

1.7   The formation of the image on the retina in (a) a   16
human eye in air; (b) a human eye under water; (c) a
seal eye under water; (d) a seal eye in air

2.1   Planktonic food of seals. (a) Antarctic krill, *Euphausia*   22
superba, a euphausiid shrimp; (b) a mysid shrimp,
Mysis; (c) a pelagic amphipod, *Parathemisto*

2.2   The food sources of four Antarctic seals. (a) The   24
crabeater seal; (b) the leopard seal; (c) the Ross seal; (d)
the elephant seal

2.3   Seal teeth. (a) Harbour seal; (b) crabeater seal; (c)   26
leopard seal; (d) ringed seal; (e) Ross seal; (f) elephant
seal; (g) bearded seal

2.4   Metabolic rates of phocid seals determined by Kleiber's   30
criteria and metabolic rates of young, growing phocid
seals.

2.5   The position of the diaphragm in a seal   33

2.6   The venous system of a seal. Redrawn from King   36
(1983)

2.7   The progressive collapse of the alveolus in the lung of a   38
seal as it dives. As the seal descends, gas is driven into
the non-absorptive region of the bronchioles and

bronchi; on further descent the alveolus closes,
trapping a small quantity of gas. If the seal remains at
depth long enough, this gas will be absorbed. Redrawn
from Kooyman (1981b)

3.1	The reproductive system of a male seal	41
3.2	The baculum, or os penis, of an elephant seal	42
3.3	The reproductive system of a female seal	43

4.1	Breeding areas and migration routes of harp seals	55
4.2	Breeding areas of hooded seals	56
4.3	The breeding lair of a ringed seal	60
4.4	The breeding cycle of the grey seal	66
4.5	Breeding locations of the southern elephant seal	67
4.6	Breeding locations of the northern elephant seal	68
4.7	The structure of an elephant seal breeding beach. The dominant male moves freely about within the crowd of females; less highly ranked males maintain a station within the females; subordinate males patrol the beaches just off shore	71
4.8	A schematic model for the evolution of pinniped polygyny. The large circles represent the two key attributes of pinnipeds; the smaller circles are attributes common to most mammals; the rectangles show attributes and functions typical of polygynous pinnipeds. The broad arrows show positive feedback loops. From Bartholomew (1970)	74

| 5.1 | The relationship of the existing seals | 100 |
| 5.2 | The relationship of seals to the carnivores | 101 |

6.1	Stone Age settlements in Europe with seal remains. From Clark (1946)	106
6.2	The 'Montgaudier baton' above, as usually depicted; below, detail of the inverted grey seals pursuing the fish	107
6.3	Map of the Kattegat region showing the locations of Hesslø and Anholt	108
6.4	Stone Age rock engravings from Rødøy, Nordland, Norway. The porpoise, strange horned seal and figure in boat suggest a hunting scene	110
6.5	Eskimo kayak harpoon. The harpoon (left) is shown ready to throw. The *tokang* is held in place by the tension of the line hooked over the peg by the hand support. After the *tokang* is fast in the seal, the tusk swivels in the *qatirn*, allowing the line to slip free of the peg	112
6.6	Cuts made in flensing an elephant seal	123
6.7	Biomass of elephant seals at various ages in the South Georgia stock. From Laws (1960)	125

7.1 A salmon bag net of a type used in the Scottish fishery   129

7.2 Possible interactions between seals, fish and fisheries.   132
After Beverton (1985)

7.3 The life cycle of 'cod worm' the parasitic nematode   136
Pseudoterranova decipiens

7.4 Location of some important seal breeding localities in   140
the United Kingdom

8.1 Distribution of mortality from 'seal plague' around the   156
North Sea to the end of September, 1988

8.2 Numbers of dead seals reported from different parts of   158
the British coast, to October 1988

9.1 Correlation between the percentage grey seal pup   172
mortality and the number of pups per 100 m of
accessible shore at the Farne Islands

Tables

1.1 Various properties of air and water compared. Values   3
     are for pure water, except the density value, which is
     for sea water

3.1 Birth weights and weight gain in a series of seals listed   48
     in ascending order of maternal weight. Modified from
     Bowen *et al.* (1985)

6.1 Quotas for harp seals and catches, Newfoundland and   119
     the Gulf of St Lawrence. After Lavigne and Kovacs
     (1988)

7.1 Calculated impact of seals on commercial fisheries in   138
     Canada. From Gulland (1987)
7.2 Culling programme for grey seals in Scotland, 1977–   143
     82
7.3 Grey seals killed in the management operation, and   144
     subsequently taken in the same area, 1977–81. From
     Harwood and Greenwood (1985)

Acknowlegements

I have drawn on a great number of sources in compiling this book. Original works are acknowledged by the inclusion of the author's name and the date of publication in the text. The bibliography at the end of the book gives the full references and will help interested readers follow them up if they so wish. In particular, I should like to thank Burney Le Boeuf, Peter Reijnders and Charles Repenning, who all found time to read and comment on chapters of this book. I value their criticisms as I value their friendship. Michael Clark has drawn many of the line illustrations with his customary skill and enthusiasm. Several of my friends have made available photographs to embellish the text. Their names are acknowledged in the captions. To all of these people I wish to record my thanks.

I am grateful to my friend and colleague in the Mammal Society, Ernest Neal, for asking me to write this book, and thereby providing the stimulus to undertake a task I had long planned but repeatedly postponed.

Without the support and encouragement of my wife throughout the last 35 years I would never have been able to spend the hours, days, weeks and months in the field that provided my personal background to the study of seals. Jennifer has not only had to put up with my protracted absences over the years, she has also had to cope with elephant seals peering in at her bedroom window and sleeping peacefully against her front door. All this she has endured without complaint. In comparison with this, her labours in checking drafts and preparing indexes seem minor, but these too have been of great value to me. I am profoundly grateful.

Nigel Bonner

For
Martin and Lucy

Series editor's foreword

In recent years there has been a great upsurge of interest in wildlife and a deepening concern for nature conservation. For many there is a compelling urge to counterbalance some of the artificiality of present-day living with a more intimate involvement with the natural world. More people are coming to realise that we are all part of nature, not apart from it. There seems to be a greater desire to understand its complexities and appreciate its beauty.

This appreciation of wildlife and wild places has been greatly stimulated by the world-wide impact of natural-history television programmes. These have brought into our homes the sights and sounds both of our own countryside and of far-off places that arouse our interest and delight.

In parallel with this growth of interest there has been a great expansion of knowledge and, above all, understanding of the natural world — an understanding vital to any conservation measures that can be taken to safeguard it. More and more field workers have carried out painstaking studies of many species, analysing their intricate behaviour, relationships and the part they play in the general ecology of their habitats. To the time-honoured techniques of field observations and experimentation has been added the sophisitication of radio-telemetry whereby individual animals can be followed, even in the dark and over long periods, and their activities recorded. Infra-red cameras and light-intensifying binoculars now add a new dimension to the study of nocturnal animals. Through such devices great advances have been made.

This series of volumes aims to bring this information together in an exciting and readable form so that all who are interested in wildlife may benefit from such a synthesis. Many of the titles in the series concern groups of related species such as otters, squirrels and rabbits so that readers from many parts of the world may learn about their own more familiar animals in a much wider context. Inevitably more emphasis will be given to particular species within a group as some have been more extensively studied than others. Authors too have their own special interests and experience and a text gains much in authority and vividness when there has been personal involvement.

Many natural history books have been published in recent years which have delighted the eye and fired the imagination. This is wholly good. But it is the intention of this series to take this a step further by exploring the subject in greater depth and by making available the results of recent research. In this way it is hoped to satisfy to some extent at least the curiosity and desire to know more which is such an encouraging characteristic of the keen naturalist of today.

Ernest Neal
Bedford

Preface

I saw my first seals in the wild from the cliffs of Cornwall, looking down on the swirling waters around the rocks of Pentire Point. Black dots in the sea were the heads of grey seals, though at the time I could say no more than that they were 'seals'. I had no better chance to study those seals more closely, but I can still remember my wonderment at how utterly at home they were in the foam and the surf. It was easy to see how seals have fascinated Man from the earliest times.

Now, fifty years later, I look back on the greater part of my life spent studying seals and find that fascination still present. In the course of this book I hope to explain some of the features of seals which contribute to that fascination, features which have made seals a chosen quarry for primitive (and not so primitive) Man, and the subject of study of a considerable number of scientists, amongst whom I number many friends. Many, if not most, of these features are associated with the fact that seals live in the sea, and the general theme of this book is seals as aquatic mammals.

Some people may be disappointed not to find reference to such favourites as the sea lion or the walrus in this book. Their omission was deliberate. I have confined the book to the true seals, the Phocidae, because these form a natural group which can be covered reasonably well in a book of this size.

Although it is not particularly difficult for the average interested person to see seals in their natural habitat, it is very much more difficult to study them systematically. Because the primary home of seals is in the water, they are intrinsically less easy to study than terrestrial mammals. Indeed, most of what we know about seal behaviour comes from those times when the seals are hauled ashore. Seals tend to be found in remote places, and this can make travelling to watch them difficult. A compensation is that the places where they live are usually of such striking beauty that the effort of getting there nearly always seems worth while.

Despite the obstacles that have made the study of seals more difficult than, for example, that of birds, we now know very much more about their natural history than we did even a quarter of a century ago. This is largely the result of the great surge of interest in marine mammals over this period, which has been the stimulus for many dedicated workers to go out into the field to study seals. Of course, it would be foolish to deny that a great deal of seal research (particularly that funded from government sources) has been undertaken because some sections of the community see seals as valuable commercial resources, or as destructive pests of fisheries. But views are changing fairly steadily and the predominant attitude towards seals in western societies is one of affectionate curiosity. I hope this book will do something to satisfy that curiosity and augment that affection.

Nigel Bonner
Godmanchester

1 What is a seal?

Everyone knows what a seal looks like, and most people will have seen one in a zoo or at a marine park. They are, in fact, amongst the more familiar animals, but despite this, the way of life of the seals and their allies is not really well known. This is a pity, for seals have much to tell us about the way an animal adapts to and exploits its environment. By looking at seals in an enquiring manner we can learn a good deal about how life on earth is forged by natural processes.

Seals are highly modified carnivores which have adopted an aquatic life. They are commonly placed in the order Pinnipedia (from Latin words meaning 'wing-footed', a term which relates to their webbed feet). When the seals are given an order to themselves in this way, the rest of the carnivores make up the Order Fissipedia ('split-footed' — referring to their feet having distinct separated toes). Some classifiers, however, simply regard the Pinnipedia as being a suborder of the Carnivora. Later in this book (Chapter 5), I shall discuss something of the possible origins and relationships of seals but for the moment I will treat the Pinnipedia as constituting a natural group which can be discussed as a whole.

In this sense the order Pinnipedia is composed of two main groupings — the suborder Phocoidea, which contains only the family Phocidae, or true seals, and the suborder Otarioidea containing the family Odobenidae, with only the walrus, and the family Otariidae, the fur seals and sea lions (Figure 1.1). As we shall see later (Chapter 5), these two suborders are not descended from a common ancestor, but though this book is concerned only with the true seals, I shall frequently make comparisons between the two groups. The term *'Pinnipedia'* is well established.

SEALS AS MARINE MAMMALS

The pinnipeds, as I have defined them here, form a remarkably similar group of about 33 species. There is much less variety within the group than is found, for example, in the rodents (think of the wood-mouse and the capybara, or the beaver and the jerboa), or the artiodactyls (the

1

Figure 1.1 The pinnipeds, or seal-like mammals. (a) a fur seal, (b) a walrus, (c) a true seal.

hippopotamus and the fallow deer, the camel and the giraffe) (Figure 1.2). The character that unites the true seals, walrus, fur seals and sea lions is that they are all marine mammals and it is their adaptive response to the marine environment that has caused all of them to look and behave so similarly.

When a terrestrial mammal takes to the water, the medium in which the vertebrates evolved, the selective pressures on it are very great. Profound changes take place and a high degree of convergent evolution is to be expected. The most striking change that the ancestors of seals encountered when they abandoned the land and took to living in the sea was in the nature of the medium that surrounded them. It is a truism that water is different from air, but it is useful to examine the nature of this difference.

Figure 1.2 Variety in mammalian orders; two artiodactyls, the hippototamus and fallow deer; two rodents the wood-mouse and the capybara.

Table 1.1 Various properties of air and water compared.
Values are for pure water, except the density value, which is for sea water.

Property	Units	Air	Water
Density	kg.m^{-1}	1.22	1,025
Viscosity	10^{6}kg.m^{-1}.s^{-1}	18	1,708
Thermal conductivity	10^{-3}W.m^{-1}.K^{-1}	1.3	16.4
Specific heat	J.K^{-1}.kg^{-1}	720	4,200
Heat capacity per unit volume	J.K^{-1}.m^{-1}	880	4,300.000
Refractive index	—	(1)	1.33
Speed of sound	m.s^{-1}	332	1,531

Water is a much denser and more viscous medium than air. It also has a much higher heat conductivity and a very much higher heat capacity per unit volume (Table 1.1). These are the factors that have most affected the evolution of seals (and other marine mammals). There are other differences, of course. One of these is the fact that sea water saturated with oxygen contains only about 8 ml of oxygen per litre, while air, being about 20 per cent oxygen, contains 200 ml per litre, and this too has affected seals, though in a less obvious way (Chapter 2). Let us examine how these physical factors relate to seals as we see them today.

Body shape

The body shape of seals is noticeably sleek and streamlined. A seal is basically elongated and spindle-shaped. The head has a pointed nose and a rounded cranium that flares smoothly into the trunk with no marked constriction at the neck. In true seals the external ears, or pinnae, are absent so the ear opening or meatus lies flush with the skin surface. In northern seals this opening may be up to about 1 cm in diameter and be very visible when the animal is listening in air, but in southern seals it is much smaller (about 2 mm) and generally concealed beneath the hair. As we shall see later, this absence of external ears does not mean that seals do not have an acute sense of hearing.

The trunk of the seal is relatively symmetrical about its midpoint. This is not true of all species — the leopard seal in particular has a well-developed thorax — but in general the animal is approximately circular in cross-section and tapers fore and aft from a point just behind the insertion of the fore flippers. The genital organs are concealed within the general body contour, so that it is not always easy to tell the sex of a seal at a glance. In the male the testes are internal. They lie outside the main muscles of the abdominal wall but within the muscles of the skin, in a position usually described as inguinal, against the pelvis and quite invisible externally. The penis likewise is invisible except when the seal is sexually excited. At rest, the penis lies in a pouch of skin with its opening between the umbilicus and the anus. This is itself concealed within a slit, very similar to the arrangement in the female, where a common furrow conceals the genital and anal openings. The nipples (either one or two pairs) are retracted at rest and lie at the level of the umbilicus. The mammary glands are composed of two sheets of tissue lying along the flanks. Even when the glands are actively secreting (and we shall see in Chapter 3 that they can be more active than those of any other mammal) they cause no protuberance on the body surface. Beneath the skin over the whole of the trunk is a thick layer of fatty tissue, the blubber. This blanket of fat has several functions; one of them is to smooth over any underlying body architeecture, so that the seal's body presents a smooth and resilient surface to its surrounding medium.

These features are not characteristic of mammals in general and we can regard them as modifications which add up to a body so shaped that it offers the minimum resistance to movement through the water. This is important to aquatic mammals because of the relatively great viscosity of water when compared with air. Only the fastest moving mammals that live and move in air need to bother about streamlining, but to a seal it is a matter of overriding importance; as active hunters, seals often need to swim down their prey and speed in the water, enhanced by their lithe form, is essential for this. In the next section we shall see how the seal generates that speed.

Limbs and Locomotion

All seals possess the normal mammalian complement of four limbs but these are much modified for life in the water. In a terrestrial mammal, a dog for example (Figure 1.3), the limbs have two main functions. They serve to support the body and carry it clear of the ground, and they provide a system of levers whereby force can be exerted on the ground which propels the dog along when it wishes to move. For the first of these functions the limbs need to incorporate a rigid column, or bony axis. In the fore-limb this column terminates at its upper extremity in the shoulder blade, embedded in the muscles at the side of the thoracic cage while in the hind limb the leg bones are connected to the axial skeleton via the pelvis. This more rigid attachment of the hind limb, which is characteristic of nearly all mammals, has led to a dominance of that pair of limbs in their second main function — propelling the animal in locomotion. In nearly all mammals it is the hind limbs that provide most of the thrust needed for locomotion.

When a terrestrial mammal walks it pushes against the ground at the contact points formed by the extremities of the limbs, which are often modified into a specialised paw or hoof. The forces needed for this are generated mostly in the limb muscles. The larger mass of muscles is found in the upper segments of each limb, the thigh and hip and the upper arm and shoulder. These muscles suffice for walking or trotting but when a dog begins to move really fast it brings another set of muscles into play. These are the muscles of the back in the lumbar region, and when they contract they flex the back strongly, allowing the hind limbs to be brought far forward, so as to lengthen the stride and increase speed. This

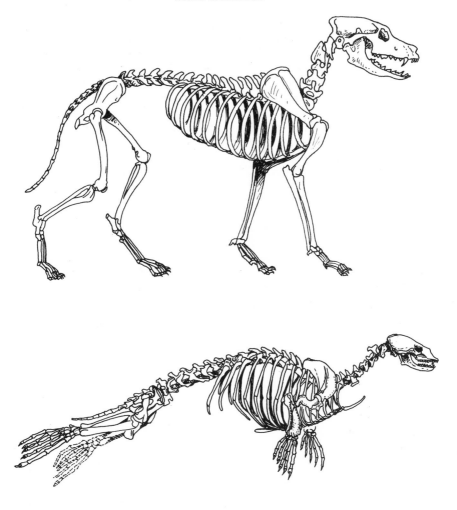

Figure 1.3 The skeleton of a typical mammal: above, the dog, and below, that of the seal.

characteristic bounding is best seen in those mammals that need to move really fast, such as the gazelle or its predator, the cheetah.

Seals have had to make use of the same basic mammalian equipment but because of the differences imposed on them by living in water their limbs and their method of locomotion have developed very differently. Because a seal in water is surrounded by a medium with a density almost identical to that of its body, its limbs have no supporting function. While all the elements of the bony axis are present they are very different from those of a typical mammal such as a dog. The fact that the seal's body is supported by the surrounding water means that the locomotory function of the limbs has to be accomplished in some other way than pushing against the ground. What has happened is that the limbs of the seal have become modified into flippers.

The two groups of pinnipeds have gone about this in different ways. Fur seals and sea lions have developed the fore limbs into a pair of broad paddles with which the animal 'rows' itself along through the water. The main locomotory muscles are consequently those associated with the upper segment of the fore limbs and the shoulders. True seals, on the other hand, rely on their hind flippers, supplemented by movements of the hind part of the body, to propel themselves through the water, much as a human diver wearing rubber fins does. In consequence, the true seal's locomotory muscles are concentrated at the hinder end of its body.

Before going further in explaining the mechanics of movement, it is necessary to describe the limbs. Brazier Howell, an American anatomist, provided an excellent account (Howell, 1930) of the functional anatomy of the seal's limbs. A more recent and accessible work is Judith King's *Seals of the World* (1983), which gives a general account, but is especially strong in anatomy. Although much modified, the basic elements of the mammalian limb are all present in the seal, though this is not obvious from external inspection. Seal limbs appear short in comparison with body size and this impression is heightened because the upper segments of the limbs are concealed within the general body contour. The 'armpit' and 'groin' in a seal occur at the level of the wrist and ankle respectively. Furthermore, the bones of the limbs are short and sturdy (Figure 1.4). The hind flippers of all true seals are built on much the same pattern. The femur is a very short, stout bone arranged almost at right angles to the long axis of the body. The bones of the shank, the tibia and fibula, are

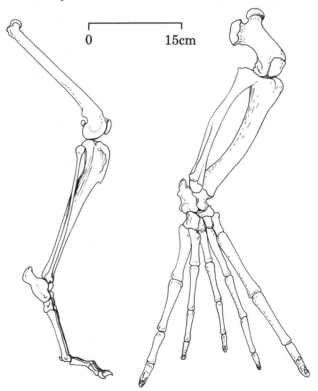

Figure 1.4 Limb skeletons of dog (left) and seal (right).

relatively elongated but are nevertheless sturdy. In all except the very primitive Hawaiian monk seal these bones are fused together near the knee joint where they articulate with the femur. The ankle is made up of seven tarsal bones (astragalus, calcaneum, cuboid, navicular, external cuneiform, middle cuneiform and internal cuneiform, for those that wish to know their exact names) and it is at this level that we reach the part of the limb that projects from the surface of the body, the hind flipper as we see it in the living seal. The remaining bones of the foot are all elongated, with the first and fifth toes the most so, and the middle toe the least. The toes are joined by a web of skin to form a broad fan and in the southern phocids this is further widened by the development of lateral expansions of fibrous tissue. Northern phocids have strong claws on each toe but in the southern seals these are reduced or practically absent. The hair covering of the body is extended down over the flipper on both surfaces and it is not possible to distinguish a definite sole to the foot.

Despite the tapering of the posterior part of the body, the flippers are relatively widely spaced. This is the result of the thigh-bones being arranged, as noted above, almost at right angles to the body. The space between the flippers is filled by a short, broad tail.

In the fore limb the humerus, like the femur, is a short, stout bone (Figure 1.4). It articulates proximally with the scapula or shoulder blade which, as in all mammals, is embedded in the shoulder muscles, rather than being joined directly to the spinal column. There is no collar bone, or clavicle, in any seal. The bones of the forearm are also short and stout. There are six carpal bones in the wrist, the scapholunar, cuneiform, unciform, magnum, trapezoid, and trapezium, together with an associated sesamoid bone, the pisiform. This structure of the wrist is similar to that of the fissiped carnivores and links them to that group. The remaining bones of the hand, the metacarpals and phalanges, are not so elongated as the corresponding bones of the foot. Externally, the fore flipper in northern phocids is short and broad. The first digit is the longest with the others progressively shorter, but only gradually so. The arctic bearded seal is known to Canadians as the 'square flipper' because it departs from the usual pattern, having the middle digit slightly longer than the others, giving a rather square-ended appearance. Each digit in northern phocids carries a large claw. Southern phocids have much more variable fore flippers, with a tendency to develop a pointed shape resulting from the rapid decrease in length of the digits from the first (longest) to the fifth. This is most marked in the leopard and Ross seals, and these species also have reduced claws, while other southern phocids have moderately well-developed claws. As in the hind flipper, both surfaces are covered with hair.

How are these limbs used? As we saw earlier, it is the hind limbs that propel the true seal through the water. Swimming is by means of alternate, inwardly directed strokes of the hind flippers, the digits being spread on the inward power stroke so that they form with the interdigital webs a broad concave surface to react against the inertia of the water. On the outwardly directed recovery stroke the digits relax, the webs contract and the flipper presents a reduced convex surface (Figure 1.5). The movements of the flippers are accompanied by lateral swinging of the hinder third of the body. Probably most of the power output comes from long muscles in the lumbar region of the back (the iliocostalis and

Figure 1.5 The hind flippers of a seal in the power and recovery strokes.

longissimus dorsi muscles) which are very well developed. The muscles of the limb itself serve mainly to maintain the position of the flipper relative to the body and control the spreading and closing of the digits. Three hamstring muscles on each side (the gracilis, the biceps femoris and the semitendinosus) firmly secure the shank close to the pelvis and nearly parallel to the vertebral column. This facilitates the transmission of the power generated by the lumbar muscles to the flipper, but at the same time makes it impossible for the seal to bring its flipper forward beneath its body.

The fact that a phocid seal generates its swimming power at the hinder end of its body has imposed other constraints on its anatomy. As an active hunter, a seal needs to retain a great measure of flexibility at the forward end of its body so that it can manoeuvre its jaws to catch prey. A long, mobile neck, with a heavy head at the end, would be dynamically unsound for an animal swimming in water. We noted earlier that seals have no obvious neck when looked at from the outside, yet internally the normal mammalian complement of seven cervical vertebrae are present. The neck length is masked by the heaviness of the muscles in this region which help to maintain the dynamically advantageous torpedo shape when swimming, but allow a wide range of movement for seizing prey.

Normally when a seal is swimming or at rest the neck is retracted and bent into a downwardly directed U. This allows a sudden extension of the head (and jaws) when the seal wishes to seize a fish or repel an intruder.

During active swimming it is generally believed that the fore flippers are held passively against the sides of the body. The blubber layer is thinner here, so that there is a shallow depression on each side into which the flipper can fit, thus maintaining the streamlined form. However, when swimming slowly and probably when manoeuvring at speed, the fore flippers are actively used. There are powerful muscles associated with the shoulders, and in the wild a seal probably makes considerable use of its fore limbs. Unfortunately, direct observation in the wild is difficult as human divers are quite unable to keep up with a seal swimming even moderately fast.

How fast do seals swim? It is hard to answer this question as far as seals in the wild are concerned. Terrie Williams and Gerry Kooyman (1985) trained a harbour seal to swim at its top speed in a tank by rewarding it for leaping towards a target suspended over the water. The seal swam over a course about 10 m long, taking about 2.5 seconds from a resting start. The target was progressively raised as the training proceeded until the animal's limits were reached. At this maximum velocity, underwater videotape recordings made against a calibrated background showed that the seal was doing 4.9 m/sec. This may not seem very fast, but to achieve it the seal had to swim flat out, even using its fore flippers to aid its propulsion.

The seal that Williams and Kooyman trained was an adult harbour seal, weighing 70–90 kg and measuring 165 cm from its nose to the tip of its hind flippers. Larger seals, benefitting from their reduced relative surface area (page 11), and hence reduced drag, should be able to swim faster. A leopard seal of 275 kg can easily leap from the water to land on an ice floe 2 m above the surface. This implies an exit speed of approximately 6 m/sec, and this may not be its maximum.

Seals are wonderfully lithe and agile in the water. To achieve this, as we have seen, has required considerable modification of their body form and this has markedly reduced their capabilities on land. Because the hind limbs cannot be rotated forwards under the body to carry its weight, a seal must heave itself forward with its fore limbs or by 'humping' movements of the back. If we analyse this movement we see that the seal drags its body over the ground using as the hinder point of traction the lower abdominal and pelvic region and as the forward point the chest. Flexing the back brings these closer together and if the weight is thrown back to the hinder traction point, extension of the back will result in the chest being thrust forward. Moving this weight forward will allow the pelvis to be brought forward when the back is next flexed. All seals can move in this way, with the fore flippers closely pressed against the sides, but the larger ones, and often the smaller ones as well, will use the fore flippers to provide additional thrust. The palms are placed on the ground and the body heaved forward over them. This clumsy method of locomotion restricts the activity of seals ashore and has caused them to adopt characteristic behaviour patterns which I shall discuss later.

However, one should not always assume that seals are slow movers when out of the water. Ribbon seals can move over the ice as fast as a man can sprint (Burns, 1981) and O'Gorman (1963) estimated the speed of a crabeater seal on ice at 25 km/h, progressing by a sinuous movement involving alternate backward strokes of the fore flippers and vigorous side-to-side flailing movements of the hindquarters.

The fur seals and sea lions have been less affected in this way. Because their locomotion in the water is effected by the fore limbs their hind limbs are less modified. In particular the shank is not bound as rigidly in a posteriorly directed position as in the true seals. This means that a fur seal on land can bring its hind flippers forward and waddle on its heels. Because the limb bones are shortened and the limbs mostly within the body contour, the steps it can take are very short but when really exerting itself a fur seal can break into a gallop, bringing its hind flippers forward simultaneously and covering the ground at a surprising pace.

Heat Balance

In the previous paragraphs I have described some of the principal modifications of the seal's anatomy that can be related to the greater density and viscosity of water when compared with air. The second set of physical properties that have markedly affected seals are the thermal properties of water: its greater thermal conductivity and its much greater thermal capacity.

Sea water is always colder, and usually very much colder, than the approximately 37°C at which mammals keep their blood. Hence, seals need adaptations to avoid excessive heat loss across the temperature gradient between the body core and the surrounding water. Many seals live in exceedingly cold regions, where air temperatures drop far below the minimum that can occur in sea water (which freezes at about −1.8°C), but the problem, while not negligible, is not so acute in air. This is because air has a much lower thermal conductivity than water, so heat leaks out from the body more slowly; and because air has a far lower heat capacity than water it can be warmed up so as to reduce the temperature gradient for a smaller expenditure of heat loss from the body core (Bonner, 1982).

Seals have had to develop solutions to this problem. An uncompensated loss of heat, which would lead to a lowering of the body core temperature, such as occurs in an inadequately clad human diver who stays in the water too long, cannot be tolerated. The physiology of higher mammals is finely tuned to a constant, and high, internal temperature. Even small decreases result in a significant depression of brain activity, which would be quite unacceptable to an active hunter. Nor can a high rate of heat loss be compensated for by increased heat production, since in the long term this would be energetically inefficient. The seal is left with two solutions.

The first of these is to reduce the amount of surface across which heat can be lost. For a given volume, the shape that has the least surface is a sphere. A spherical seal is dynamically impractical, but the smooth torpedo shape of the seal with the reduction of projecting appendages we noted earlier, is economical of surface. The hydrodynamic properties which were important in streamlining prove to have an additional advantage in heat conservation.

A further reduction in surface area can be achieved by taking advantage of the surface/volume relationship (Figure 1.6). Because the

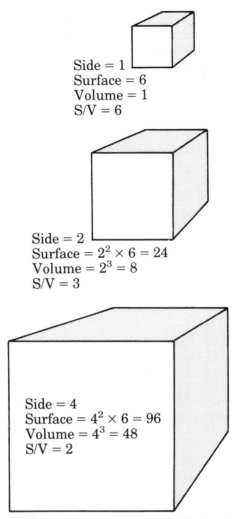

Side = 1
Surface = 6
Volume = 1
S/V = 6

Side = 2
Surface = $2^2 \times 6 = 24$
Volume = $2^3 = 8$
S/V = 3

Side = 4
Surface = $4^2 \times 6 = 96$
Volume = $4^3 = 48$
S/V = 2

Figure 1.6 The surface volume relationship. As the volume of a body increases the ratio of surface to volume becomes less, hence larger bodies have less relative surface area.

surface of a body increases as the square of its linear dimension, while its volume increases as the cube, it follows that for bodies of the same general shape, the larger ones will have relatively less surface area. Seals have exploited this strategy to reduce heat loss and seals are all large mammals in a literal sense, there being no small seals as there are small rodents, small carnivores or small artiodactyls.

The other way to conserve heat is to insulate what surface there is. The basic mammalian way of doing this is by the hair covering over the body. All seals have a hair coat and in some of the otariids, the fur seals, this is very luxuriant indeed. In the true seals, however, the hair coat is composed of rather stiff and not very dense hair. The northern fur seal, for example, may have 57,000 hair fibres per cm^2 (Scheffer, 1962) while the harp seal, which lives in just as cold, if not colder surroundings, has only about 1,800 (Tarasoff, 1972). A hair coat is an effective insulator in air for it traps a layer of stationary air within it and, as we have seen, this minimises the loss of heat. However, it is much less effective in the water if the water wets the hair and penetrates to the skin surface. Fur seals avoid this happening. Their coat consists of two types of hair fibre, long stout guard hairs and much finer and shorter underfur fibres. These are arranged in groups, a single guard hair being associated with up to about 50 underfur fibres emerging from the same hair canal. The oily secretions of the sebaceous glands render these fur fibres water repellent so that when the seal submerges the water penetrates the coat only as far as the zone where the guard hairs emerge from the underfur layer. The strong shafts of the guard hairs support the underfur layer and prevent it from collapsing under the pressure of the water at moderate depths.

True seals do not have such a fur coat (and neither do the other section of the otariids, the sea lions). When they dive the water penetrates the hair and the skin is wetted. Even so, the hair layer probably has some insulative effect under water; it will serve to slow down the exchange of water at the skin surface. The shafts of the hair are all inclined backwards, towards the posterior end of the body, at an angle of about 45°, and the hairs themselves are curved and slightly flattened so that their tips form a pattern rather like the tiles on a roof. This not only helps to promote the flow of water past the hair surface, reducing drag, but also helps to retain the water layer beneath.

The main means of insulation in true seals, however, is the blubber layer. Fat is a poor conductor of heat and a blubber layer is about half as effective an insulator as an equal thickness of fur in air. However, unlike fur which collapses, eliminating its insulative layer of air when the fur seal dives, blubber, being incompressible, is unaffected by the depth to which the seal descends. Seals commonly have from 7 to 10 cm of blubber over their bodies, which effectively prevents loss of heat from the core.

Blubber, or hypodermal adipose tissue, consists of a layer of fat-filled cells lying beneath the skin. Unlike whales, which also have blubber, there is very little fibrous tissue present in seal blubber. Bryden (1964) has shown that seal blubber is a better insulator than whale blubber, probably because of its lack of fibrous tissue. Elephant seal blubber has a conductivity of 0.00017 cal cm/sec cm^2 (about the same as asbestos fibre), while whale blubber has an equivalent value of 0.00050 cal cm/sec cm^2.

In seals almost all the fatty tissue present, apart from a little behind the eyeball, is in the blubber. There is no visceral fat as in most other mammals. Chemically, the fats are present as the glycerol esters of fatty acids with carbon chain lengths of 16 and 18 carbon atoms. This is generally true of the fats of marine mammals (Bryden and Stokes, 1969) and seals show no special adaptation in this respect.

Besides acting as an insulation, blubber has other roles. We have seen how it serves to aid the smoothing of the body outline and assist streamlining. It is possible that it is even more effective in reducing drag. When a dolphin is swimming fast transverse corrugations at right angles to its direction of movement appear on the skin (Essapian, 1955). These mark areas where the pressure of the water at the surface of the body differs and thus indicate incipient areas of turbulence. However, instead of turbulence developing, as it would in the case of a rigid-hulled ship, the surface of the dolphin's skin responds to the pressure differences by changing its shape, eliminating the turbulence as it develops. This phenomenon has not been observed in seals but it seems probable that the same would apply.

Another function of blubber which is well proven is as a food reserve. Fat is the most concentrated form in which energy can be stored and its metabolism produces not only energy but also water. Both these properties are of significance, as we shall see later.

The blubber layer is not continuous over the whole body of the seal; for hydrodynamic reasons, the flippers are free of blubber and the anterior part of the head, with its battery of sense organs, nostrils and jaws, is also blubber-free. Whales, which face similar problems, avoid excessive loss of heat from their flippers by using a device, the counter-current heat exchanger, that is quite familiar to heating engineers. The counter-current exchanger works by extending the average heat gradient between the hot and cold flows. In order that the tissues of the flipper may stay alive and functional and not freeze solid, the whale has to maintain some blood circulation through them. The vascular supply to the flippers is arranged so that the main arteries, carrying blood to the periphery, are closely surrounded by veins, bringing the blood back to the body core. What happens in the counter-current exchange is that the cold blood coming from the surface in the veins extracts heat from the arterial blood coming from the body core, so that by the time the arterial blood reaches the surface nearly all its heat has been given up (exchanged) and not much more cooling can take place with irrevocable loss of heat. Such counter-current heat exchangers have not, so far as I know, been described in seals but the gross appearance of the blood vessels to the flippers suggests that heat exchange could occur in this way.

A seal ashore is not likely to be suffering from the cold. The adaptations which ensure that it remains warm in the water will be more than sufficient to ensure that in most conditions a seal will not be at risk in air. On the Ross Ice Shelf a Weddell seal may encounter temperatures as low as $-50°C$ which, with the strong winds that are common there, may produce a chill factor of $-100°C$ to $-150°C$. In these circumstances the seal is likely to return to the water (which will never be colder than $-1.8°C$), and accept the greater thermal capacity of the latter.

On the other hand, seals are quite likely to suffer from overheating when ashore. A bull elephant seal, lumbering about to defend his harem (Chapter 4), may visibly steam even on a cold day. We can easily understand how an animal that may weigh up to 3 tonnes can overheat when moving violently; what is more surprising is the fact that a seal at rest even in subzero temperatures in the Antarctic can also warm up. On a clear day in the Antarctic summer, despite the low elevation of the sun the radiation at ground level can reach a value of up to 1,000 watts per square metre as a result of the extreme clarity of the atmosphere which contains very little water vapour. A seal lying on the ice acts as a 'black body' and absorbs this radiation, as it basks, with significant warming. Seals meet such situations by physiological and behavioural responses. In temperate regions seals will retreat to the water on very hot days; monk seals in the tropics will seek whatever shade they can find on a beach; elephant seals in California will flip sand onto their backs. Such responses, however, are not always adequate or possible and seals have a physiological method for losing excess heat. Blubber is not a passive insulator, like a roll of asbestos lagging round the body. It is a vascular tissue, permeated by blood vessels; modification to the architecture of these blood vessels allows considerable control of the heat balance.

Normally, the heat balance is such that the seal is warmer than its environment. In these circumstances the blood vessels external to the blubber layer are constricted, so that the flow of blood to the skin is reduced and heat is conserved. If however it becomes necessary for the seal to lose heat a special mechanism comes into play. Typically, the pattern of arrangement of blood vessels in the skin is for an artery to divide into arterioles which in turn divide into the very fine capillaries. These unite to form first venules and then veins which convey the blood back to the heart. Flow through the capillaries is limited by their very narrow bore and, in a seal in a cold environment, by constricting the arterioles as well. However, when too warm seals can increase the rate of blood flow through their skin by dilating special vessels which join arterioles directly to venules, bypassing the capillary bed. These bypasses are very near the surface so the increased flow of blood allows heat to be lost to the environment. The bypasses are known as arteriovenous anastomoses, or AVAs for short. AVAs are found in a number of animals that may have a problem in losing excess heat. They occur, for example in the skin of the legs of sheep or on the ears of rabbits. Their presence in seals was first shown for the Weddell seal and later for the elephant seal (Molyneux and Bryden, 1975, 1978). Subsequently, it was shown that AVAs were present also in fur seals and sea lions, but in these they were concentrated on the flippers, which being the only parts of the body free of the insulating fur layer were the only areas where heat could be lost in this way.

We have seen that its blubber layer ensures that an adult seal is not likely to suffer from heat loss on land but this is not true of a new-born seal pup. Seals, like all other mammals, have minimal fat deposits at birth. A Weddell seal pup leaves its mother's uterus at a constant 37°C to emerge, wet and blubberless, onto the Antarctic ice. Its wetness is not a major problem; it loses little heat by evaporation, since the moisture on its fur soon freezes (releasing a few calories as it does so, as Kooyman (1981b) pointed out) and drops away as ice. The young pup is now revealed in a very dense furry coat. This first coat, the lanugo, is made of finer hair than the adult coat. It is denser than the adult coat because the young seal when born has all, or nearly all, of its hair follicles already present and as these are spread over a much smaller area, it follows that the hairs are closer together. Nevertheless, the insulation provided by the lanugo is not in itself always sufficient to maintain a heat balance and pups can often be seen shivering before they accumulate a blubber layer from their mother's milk. Until this comes about, the pup has yet another means of preventing dangerous cooling. This is a specialised adipose tissue called brown fat. When activated, brown fat can take up large amounts of oxygen, producing heat, a process known as non-shivering thermogenesis. Brown fat is concentrated in the neck and pelvic regions of the pup and in association with venous plexuses developed about the pericardium and kidneys (Blix *et al.*, 1975). Even with such adaptations, the pup seal's best defence against freezing to death is still its blubber layer, and we shall see later (Chapter 3) how rapidly this develops.

Senses

A seal, like any other mammal, has to provide itself with a constant stream of information about its environment and this it does through its sense organs. Most of this information is acquired by four senses — sight, hearing, smell and touch. Each of these is affected to a greater or lesser extent by a marine environment.

The mammalian eye, like other mammalian sense organs, evolved to function in air. Air has a low refractive index and it is a particularly transparent substance, that is to say it absorbs very little light and it does so relatively unselectively. Water has a higher refractive index than air and it absorbs light much more readily. This means that light will penetrate much less far through water. In the sea at 10 m depth some 90 per cent of the light has been absorbed or reflected at the air-water interface and this rises to 99 per cent at 40 m. At 600 m it is pitch black to human eyes, virtually all the light having been absorbed. Furthermore, the different wavelengths of light are absorbed at different rates, the longer wavelenths (corresponding to red colours) being absorbed first and the short (blue) wavelengths last.

This means that vision is not a particularly useful sense for gathering information at long distances beneath the water and we shall see that seals have other means of doing this. However, it is still a very useful sense and no seal has allowed its eyes to degenerate, as those of some other mammals, such as moles, mole rats or some river dolphins, have done. Seals in fact have well-developed eyes and it is clear that they make much use of them. The eyes are large, both absolutely and in relation to the size of the animal. Judith King (1983) has pointed out that many seals have eyeballs about 40 mm in diameter; the largest eyes are those of the Ross seal and the elephant seal (about 60 mm in diameter). A large eye, like a large camera lens, means that it has greater light-gathering power and can hence operate efficiently in low light levels under water.

If we examine the seal's eye anatomically we find several modifications that are clearly associated with underwater activity. The most immediately obvious of these is the shape of the lens (Figure 1.7). In seals, as in whales, this is nearly spherical and the reason is the same in both groups. In air the curved surface of the cornea has a powerful refractive effect and the lens has only a subsidiary and fine focusing role. However, when submerged in water, which has nearly the same refractive index as the cornea, the refractive effect of the latter is lost and in order that light rays may be brought to a focus on the retina the lens has to be more powerful and develops its spherical shape.

The retina of seals is similar to that of terrestrial carnivores. Two types of sensory cells are present in the typical retina: rods, which function at low light intensities and are insensitive to hue discrimination, and cones which function in bright light and provide detailed vision and colour vision in some animals. In the seal retina, microscopic examination reveals only rods, and from this it is deduced that seals live in a monochromatic world. Colour discrimination has been reported in one seal (Wartzok and McCormick, 1978) but Schusterman (1981) suggests that seals, like cats, tend to respond to brightness rather than hue. However, it is not a simple matter. Tests on harp seals (Lavigne *et al.*,

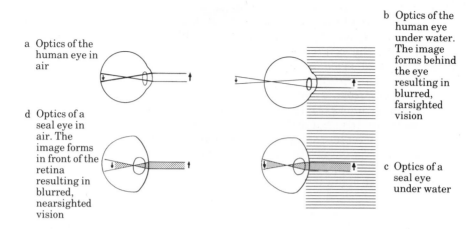

Figure 1.7 The formation of the image on the retina in (a) a human eye in air, (b) a human eye under water, (c) a seal eye under water, (d) a seal eye in air.

1977) have shown that in that species two types of photopigment are present, which implies the functional presence of cones. It is likely that one pigment (corresponding to the 'cone' one) functions in bright light at the surface or when ashore, while the other functions in dimmer light when submerged.

The elephant seal, which is a deep diver, has been shown to possess a modified photopigment, resembling that of deep sea fishes (Lythgoe and Dartnall, 1970). The Weddell seal, another deep diver, does not have this modification and it has been suggested that the elephant seal uses its modified photopigment to respond to the illumination of the bioluminescent squids on which it feeds. Its absence in the Weddell seal perhaps indicates that they may have another means of finding their prey at depth.

Because when the seal dives deeply there will be very little available light, it has to make the best use of all the light that enters the eye. The absolute size of the eye has already been mentioned but the seal has another way of ensuring that the light is fully utilised. Behind the layer of sensory cells in the retina is a layer of reflective cells — the tapetum. This serves to reflect back any light that passes through the sensory cell layer so that there is a second chance for it to be absorbed and stimulate a sense cell. The tapetum is found in many nocturnal mammals — the reflection of a car's headlamps in the eyes of a prowling cat at night will be familiar. In the seal, which is basically a diurnal mammal, it functions when submerged rather than at night.

A seal does not, of course, spend all its time submerged and hence it needs eyes that will function efficiently in air as well as in water. An eye that is designed to operate under low light conditions can be embarrassed by too much light and a seal on snow in bright sunlight might be expected to suffer. In fact, seals can protect their eyes very efficiently by closing the pupil, the deeply pigmented brown iris contracting first to a vertical slit and then to a tiny pinhole (Jamieson and Fisher, 1973). But excess light is not the only problem. The refractive apparatus of the seal's eye is developed to operate under water. In air the cornea will have its usual

16

effect and this added to the refraction from the spherical lens will result in the light being brought to a focus short of the retina — in other words, the seal would tend to be short sighted. This is not the only problem arising from the refraction from the cornea. The surface of the seal's cornea is not spherical but has different curvatures in the horizontal and vertical planes. This difference in curvature may be a result of adaptation to reduce the pressure on the eye when the seal is swimming fast under water (Jamieson, 1971). In air, however, it results in the seal being not only short-sighted, but astigmatic as well. However, the vertical slit pupil parallel to the astigmatic axis has the effect in bright light of focusing to a point on the retina. Contraction of the pupil will also minimise the myopia. The result is that a seal will see clearly in air only when the light is reasonably bright.

This does not mean, however, that seals do not rely to a considerable extent on vision on land. Even if their eyes do not allow them to define detail they are very responsive to movement and a person stalking a seal ashore needs to move very cautiously, though he need take no special care to conceal his outline. Anyone who has watched a group of harbour seals* will have noticed how frequently a member of the group will raise its head to scan the scene. It is clear that vision is an important sense to them in avoiding predators.

Hearing is another sense that operates rather differently under water than in air. While water is less favourable for the transmission of light than air is, the opposite applies to sound. Sound travels faster (about four times as fast) in water than in air and, more importantly, it is attenuated less, so sounds travel further.

In a terrestrial mammal in air there is a great difference in acoustic impedance between the air and the tissues of the head. This results in 90 per cent of the sound being reflected away from the head. However, at the external ears sound is reflected down the trumpet-shaped pinna to the ear drum where it actuates a series of tiny bones resulting in the stimulation of sense cells in the inner ear. A terrestrial mammal can determine the direction of the origin of a sound by computing the difference in time for the sound to arrive at each ear. The 'sound shadow' cast by the skull and tissues between it and the opposite ear gives additional clues as to the direction of the sound. Neither of these methods works well in water. Because of the increased speed of sound in water small differences are more difficult to detect and the method using sound shadows will only be efficient if the ears can operate independently. This is difficult if the head is immersed in water; a human diver, for example, has great difficulty in localising sound. The reason for this is that because there is little difference in acoustic impedance between water and the tissues of the skull sound waves arrive at the inner ear by bone conduction from all directions and localisation is lost.

Seals have modified the bones of their skulls so that this property of bone conduction can actually be turned to advantage in localising sounds. One of the bones that is associated with the ear, the squamosal, is

---

* This is *Phoca vitulina*, the animal usually known as the common seal in the United Kingdom. I prefer the name harbour seal, since 'common seal' can be ambiguous where other species are more abundant, as for example, in Orkney.

enlarged and has a large flat surface facing upwards and to the front (in approximately the same direction as the eyes look out). Sound waves arriving normal to this surface are transmitted into the squamosal and through it to the inner ear. Waves which arrive obliquely to the squamosal are reflected (King, 1983). By making scanning movements of its head the seal can localise the source of the sound. This is a more sensitive system than might be supposed. It has been shown (Møhl (1964) as interpreted by Schusterman, 1981) that a harbour seal can separate two sound sources only 3° apart. The tiny bones of the inner ear, the ear ossicles, of phocids are much more massive than those found in other mammals. In the harp seal they may weigh 227 mg. It is believed that this character is used in the general reception of sound. Because in water sound will act on the whole head the entire skull will vibrate, but the inertia of the loosely attached ossicles sets up the impulses that activate the sense cells (Repenning, 1972).

It is possible that this specialisation for underwater hearing has been to some extent at the cost of hearing in air, for all phocids are more sensitive to sound under water than they are to sound in air (Schusterman, 1981). It is difficult to express hearing ability in terms that are meaningful to non-specialists, but it can be said that a seal under water hears as well in the frequency range of 1 kHz (at least) to 90 kHz as a human in air hears in the range 0.5–15 kHz. Within these limits, other hearing attributes are probably the same (Terhune and Ronald, 1974).

Not only do seals use sound to orientate themselves beneath the surface, they also use it to communicate with each other and it has been suggested that they use it to echolocate as dolphins do. Weddell seal vocalisations underwater can be surprisingly loud and can be detected nearly 30 km away. They consist of trills, each composed of a series of pulses of decreasing frequency, which probably function as dominance signals; chirps, which sweep through a range of frequencies; and growls, usually below 0.2 kHz, which function as threats (Watkins and Schevill, 1968). The trills have the same character as the pulses used in echolocation by dolphins and it is likely that they are used for the same purpose, but this has not been proved. Tests on a harbour seal locating a ring in the dark in a small (7.5 m diameter) tank (Renouf and Davis, 1982) seemed to indicate an echolocating ability but the experiment was not entirely conclusive; the seal produced only a few faint clicks and was able to discriminate in only 90 per cent of cases (Renouf, 1984). Perhaps reverberations from the edges of the tank confused the animal.

The mechanism of sound production by seals underwater has not been much studied. Presumably it involves circulating a relatively small volume of air through the larynx and over the vocal cords, or by movement of air between the larynx and trachea causing the tracheal membrane to vibrate. As we shall see later (Chapter 2), seals do not take down large quantities of air when they dive, though many seals may make communication calls near the surface where air supplies would be easily replenished.

Seals are often very vocal in air. Some of the sounds are similar to those produced under water, like the trills and throbs of Weddell and Ross seals, but some are used only on land. Elephant seals produce a wide range of grunts, roars and belches. Some of these are simple coughs and snorts but the roars of adult bulls play an important role in establishing dominance on the breeding beaches (Chapter 4).

It is difficult to evaluate seals' sense of smell. Scents are detected in mammals by the olfactory epithelium that covers the scroll-like turbinal bones in the nose. The sensory epithelium is irritated by contact with water, so odours can be detected only in air. Seals have very well developed turbinals but the parts of their brains connected with smell are quite small. Nevertheless, it is clear that scent plays an important role in the life of seals. Many seals have strong and very characteristic scents — the ringed seal was once known as *Phoca foetida*, the 'stinking seal' — and it is hard to believe that they cannot detect these. The important bond between mother and pup seems to be established through scent. A mother grey seal, returning to her pup on a crowded beach will first call and listen for her pup's answering call, but will always finally identify it by sniffing at its muzzle (Fogden, 1971, Burton *et al.*, 1975).

Touch is the last of the four main senses that seals use to obtain information about their environment. The skin of seals is not obviously more or less sensitive to touch than that of other hairy mammals. A biologist will often need to creep up behind a sleeping seal to read a numbered tag previously inserted in the web of its hind flipper. It may turn out that the tag is number-side down but it is possible to turn the flipper over very gently and read the tag without waking the seal. Once awake, however, the lightest touch will alert it and the chance of reading the tag is lost. On the other hand, I have watched a scavenging sheathbill on the beach in South Georgia in winter pecking away at a sore on the flipper of a leopard seal without apparently disturbing the animal at all. Perhaps this was stoicism rather than lack of sensitivity.

Whiskers are important tactile receptors in many mammals. All seals have well developed whiskers. In the bearded seal the whiskers are sufficiently prominent to have given it its name. Whiskers, or vibrissae, are arranged in definite groups. There are the mystacial vibrissae, arranged on the upper lip, the superciliary vibrissae, above the eyes, and the nasal vibrissae, usually only a single pair of hairs on top of the nose. Their precise arrangement and abundant innervation indicate that they are functional organs. Whiskers ought to be important to a marine mammal because of the physical properties of vibratory transmission in water. Objects which oscillate with a relatively large amplitude, such as the tail of a swimming fish, should produce a vibration which could be detected by a seal's whisker at a range of roughly 0.5 m (Renouf, 1979).

In a series of patient observations on captive seals Deane Renouf (1980) has shown that harbour seals in murky water took longer to capture live trout if their whiskers had been clipped than if their whiskers were intact. This effect was not noticed in seals captured as pups but Renouf suggested that seals experienced in capturing fish at sea rely in some way on information received by their vibrissae when they chase and capture their prey. A seal pushes its whiskers forward when chasing fish, usually to a considerable extent, and they could detect water displacements created by the swimming movements of fish, allowing the seal to position its head correctly so as to seize the fish in its jaws.

It is certain that seals are able to locate and capture prey in conditions when the use of sight is impossible. Many seals inhabit very murky estuarine water where visibility must be minimal, and the Weddell seal deep under ice in the darkness of the polar winter can scarcely use its eyes to find its prey. But the most conclusive evidence, perhaps, comes from the many reports of blind seals, and animals which give every indication of having been blind for long periods, which are found in good condition. Such a blind grey seal was seen at the Farne Islands in three successive years when she hauled out to pup in the same position each year. Though both her eyes were white and opaque she appeared to be in as good condition as the other seals present there.

In discussing the senses of seals I have said nothing of the proprioceptive sense — that internal sense that gives an animal information about the attitude of various parts of the body. We know nothing about this in phocid seals. However, such a sense is likely to be of particular importance in a aquatic mammal which has to orient itself in a three-dimensional medium. California sea lions are notable circus performers, showing an astonishing ability to balance objects on their snouts. I believe that this is a manifestation of a very precisely developed proprioceptive sense and though this has not, so far as I am aware, been demonstrated in phocid seals I am sure that they possess the same ability.

2 Feeding and diving

FOOD SOURCES IN THE SEA

The average person on being asked what seals feed upon would probably unhesitatingly answer: fish. In many cases this would be true, but it is not the whole story. Probably all pinnipeds do eat fish at some time but for some of the most abundant and successful species, fish is not the principal food. Nevertheless, seals are all flesh-eaters. Their high energy requirements to maintain their activity and heat balance necessitates their feeding on the concentrated energy sources that are found in animal tissues. Usually the food organisms of seals are rich in fat, which itself is the most concentrated energy substrate available to mammals.

We can note that of the three groups of mammals that have adopted an aquatic existence, the cetaceans, the sirenians (or sea cows) and the seals, only the sea cows are vegetarian. These sluggish creatures all inhabit tropical waters where thermal stress is less than at high latitudes. A recently extinct exception to this was Steller's sea cow, which lived in the frigid waters around the Bering and Commander Islands. However, Steller's sea cow aptly demonstrated the thermal advantage of size — these huge creatures were five or six times as large as the existing tropical sirenian species. Sea cows are a conspicuously less successful group than either the cetaceans or the pinnipeds and it is perhaps justifiable to speculate that their less nutritious diet, which forces them to spend much of their time grazing and digesting their food, is connected with this.

The ocean provides food in many forms, ranging from planktonic organisms weighing a fraction of a milligram to large vertebrates, including seals themselves. Seals take their food from almost the entire spectrum, neglecting only the smallest plankton. This involves seals feeding on many different classes of animals, ranging from planktonic crustacea, through molluscs to fish and even higher vertebrates. Most seals are rather general feeders, taking a variety of prey and having the ability to switch from one prey item to another, depending on availability.

The Weddell seal, for example, has been shown (Clarke and McLeod, 1982) in the Antarctic Peninsula region to feed largely on cephalopods, taking mostly squids in March, but switching to octopus by July. On the other hand, in the Ross Sea, on the other side of the Antarctic continent, Weddells feed mainly on fish (Kooyman, 1981a). Twenty-nine species of fish have been found in grey seal stomachs from around the British Isles. From seals taken near salmon fishing stations, salmon remains are frequent; however, from a sample of 17 stomachs with recognisable food remains taken from seals in the Southern and Outer Hebrides, none contained any salmon remains, though four contained mackerel, which had not been found in any of 40 stomachs from the mainland (Harwood and Greenwood, 1985). I might remark in passing that this discrepancy aptly illustrates the problems encountered in trying to describe the diets of seals in the wild. Similar differences have been shown in the diet of harbour seals and would no doubt be available for other species if sufficient sampling had taken place.

Although we may think of the majority of pinniped species as being generalist feeders, we should be aware that this may conceal our ignorance of the real feeding patterns which may be more closely controlled by seasonal or other factors than we think. However, it is clear that many seals are capable of feeding on a sufficiently wide range of prey

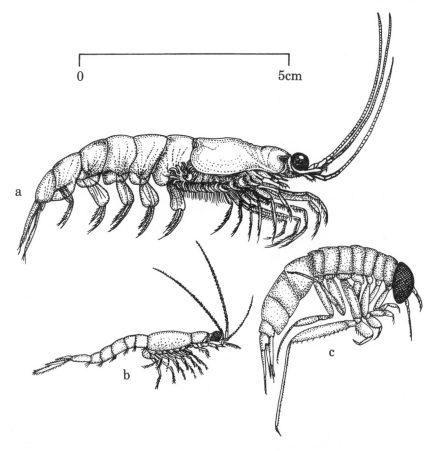

Figure 2.1 Planktonic food of seals. (a) Antarctic krill, Euphausia superba, *a euphausiid shrimp; (b) a mysid shrimp,* Mysis; *(c) a pelagic amphipod,* Parathemisto.

species to avoid adverse effects should one particular stock suffer depletion.

Another Antarctic seal, the crabeater, is a good example of a seal which has departed from the generalist pattern to become a specialist feeder. Despite its popular name, the crabeater does not feed on crabs (crabs and lobsters are absent from the seas where the crabeater is found). Instead, it feeds almost exclusively on a small shrimp-like euphausian crustacean called Antarctic krill, *Euphausia superba* (Figure 2.1). Krill is an astonishingly abundant organism. It has been suggested that krill makes up approximately 50 per cent of all the zooplankton in the Southern Ocean. This quantified claim is scarcely justified by the evidence, as it has up till now proved impossible to determine with any precision the abundance of krill in the ocean. However, it is clear that krill does form the key organism in the Antarctic marine food web. Krill is best known as the principal food of the baleen whales; besides these it also supports the majority of the Antarctic seabirds. But it is the crabeater seal that of any single species consumes the largest amount of krill, the population of some 15 million seals taking about 62 million tonnes of krill yearly. Krill clearly represents a huge resource and the evolution of a seal species to exploit it is not surprising.

Crabeater seals themselves also represent a large resource, so it is not surprising that another Antarctic seal, the leopard seal, has evolved as a specialist crabeater seal predator. Adult crabeater seals frequently show characteristic pairs of parallel scars on their flanks. These were at one time thought to be caused by killer whales, which are known to hunt them, but the marks left by killer whale teeth are closer together and more numerous than the paired scars. Fresh paired scars on adult crabeaters are rare, and most are on animals less than 18 months old. By measuring the spacing between the scars, and allowing for bodily growth, Dick Laws was able to show that these scars correspond to the average spacing between leopard seal canine teeth and are almost certainly inflicted by these seals when the victims are four to five months old (Laws, 1984).

Although the leopard seal can be regarded as a specialist crabeater seal predator, this is a rather seasonal habit since as the crabeater pups mature they become more adept at escaping the predator (and hence acquire the scars that bear witness to what was, from their point of view, a successful encounter with a leopard seal). Leopard seals must therefore have other food bases. An analysis of the available records (Laws 1984) showed that leopards take about 50 per cent krill, 20 per cent penguins, 14 per cent other seals (mainly crabeater pups), 9 per cent fish and 6 per cent squid (Figure 2.2). On this basis one could almost claim that the leopard seal is a specialist krill-feeder, and so it is, but its habit of feeding on red meat is a specialisation that has left conspicuous marks on its anatomy, as we shall see later. We should, in any case, beware of reading too much into a detailed analysis of this type. Sampling techniques are not really adequate for us to say with certainty what any individual seal eats in the wild, or what the population as a whole consumes. Presumably only large, mature leopard seals can successfully prey on crabeater seals. Younger ones may take a larger proportion of krill.

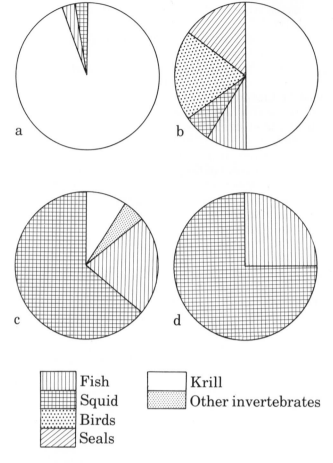

	Fish		Krill
	Squid		Other invertebrates
	Birds		
	Seals		

Figure 2.2 The food composition of four Antarctic seals, (a) the crabeater seal, (b) the leopard seal; (c) the Ross seal; (d) the elephant seal.

Another pair of Antarctic seals, the Ross seal and the elephant seal, seem to have become specialist feeders on squid (Figure 2.2). Squid and their relatives, cuttlefish and octopus, are an abundant marine resource whose importance in the ecosystem is often overlooked. Many squid feeders, like the beaked whales and the elephant and Ross seals, seem to be deep divers and it is probable that much of their feeding is done away from the surface.

FEEDING ADAPTATIONS AND METHODS

A generalist feeder, like a grey seal, is a pursuit hunter, locating and then hunting down its prey till it can be seized with the mouth and dispatched. Unfortunately, because of the difficulty of observing a fast-moving aquatic predator like a seal, there are few direct observations on pinniped feeding behaviour. Most of what we know is derived from a study of anatomy or indirect observations, with a certain amount of evidence from captive animals.

We have already seen how the modifications of the body form of seals have rendered them powerful and manoeuvrable swimmers. Their large size gives them an advantage in swimming fast for here again the surface/volume relationship comes into play. The muscle mass which generates the power needed for locomotion will vary as the cube of the linear dimension, while the drag (the chief impediment to movement through the water) will depend on the surface area of the animal, which varies as the square. In general terms this means that larger animals will swim faster than smaller ones and, as we have seen before, seals are all large mammals.

Besides their abilities as swimmers, pinnipeds are equipped with an array of sensory organs that allow them to locate and follow prey (Chapter 1). A harbour seal feeding on a moderate-sized fish, sea trout for example, will thus locate it, probably using its eyes but perhaps also its vibrissae, chase it, and when it is close enough, seize it with its jaws. For this the teeth are important.

The Teeth

Although there are some striking aberrations in the specialist feeders, most seals have a rather simple dentition. The teeth at the front of the mouth, the incisors and canines, are always well-developed. There are three upper incisors and two lower (two upper and two lower, or two upper and one lower in some species) and these, together with the canines, are capable of exerting a firm grasp on the prey. The cheek teeth, on the other hand, are less impressive in the general feeders. There is no obvious distinction between premolars and molars; the teeth form an even series from the front to the back of the jaw. The teeth are peg-like or conical, sometimes with a lobulated structure (Figure 2.3a). Teeth such as these cannot be used to shear through flesh or grind up food. If our harbour seal catches its sea trout, it will have to bring it to the surface and thrash it about to break it up into pieces small enough to be swallowed. Some phocid seals, the grey seal for instance, will use the strong claws on their fore flippers to assist in tearing up the food. Southern phocids, which lack these claws, are unable to do so.

The incipient lobulation seen in the teeth of some of the generalists reaches its climax in the extraordinary teeth of the crabeater seal (Figure 2.3b). The ten cheek teeth on either side of the mouth intermesh to form an effective sieve for separating the krill from the water taken in with the food. We do not know how the crabeater seal feeds in the wild but we can make reliable inferences from what we know of its anatomy and from some limited observations on a couple of young specimens that were kept for a short while in the Port Elizabeth Oceanarium (Ross et al., 1976). Despite some earlier accounts (Racovitza, 1900; King, 1961), crabeater seals do not feed like whales, taking in huge mouthfuls of sea water with its plankton, and then straining out the water through an extensive filter bed. To feed successfully in this way a crabeater seal would have to have a much larger mouth in relation to the size of its body, as indeed whales do. Instead, I believe a crabeater seal, having located a swarm of krill, will swim into it and then direct its snout towards an individual (perhaps using its whiskers to do so), and when close enough, suck it in by

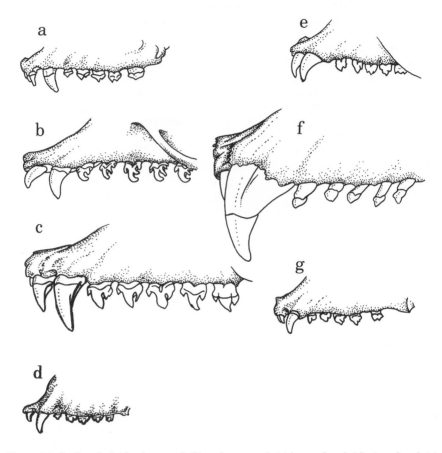

Figure 2.3 Seal teeth: (a) harbour seal; (b) crabeater seal; (c) leopard seal; (d) ringed seal; (e) Ross seal; (f) elephant seal; (g) bearded seal.

depressing the floor of its mouth in the same way that a predatory fish like a pike engulfs a minnow. Once the krill is inside the seal's mouth the jaws close and the tongue is raised, expelling the water taken in through the grid formed by the interlocking lobulated teeth and out through the sides of the mouth. The process is repeated until sufficient krill is accumulated inside the mouth to make up a mouthful or bolus, which is then swallowed. Because the crabeater seal feeds selectively, in a directed manner, the proportion of water taken in with the prey is much less than is the case with baleen whales, and a less extensive filtering area is needed.

The average meal size of a crabeater seal is probably about 8 kg of krill (Øritsland, 1977). A krill weighs about a gram, so the crabeater has to make many captures to satisfy its needs. Only the relatively large size of krill (for a zooplankton organism), and its habit of swarming, makes it suitable to support a large mammalian predator in this way.

Leopard seals, as we have seen, also feed extensively on krill, and they too have very complex teeth (Figure 2.3c). While the crabeater's teeth may be described as lobulated, those of a leopard are divided into a series of very sharp points. However, they probably function in the same way, though the points may also be useful for grasping a struggling fish or penguin.

None of the northern seals show the same extreme specialisation in a plankton diet as do the southern species discussed here, but many northern seals do feed for at least part of the time on plankton. Ringed seals, for example, feed on a variety of small pelagic crustaceans, such as the amphipod shrimp, *Parathemisto*, or the mysid shrimp *Mysis*. Their teeth (Figure 2.3d), though more divided than those of other northern phocids, are nothing like as complex as those of the crabeater. Ringed seals also feed on fish and we do not know how important plankton is in their diet; it may be that they are not highly specialised in feeding in this way because plankton is only a small part of their year-round diet. Perhaps the small size of ringed seals (they weigh at most around 110 kg while the average crabeater seal weighs 193 kg) is associated with the limitations imposed by their method of feeding.

Squid are soft bodied creatures which are usually swallowed whole by their predators. No special modifications of the dentition are required for squid eating and we find that the cheek teeth of the Ross and elephant seals are small in comparison with the animals' size (Figure 2.3e,f). The teeth at the front of the mouth have other uses, particularly in the elephant seals where the males have enormously enlarged canines for sexual fighting, and so are still large.

A feeding speciality found in the north which is not represented in the Southern Hemisphere is exhibited by the bearded seal. This large seal (it weighs up to 260 kg) feeds on bottom-dwelling (benthic) molluscs, crustaceans, sea cucumbers and fishes taken in shallow water down to 130 m or less. The teeth of the bearded seal (Figure 2.3g) are rather feebly developed; they are loosely rooted, soon wear flat and drop out. It is probable that like the walrus, with which bearded seals share many similarities, and which also feeds on bottom-dwelling animals, the bearded seal obtains much of its food by suction. They show a special fondness for whelks, yet the shells are never found in the seals' stomachs. The circumstances in which a living whelk can be sucked out of its shell baffle the mind!

The Digestive Tract

The digestive tract in seals is, as in most carnivores, uncomplicated. Because seals usually eat their food whole, the oesophagus is provided with longitudinal folds so that it can dilate to accommodate bulky items. This leads to the stomach, which is capacious. The stomach is a simple bag, with no subdivisions such as are seen in ruminants or whales. The gut beyond the stomach is differentiated into a small intestine and a large intestine. There is a small pouch-like caecum at their junction. The final part of the large intestine forms the rectum, but this is small. Seals produce frequent, watery faeces, and there seems to be no special function in the large gut for the withdrawal of water from the faeces before evacuation as in many other mammals.

The most striking feature of the seal's digestive tract is the remarkable length attained by the small intestine in some species. One might expect the gut of a meat-eater to be fairly short. Meat requires only a short digestion compared with vegetable matter, and most carnivores have relatively short guts, typically five or six times the body length (King, 1983). This is not the case with seals, however. Dick Laws (1953b) measured the length of the small intestine in 89 elephant seals and found it was mostly between 20 and 25 times the body length of the animal. In one very large specimen the small intestine was 202 m in length, or 42 times the body length. The reason for the remarkably long gut of the elephant seal is not known. It is almost certainly not associated with its squid-eating habit, for the other Antarctic squid-eater, the Ross seal, has one of the shortest relative gut sizes (4.5–11.3 m, or 2.3–4.9 times body length — King, 1983) of any seal.

Fasting

One of the characteristic features of the feeding pattern in seals is the occurrence of periods when it ceases to feed and fasts. In some seals, such as the elephant seals, it is easily observable that during the breeding and moulting periods, both sexes abstain from food. The seals remain on shore during these times and have no opportunity to take either food or water. For seals which spend less continuous periods on land, such as harbour seals or the ice-breeding seals, it is hard to be certain that no food at all is taken at these times, but all the evidence suggests that no seals feed during the breeding season and probably few feed while moulting.

The key to the seal's ability to fast is, of course, its blubber layer. Seals are able to utilise the lipids stored in their blubber to maintain a fasting metabolism, either directly or after conversion to glucose which can be utilised by the brain, without having to break down muscle protein in the process of gluconeogenesis as in a fasting man. Deprivation of water during the period of fasting is less important to a seal since its energy source is fat, which during oxidation provides a source of 'metabolic water'. Newly weaned northern elephant seal pups fast for about twelve weeks before they begin to feed for themselves. During this time they obtain all the water (and energy) they need from the breakdown of fat in their blubber. In fact, their needs are not great, for they have an exceptionally low rate of water turnover (Ortiz et al., 1978).

Even when feeding seals do not seem to drink water. Normally the only water available to them is sea water, with its heavy concentration of about 3.5 per cent salt, and while their kidneys are capable of excreting salt by producing a urine more concentrated than this they do not need to do so. Harbour seals feeding on herring take 80 per cent water with their food. The amount of herring needed to produce 100 kilocalories (1,250 g of fish) would contain 1,000 g of water. The oxidative breakdown of the fat and protein in the fish would produce another 121 g of metabolic water, making 1,121 g in total. Water losses from the lungs in breathing (106 g) and in the faeces (200 g), would total 306 g, leaving 815 g of water for the urine, a quantity sufficient to dispose of the nitrogenous wastes and excess salts at a concentration of the order of that found in seal urine (Irving et al., 1935).

A curious phenomenon that has been associated with fasting is the presence of stones in the stomachs of seals. Laws (1956a) found that 84 per cent of the stomachs of the elephant seals he examined contained sand and stones, in amounts of up to a kilogram or more. This material must have been deliberately swallowed, as it was very unlikely to have been taken in with the food, which consists of free-swimming organisms. Laws discounted suggestions that the stones had been eaten to help grind up the food, or to destroy parasites. He showed, however, that the incidence of stones in the stomachs, month by month, indicated that the seals ate the stones just before they came ashore and eliminated them when they returned to sea. He concluded that the stones served to alleviate the hunger pangs resulting from prolonged fasting, by providing the stomach muscles with 'bulk' on which they could contract. I am not entirely convinced of this. Fasting is such a basic and long-established feature of seals' lives that I cannot believe that they require stones to offset the discomfort of an empty stomach. Furthermore, the amounts found are usually trivial in relation to the size of the stomach. Perhaps we should admit that here is another of those mysteries associated with the life of seals which at present we do not understand.

FOOD CONSUMPTION, METABOLISM AND ENERGETICS

There is a general belief, at least amongst fishermen, that seals have prodigious appetites. Certainly they can take very large meals on occasion, but this is a common characteristic of carnivores and does not in itself imply that food consumption, averaged over the year, is unusually high. It is, in fact, very difficult to measure the consumption of any mammal in the wild and these difficulties are greatly increased when the mammal concerned does its feeding at sea. Many estimates of food consumption were based on the examination of the stomachs of shot seals. Those containing the largest amounts of food were generally considered to contain a 'complete' meal and consumption was then calculated by making assumptions about the frequency with which such meals were consumed. Even more hazardous were estimates derived from fragments of prey found in the stomach, which were then considered to represent whole organisms. Examination of stomachs can certainly yield valuable information about feeding; indeed, this may in some cases be the only reliable method of obtaining any information at all. But without adequate information about frequency of feeding and a knowledge of fasting periods (which seem to play an important role on both a short-term and long-term basis in many, if not all, seals) it cannot tell us how much seals eat.

Even more misleading may be estimates based on the rations consumed by seals in captivity. The animals are rarely living under conditions that even approximate to the wild state and the food offered may have very different nutritional values from that which would be taken by the seal hunting for itself.

Another approach is to estimate food consumption from the energy requirement of the animal, by constructing an energy budget which takes into account its various activities, growth, reproduction and losses associated with faeces, etc. David Lavigne and his co-workers in Canada have been foremost in developing this approach.

Until quite recently it was generally believed that seals, and other marine mammals, had metabolic rates that were significantly higher than those of more normal terrestrial mammals. For these, the relation between metabolic rate and body mass, when plotted logarithmically, produces a straight line over a wide range of body masses — the so-called 'mouse to elephant' curve. The available data from seals clustered above this line, giving a strong impression that seals had metabolic rates around twice those of the others. However, as Lavigne and his colleagues (1986) pointed out, the values used are only meaningful if the measurements are made under standard conditions. Because seals are aquatic mammals, this was rarely the case. When all the seal data obtained under non-standard conditions were eliminated it became clear that seals lay on the generalised mammalian line (Figure 2.4).

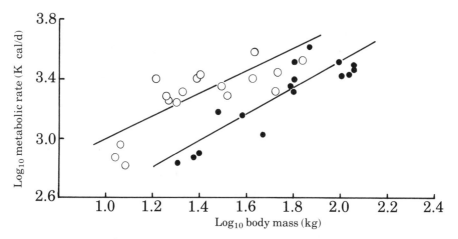

● Metabolic rates of phocid seals determined by Kleiber's criteria
○ Metobolic rates of young, growing phocid seals

Figure 2.4 Metabolic rates of phocid seals as determined by Kleiber's criteria (●); metabolic rates of young, growing seals (○).

The observation that the metabolic rates of seals are similar to those of other mammals raises an interesting question. Seals have a thick layer of relatively inert fatty tissue, the blubber, investing their bodies. If the whole seal has a similar metabolic rate to that of other mammals and its blubber has a lower one, must it not be the case that the remaining tissues of the seal do indeed have a high metabolic rate? The answer, rather surprisingly, is 'no'. Seals concentrate their fat in the blubber layer. Almost no storage fat is found elsewhere in their bodies. In fact, the total fat content of seals may not be as high as other mammals. A seal in peak condition may have up to 60 per cent of its body weight as blubber. On the other hand, a fit human has between 15 and 20 per cent fat and an obese person may have up to 85 per cent fat, leaving the seal looking relatively slim.

Lavigne and his group (1985) produced a generalised model of the energetics of a hypothetical harp seal population. This population consisted of a million animals, from pups of the year to animals up to age 30. Mortality was subtracted from the population at two-weekly intervals so as to create a realistic age structure. The energy budget for an individual harp seal, from birth to age 30 was then constructed. This varied with age, depending on whether the animal was immature or mature. For mature animals the budget also varied with sex and reproductive state. Energy required for growth was calculated and fed into the model.

Starting at birth, the growth due solely to the energy contained in its mother's milk was calculated. At weaning, nine days after birth, the pup begins a five-week fast. During the sixth week it begins to feed again and regains body weight. Growth was then assumed to continue till the animal reached sexual maturity. After the onset of sexual maturity the lean body mass was considered to continue to grow for some time, whereas the blubber mass was assumed to follow the observed pattern of seasonal growth.

Energy costs of basal metabolism and activity (based on laboratory observations) were estimated for each fortnight in the year, while for mature females the costs of reproduction, growth of the foetus, the heat increment of gestation and lactation were calculated. The energetic costs of feeding were calculated as 20 per cent of the metabolisable energy. Faecal and urinary energy losses were deducted. The energy requirements of known-age individuals were then multiplied by the age distributions in the theoretical population to give the energy budget for the entire population.

Having built this model, manipulating the parameters allowed some interesting conclusions to be drawn. Changes in natural mortality, fertility and mean age of maturity produced only small changes in the *per capita* energy requirements of an unexploited population with a stable age structure. *Per capita* requirements varied from 2.63 million to 2.76 million kcal per year. Estimates of population energy requirements varied with changes in the population size, basal metabolism and the energy cost of locomotion. For the entire population, a 10 per cent change in population size resulted in a 10 per cent change in population energy requirement, as would be expected, but it required a 19 per cent change in basal metabolism, or a 23 per cent change in activity to cause about a 10 per cent change in energy requirements.

While this tells us quite a lot about a seal's energy requirements it does not take us much further in answering the question we posed at the beginning of this section: How much does a seal eat? But now we can see that this was not a very meaningful question in the first place. A seal, like any other animal, requires a certain amount of energy for its vital activities. This energy may come in different packages and these will decide how much food is actually consumed.

Harp seals feed extensively on the shoaling fish, capelin. Capelin sampled in January have an energy content, or caloric density, of 2.60 kcal/g. On this basis, the average energy requirement through the year would be satisfied by a consumption of between 0.08 and 0.91 tonnes of capelin per year for each seal (assuming that the seal realised about 88 per cent of the energy contained in its food). But the energy content of capelin varies considerably throughout the year, from a maximum of 2.79 kcal/g in December to a minimum of only 0.91 kcal/g in June and July. Such changes in energy content will affect the seal's appetite — the less satisfying the food, the more it will eat. Moreover harp seals do not feed only on capelin. Other fish and invertebrates have different energy contents, and differing proportions of these energy contents can be made use of by the seal. Lavigne has calculated that the biomass of food consumed per year for his average harp seal might vary from 0.9 tonnes if it were feeding exclusively on fish to 2.8 tonnes if it fed exclusively on invertebrates.

The question 'How much does a seal eat?' is unanswerable in a general sense. What we can say with some certainty is that the amount of food consumed by seals is not in any way exceptional for a carnivorous mammal in similar conditions. Seals are not, as has often been suggested, especially heavy eaters, or poor converters of fish flesh.

DIVING

In order to exploit the food that exists at various levels in the ocean it is necessary for seals to be proficient divers. Their locomotory adaptations make them fully mobile in all three dimensions of the watery environment but for the depths to be fully exploited, the seal's body needs to have modifications to enable it to stay beneath the surface for extended times and to deal with the effects of pressure at depth.

Although mammals absorb oxygen from solution in the fluid film that coats the respiratory epithelium lining the alveoli, the terminal divisions of the lungs, no mammal can obtain its oxygen from solution in a watery environment as fish do. Vertebrate lungs will operate effectively only in the presence of high concentrations of oxygen; air contains 21 ml of oxygen per litre while sea water saturated with oxygen contains only 8 ml per litre. Lungs, which are essentially greatly-divided sacs, cannot be filled and emptied fast enough to extract the required amount of oxygen from such low concentrations. The gills of an active fish, such as a mackerel, are bathed in a continuous stream of water; the faster the fish swims, the greater the flow over the gills and the greater the rate of oxygen extraction. Such compensation would not be available with a lung in water and hence we find that lungs are effective only in air.

In consequence, seals like other marine mammals have to rely on enhanced breath-hold capacity to sustain them while diving. This has been achieved through both anatomical and physiological adaptation.

As a first necessity, seals must be able to keep water from entering their lungs and respiratory passages when submerged. When a seal dips its head beneath the surface, its nostrils close automatically. Indeed, this is the relaxed position, the nostrils normally being held closed by the tone of the muscles; contraction of a pair of muscles (the nasolabialis and the maxillonasolabialis) opens the nostrils when the seal wishes to take a breath. When submerged the pressure of the water acting on the slit-like nostrils closes them even more securely. When it is necessary for a seal to open its mouth under water as when, for example, it seizes prey, the back of the mouth is closed off by the soft palate and the tongue. The flat medial surfaces of the two arytenoid cartilages of the larynx press against the epiglottis to prevent food entering the trachea when swallowing; this mechanism effectively keeps the glottis watertight, but there is anyway probably very little water in a seal's mouth when it swallows.

The lungs of a seal are not very obviously different from those of a terrestrial mammal, but there are some subtle differences. The seal's lungs tend to be relatively slightly larger; this is associated with the fact that the thorax, having fifteen pairs of ribs, is slightly longer than that of the average mammal, which has thirteen pairs. The lungs are approximately equal in size and have three main lobes, the right lung having a small additional lobe. The trachea branches into the two bronchi just before entering the substance of the lungs. These bronchi divide into bronchioles which after further branching finally terminate in the alveoli where the gaseous exchange takes place. The final two or three generations of branches of these small airways have their walls reinforced with muscle and irregular rings of cartilage, similar to, but on a smaller scale than, those that reinforce the trachea.

A final feature of the respiratory system that is characteristic of seals is the very oblique diaphragm (Figure 2.5). This is attached posteriorly to the dorsal wall of the abdominal cavity at about the level of the second lumbar vertebra and anteriorly to the xiphisternum, the last element of the breastbone or sternum. Because the bones of the sternum are very short and the thorax is not very deep the diaphragm assumes an oblique position in the body cavity. We shall see the significance of this shortly.

Breath-hold capacity can be increased by taking more oxygen down with each dive. A human diver will breathe deeply — hyperventilate — before diving, and descend with lungs full of air. There are disadvantages in this. For a start, full lungs increase buoyancy and so make it more difficult to descend; secondly, there are pressure problems associated with diving with full lungs. Seals hyperventilate before diving, but they expel most of the air from their lungs before they go down, and hence they do not depend on air in the lungs for their oxygen supply when they dive.

Besides being stored as a gas in the lungs, oxygen can be carried in physical solution in the blood and tissue fluids, or chemically bound to haemoglobin in the red blood cells or to another respiratory pigment,

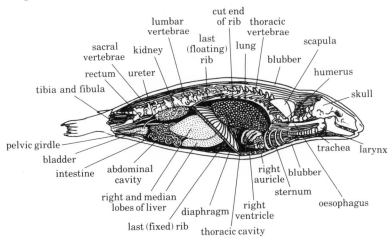

Figure 2.5 The position of the diaphragm in a seal.

myoglobin, in the muscles. In seals the major store is carried in the blood. Seals have greater blood volumes than terrestrial mammals. A Weddell seal, for example, has about 150 ml of blood per kilogram bodyweight, about twice the value for Man. Furthermore, seal blood contains more haemoglobin than human blood — about 1.6 times as much. The combined result of this is that the blood oxygen store per unit of body weight is about three or three and a half times that of Man. Gerry Kooyman (1981) has pointed out that because blubber is more or less inert and represents about 30 per cent of the seal's body weight, a more realistic comparison might be to lean body weight, in which case a seal's blood oxygen store would be about 5.3 times that of Man (though it should be borne in mind that an obese human may have about the same proportion of fat — though differently distributed — as a seal). Not only does the seal have more haemoglobin in its blood than Man, it also has very much more myoglobin in its muscles. This protein, which resembles haemoglobin in its ability to combine loosely with oxygen, is what gives muscles their red colour. Weddell seal muscle, containing about ten times the myoglobin concentration of human muscle, is almost black.

The diving capacity of seals is prodigious. Average dives of small species such as harbour seals and harp seals last in the order of five minutes, increasing to ten for the larger Weddell seal and as much as 19.2 minutes for the very large northern elephant seal. Maximum dive durations are 28 minutes for harbour seals, 15.8 minutes for harps, 73 minutes for Weddells and 47.7 minutes for the northern elephant seal (Lavigne and Kovacs, 1988). Information of this sort has been obtained by attaching recording apparatus to a seal, turning it loose to swim, dive and feed freely, and then retrieving the recorder when the seal next returns to the land or ice.

This technique was developed by Gerry Kooyman, working with Weddell seals on the permanent ice shelf of the Ross Sea in Antarctica. This was a good setting for the work, as the seals were very tolerant of their human experimenters. Because access to the water and egress from it was by only a few holes or cracks in the ice, the experimenters could be fairly sure where the seal carrying their apparatus would emerge after it had been liberated, thus making the recovery of the apparatus (and the experimental data) more certain.

Kooyman's first time depth recorders, or TDRs as they became known, were very simple instruments. They consisted essentially of Bourdon tubes (the sensitive elements removed from pressure gauges), glass discs greased and dusted with fine charcoal, and one-hour kitchen timers. These were enclosed in a brass case and fitted to the seal with clips. The first seal Kooyman experimented on was captured at Cape Armitage and transported to a hole Kooyman had made in the ice near his base at McMurdo Station. Here it was fitted with the TDR and put back into the water. The seal made a short dive of about three minutes, returned for a few breaths and then disappeared. It seemed the seal and the instrument pack had gone for good but, by great good fortune, a colleague of Kooyman's was counting Weddells at an ice crack at Cape Armitage where the experimental animal had been captured. He was surprised to see a seal emerge from the water with a TDR on its back, but acting with commendable initiative, removed the instrument and returned it to Kooyman. The recorded profile, scratched by a stylus on the carbon-dusted glass plate as it rotated on the timer, showed that the seal had swum the 1,500 m from its release point back to Cape Armitage beneath the ice in 26 minutes, at variable depths, but not exceeding 55 m (Kooyman, 1981).

Later TDRs were much more sophisticated instruments and combined several functions. It is now possible to monitor not merely time and depth, but heart rate, blood gas levels, hormone levels and brain activity and to record all these observations electronically. The instrument packages are contained in small pressure housings fitted by harnesses to the seals. A very great deal of what we know of the underwater activity of seals has come from these studies on instrumented Weddells swimming free beneath the ice.

Weddell seals make two kinds of dive. One type, identified as exploratory dives, consist of relatively shallow dives, with an average maximum depth of 130 m and durations of between 20 and 73 minutes. Hunting dives last 8–15 minutes and descend to between 200 and 400 m. A few dives were deeper than this, near 600 m, but these are rare (Kooyman, 1966).

Other seals have been investigated in a similar way, but few are so easy to capture and recover as Weddells. Seven Hawaiian monk seals were fitted with TDRs at Lisianski Island and over 4,800 of their dives recorded. Most were in the range 10–40 m but some were as deep as 121 m. The depths to which the seals dived corresponded with the depths at which known prey of monk seals occurred (DeLong et al., 1984).

But the most remarkable results have come from a TDR that was fitted to a female northern elephant seal at Año Nuevo Point, California. In 1983, two lactating cow elephant seals were immobilised with ketamine injected with a dart-pistol. A TDR was attached to the ankle of one and a depth histogram recorder (DHR) to the ankle of the other. Both cows in due course weaned their pups and returned to feed in the sea. They were away rather longer than expected, the TDR animal being absent for 127 days and the DHR animal for 93 days. Whether this was the result of the attachment of the instruments is not known, but it does not seem very likely. The TDR record yielded quite remarkable information. From the time the seal went to sea until the TDR ran out of recording film eleven days later, the seal dived repeatedly and continuously for a total of 653 dives. On average, she dived 61 times a day, each dive lasting about 20 minutes followed by 3 minutes (plus or minus 1 minute) at the surface. The maximum dive time of 32 minutes was more than 50 per cent longer that the mean dive time. The mean depth of the dives was 333 m (plus or minus 43 m) with a maximum of 630 m, the greatest depth recorded for any seal. The dives gradually became deeper on the record by about 10 m increments until dives 12, 13 and 14 when the depths reached 108 m, 234 m and 338 m respectively. It was probably at that stage that the seal reached the edge of the continental shelf and was diving into deeper water. The DHR showed grouped records of 510 dives. Forty five per cent were between 199 and 442 m and 14 per cent between 442 and 667 m (Le Boeuf et al., 1986).

These results raise some interesting questions. Does the continuous diving for 11 days mean a non-stop feeding effort? Why did the seal dive as deeply during the night as during the day, for their prey (squid) is believed to migrate nearer the surface at night? Do these seals ever sleep, or do some of the dives represent sleep activity? Perhaps sleeping at depth is the safest strategy for a seal that is sometimes preyed on by the great white shark. Sharks' eyes are on the top of their heads and they may find their prey because it is silhouetted against the surface. By sleeping at depth the elephant seal might avoid such attacks (Le Boeuf *et al.*, 1986). One factor stands out: elephant seals at sea spend very little time — only 11 per cent — near the surface. This provides confirmation, if any were needed, that it is very difficult to make offshore observations of these animals.

But let us return to Gerry Kooyman's Weddell seals and review his summary of the physiology of their diving. In a 450 kg Weddell seal there are about 67 litres of blood, of which 23 litres are arterial blood about 95 per cent saturated with oxygen. The oxygen carrying capacity of the blood is 35 volumes per cent and metabolising tissues could extract some 19.1 litres of oxygen from this store. Another 11 litres of oxygen are stored in the myoglobin in the muscles, giving a total store of 30 litres. The average oxygen consumption rate is 250 ml per kg per hour, or a requirement of 1.9 litres per minute for our 450 kg animal. Hence, the 30 litres of oxygen should be consumed in about 16 minutes. However, we know from the TDRs that breath-holding can last for at least 73 minutes, so some special mechanisms must come into play.

What happens during an extended dive is that the seal functions as a heart-brain-lung system in which circulating blood is limited to these organs. All other tissues derive their energy from the usual aerobic pathways until the oxygen stored in the tissue is exhausted; they then have to function anaerobically for the remainder of the dive. They can do this because of modifications to the vascular system of the seal. No one who has opened the body of a seal will have failed to have been impressed by the structure of the blood vessels revealed. The veins around the liver form a huge baggy hepatic sinus, while the posterior vena cava forks into a great distended vessel like a pair of traditional Dutchman's trousers. Where these vessels combine to pass through the diaphragm there is a muscular cuff, the caval sphincter, which can control the return of blood

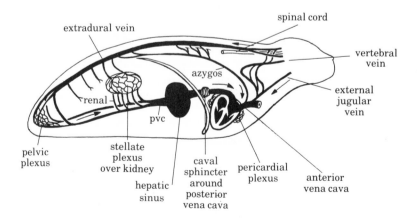

Figure 2.6 The venous system of a seal (Redrawn from King, 1983).

to the heart. What is not apparent, but equally significant, is that the return of blood from the head is mainly via a large vein lying above the spinal cord within the bony arches of the spinal column. This extradural vein is a speciality of seals (Figure 2.6).

When a Weddell seal embarks on a prolonged dive its heart rate falls from between 50 and 60 beats per minute to as little as 15 beats per minute. (In seals which are restrained and forcibly dived the heart may slow to as little as 4–6 beats per minute.) This is the phenomenon of bradycardia. Arteries to the peripheral parts of the body constrict, reducing the flow of blood through them. The blood flow to the brain, however, is unimpeded and remains nearly constant, though that to the viscera, skeletal muscle, skin and flippers is reduced by about 90 per cent (Zapol *et al.*, 1979). Venous blood, returning via the extradural vein, pools in the hepatic sinus and posterior vena cava, its return to the heart being controlled by the caval sphincter. In this way the best use is made of the oxygen stored in the blood; its flow is restricted to those tissues, the brain and heart, that cannot tolerate lack of oxygen. Once their oxygen stores are exhausted, the tissues outside the heart-lung-brain system must derive their energy from glycolysis, the process of converting glycogen to lactic acid, which does not require oxygen. This is a normal process in exercising muscles, even in conditions of plentiful atmospheric oxygen, for when a muscle exercises vigorously the blood may not be able to supply sufficient oxygen. However the accumulating lactic acid causes fatigue and there is a limit to how far glycolysis can continue. What differs in the diving seal is that the lactic acid can be tolerated and allowed to accumulate in the tissues without the ill effects that would occur in a less well adapted mammal.

Using blood samples obtained from the seals, Kooyman was able to show that no significant increase in blood lactate occurs until the dive time exceeds 25 minutes. For longer dives the lactic acid accumulates, reaching a value of about 230 mg per cent for dives of 60 minutes duration.

This indicates that the shorter dives made by Weddell (and probably other) seals are aerobic. The seal simply holds its breath and uses its oxygen stores as economically as possible. Of 4,600 dives measured, Kooyman found that only 3 per cent were in excess of 25 minutes. Only in the longer, exploratory, dives does the full diving response of bradycardia and anaerobic metabolism come into play. These longer dives require a protracted recovery time. A dive of 45 minutes results in a surface recovery period of 105 minutes, during which time the heart rate increases (tachycardia), oxygen stores are replenished, and the metabolites of anaerobic metabolism (mainly lactic acid) are disposed of by oxidation.

Another problem associated with diving, and not only with protracted dives, is the effect of pressure. A seal at 600 m below the surface is subject to a pressure of 60 atmospheres, or about 64 kg per square cm. This enormous pressure has little effect on the tissues of the seal's body. These are, in effect, liquids and are virtually incompressible, but difficulties arise wherever there are gas spaces in the body. The principal gas space in a mammalian body is the respiratory tract. However, the seal avoids problems here firstly by expelling most of the air from its lungs before it dives and then allowing its lungs to collapse, the space they previously

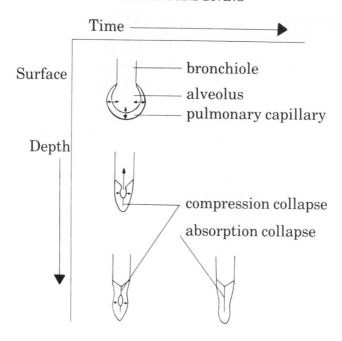

Figure 2.7 The progressive collapse of the alveolus in the lung of a seal as it dives. As the seal descends, gas is driven into the non-absorptive region of the bronchioles and bronchi; on further descent the alveolus closes, trapping a small quantity of gas. If the seal remains at depth long enough, this gas will be absorbed. (Redrawn from Kooyman, 1981b).

occupied in the rib cage being taken by the abdominal viscera which bulge against the oblique diaphragm. As pressure increases, air spaces in the middle ear and external auditory meatus are filled by the engorgement of blood vessels in cavernous tissue surrounding these spaces. This is an automatic reaction, depending simply on the external hydrostatic pressure. This is a contrast to conditions in a human diver, who must equilibrate pressures by passing air into the middle ear via the eustachian tubes. Should these be blocked, the human diver will suffer severely, for not only will the ear drums be subject to the external pressure of the water outside but so too will the cranial sinuses. The seal has no cranial sinuses and so is not affected in this way.

Direct pressure effects are therefore not serious for seals. What about the indirect effect that can have such catastrophic effects for human divers, the bends? A human diver breathing air at pressure gradually accumulates nitrogen in solution in his blood. A bend occurs when the nitrogen bubbles out as the pressure is reduced. The bubbles, when they occur in a joint, can give rise to excruciating pains. Bubbles in blood vessels can be even more serious, for they can cause a blockage to the blood supply which in a vital organ like the heart or brain can be fatal. But it has been found that bends can be caused in man not only by breathing air under pressure, but also by making repetitive dives with only short surface intervals between. Kooyman calculated that this could occur also for a Weddell seal even on a single dive if there were not some protective measures. He carried out experiments with a pressure chamber and found that the nitrogen tension in the blood always remained at the same low value, irrespective of the external pressure applied (Kooyman *et al.*, 1972). The reason for this was that the collapse of the lungs, as the abdominal viscera bulged against the diaphragm, drove the air out of the absorptive alveoli of the lungs into the non-absorptive bronchioles and bronchi (Figure 2.7). In this way the opportunity for nitrogen absorption is greatly reduced and this, coupled with the low absolute amount of nitrogen a seal takes down with it on a dive, provides the necessary protection against the bends.

3 Reproduction and growth

The time of birth is a critical one for all mammals and the crisis is exacerbated for a mammal that normally lives in the sea. The Cetacea and the Sirenia have solved this problem, and both give birth in the water. No seal normally does so, and so their reproduction more resembles that of conventional mammals, though in general it is modified so as to reduce the vulnerable time that must be spent ashore during the period around birth. Many of these modifications are behavioural in nature and affect the social structure of the seals, the subject of the next chapter. Others, however, affect the physiological aspects of reproduction and are dealt with here.

ANATOMY AND PHYSIOLOGY OF REPRODUCTION

The reproductive system of the male seal is relatively simple (Figure 3.1). As noted earlier, the testes are not contained within a scrotum, but are embedded in the groin, between the abdominal musculature and the muscle layer and blubber of the skin. Even when fully active, they are not visible externally. Since they are so well concealed, it seems strange that they are, in fact, nearly at the level of the seal's knee, but this, of course, is accounted for by the extreme shortness of the seal's thigh. The absence of a scrotum in seals may be associated with their humping method of locomotion on the ground. Scrotal testes could be at some risk when the seal was moving. On the other hand, in most mammals the testes lose their ability to produce viable sperm unless they are kept a few degrees cooler than the body core temperature, and this is usually done by suspending the testes in the scrotum. Seals have evolved a cooling method for their testes that involves a heat exchanger. The testes are enveloped in venous plexuses that communicate with the veins coming from the hind flippers. These supply relatively cool blood to the gonads. Blix and his colleagues (1983) showed that in the harp seal, where the testes lie beneath some 8 cm of skin and blubber, their temperature is 1–4° C lower than that of the body core.

The only accessory sex gland in the male seal is the prostate, which encircles the urethra just below the neck of the bladder. This has the

40

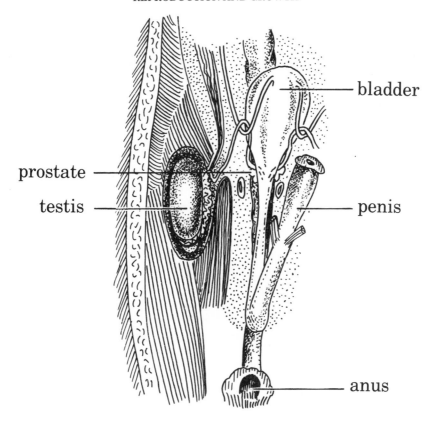

Figure 3.1 The reproductive system of a male seal.

spermatozoa when the seal ejaculates. The penis is contained within a pouch with the opening about midway beteen the umbilicus and the anus. Seals possess a penile bone, an os penis or baculum. This is the ossified distal part of the corpus cavernosum penis, the basal of the three blocks of tissue that make up the body of the penis. The baculum is of rather indefinite shape (Fig. 3.2), in contrast to those of fur seals, which have a characteristic architecture. Its function is not very clear. A baculum would stiffen the end of the penis in copulation; in elephant seals, at least, it seems that the penis is inserted before it is fully erect, and this would be possible only with a baculum. A baculum is present in a wide range of mammals, being found in all carnivores (except hyenas), insectivores, bats and primates (except Man). It is certainly not a marine adaptation as whales lack this bone.

The female reproductive system (Figure 3.3) conforms closely to the basic mammalian plan. The paired ovaries are each contained within an ovarian bursa, a pouch formed from a double fold of peritoneum. The fringed mouth of the fallopian tube follows a serpentine course and traverses the edge of the bursa before it joins the proximal end of its appropriate uterine horn. The ovarian bursa is voluminous and appears unnecessarily large for the gonad within it. As in all mammals, the ripe egg is discharged into the abdominal cavity before being gathered up by the fallopian tube, where fertilisation takes place. The uterus is

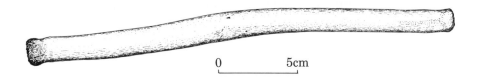

0   5cm

Figure 3.2 The baculum, or os penis, of an elephant seal.

bicornuate, or Y-shaped. The two uterine horns usually join near the uterine cervix, so that a small common uterus is present, but pregnancy occurs in one or other of the uterine horns. The two horns (and the two ovaries) alternate in function in successive pregnancies.

The cervix protrudes a short distance into the vagina. This is very stoutly built, with walls richly provided with white fibrous tissue. These thick walls may be an adaptation to the need to stretch to give birth to the large pups that seals produce, or perhaps they are a response to the presence of a baculum in the male. The vagina does not communicate directly with the exterior. There is what appears to be another equal-sized segment of the reproductive tract. This is separated from the vagina by the remnants of a hymenial fold and near its upper end can be discerned the urinary papilla and the clitoris, showing that it is an inward development of the vulva. This vestibule or urinogenital sinus opens to the exterior as a common furrow which also encloses the anus at its posterior (or dorsal) end. A similar structure exists in eared seals and in whales, and it is almost certainly an aquatic modification. Although the epithelium of the vagina and urogenital sinus mucifies when the seal is on heat, and there are many mucous glands present, there are no obviously distinct accessory sex glands in the female tract. The clitoris in many seals is strengthened by an os clitoridis, the female homologue of the baculum.

The position of the mammary glands is not obvious on casual inspection (amd their location has on occasion been known to remain a mystery even to a trained biologist). They are formed of two sheets of tissue which extend along the ventral and lateral surface of the abdomen. There is, of course, much variation in size, depending on whether or not the seal is lactating. In the Weddell seal, for example, the inactive gland measures about 30×16 cm in area and has a volume of about 0.6 litres. When lactating, the area of the gland changes little, but it becomes thicker so that the volume increases to about 2.8 litres. Most seals have a single pair of nipples, though in the bearded seal and the monk seals there are two pairs (and supernumerary nipples, either paired or unpaired, are not uncommon in many seals). Each nipple lies flat to the surface of the body, but erects when stimulated by the pup's nuzzling. Secretion of the milk is a fairly active process and milk may be seen trickling from the nipples of a lactating cow. Seal milk is white and very creamy, with a high fat and protein content. The milk sugar content is very low. When the physiology of lactation in the seal is discussed later (page 47) the reason for the peculiarly rich composition of seal milk will become clearer. Milk from the three species that I have sampled did not taste in the least fishy, but was not particularly palatable.

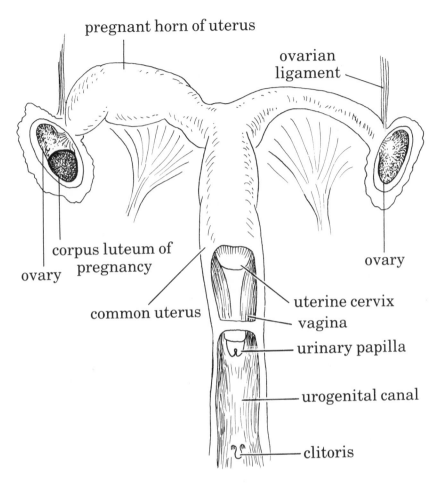

Figure 3.3 The reproductive system of a female seal.

THE SEXUAL CYCLE

Because the reproductive activity is cyclical, it is difficult to know where to start. I choose to do so with an experienced mature female that is just about to give birth. Birth itself is a very rapid process in seals. Although the new-born pup is large in relation to its mother's size, its absence of projecting limbs and generally streamlined form make it easy to expel from the uterus. The pup may be born either head or tail first and the time from the first visible onset of labour until the expulsion of the pup may be as little as fifteen minutes. The placenta may be delivered simultaneously or follow after a minute or so. Frequently the movements of the pup drag the placenta forth. The umbilical cord may break at birth, or the pup may drag the remnants of the placenta around with it until the cord is shed at the age of two or three days. The further development of the pup will be dealt with later.

Immediately after birth the female reproductive tract begins to regress and repair. The uterine horn where the foetus was established rapidly contracts and there is negligible bleeding from the placental scar. The corpus luteum that had controlled the pregnancy on that side begins to lose its glandular nature and develops fibrous tissue to become an inactive corpus albicans. In the ovary on the opposite side a follicle is rapidly maturing. The time between birth and mating is not known for all species of seal, of course, but typically it seems to be between three and four weeks. Some shorter periods, such as 8–12 days for the harp seal, are well attested, but much longer periods, such as the 2–3 months recorded for the harbour seal may be the result of misinterpretation of the habits of an animal which is difficult to observe.

As the follicle matures, other hormonal changes take place which make the female attractive to the male and lead her to accept the male's attentions. This is the period of heat or oestrus, which in suitable circumstances leads to copulation and the conception of a new foetus. In most seals copulation probably occurs several times while the female is on heat. Whether copulation induces the release of the egg from the ovary or whether this occurs spontaneously is not known for certain. The normal behaviour of seals around the breeding season would be likely to ensure successful fertilisation in either case. After fertilisation in the fallopian tube the fertilised egg cell, aided by the cilia that line the tube, moves down into the upper part of the uterine horn and divides to form a hollow ball of cells, a blastocyst.

The normal pattern in mammals is for the blastocyst to develop an intimate contact with the uterine wall, from which it draws its nourishment, so as to grow into the foetus. This does not immediately happen in seals, however. In all species for which good data are available there ensues a period after the development of the blastocyst when it lies inactive in the lumen of the uterus. The duration of this period varies from species to species, but it seems to average about three months. Meanwhile, the follicle from which the egg was shed has developed into a corpus luteum, a glandular body that produces the hormone progesterone that has an important role in controlling pregnancy. Despite the apparently active nature of the corpus luteum further development of the embryo awaits another cue.

It is not yet certain what this cue is, but in some species it seems to be associated with a change in the nutritional status of the seal, after it begins to feed again following the moult. Ian Boyd (1984) found that in grey seals the females which showed the earliest increase in body condition also had the earliest time of resumption of embryonic development. When this takes place the corpus luteum begins a phase of intense activity and hormone secretion. The blastocyst swells and develops an intimate attachment to the wall of the uterus. This is often spoken of as 'implantation' but in fact seal embryos do not implant; they remain superficial to the wall of the uterus at all stages. Nevertheless, the phrase 'delayed implantation' to describe the period of inactivity of the blastocyst has become too established in the seal biologist's vocabulary to be easily abandoned.

As the embryo develops it forms from the membranes surrounding it that characteristic mammalian organ, the placenta. Within the placenta the maternal and foetal blood vessels come in very close contact and nutrients and oxygen can be taken up by the foetus and its waste products passed to the maternal circulation, to be disposed of via the mother's kidneys. Initially, the blood vessels are separated by the epithelium of the foetal membrane (the chorion), the epithelium of the maternal uterine wall, and some deeper tissue (endothelium) investing the maternal blood vessels. However, as the seal's placenta develops, these maternal layers degenerate until only a thin layer of endothelium, less than a thousandth of a millimetre thick in many places, separates the maternal blood vessel from the foetal tissues. Richard Harrison and Judith King (1980) have speculated that the thinning of the placental barrier may be an adaptation to facilitate gas exchange if the mother dives with a slowed heart rate. The thin barrier may also allow maternal hormones to pass easily to the foetus, for it is found that in late foetal life and in new-born seal pups the gonads are greatly enlarged (Amoroso *et al.*, 1965; Bonner, 1955). These gonadotrophic hormones probably arise in the placenta itself (Hobson and Boyd, 1984).

Once a placental connection has been established the foetus grows rapidly. The placenta of seals is typical of carnivores generally. It forms a broad tubular band encircling the developing foetus and attached to the wall of the uterus near the middle of the uterine horn. Along its margins are strange lakes of degraded maternal blood — the marginal haematomata. Their function is not clear but they may be sources of iron for the foetus as the blood derivative that remains in the haematomata is a porphyrin which has lost the iron atoms of the original haemoglobin.

The purpose of the delay of implantation (or suspension of development, to use the term preferred by some workers) is not known. It has been suggested that, by allowing copulation to occur close to the time of parturition while still accommodating a period of active gestation appropriate to the size of the animal, it allows the seal to get through the two essentially terrestrial activities of its life cycle in only one vulnerable period on shore. This is plausible, but it should be noted that most seals have another terrestrial phase when they moult, and copulation could occur during this phase. Furthermore, many seals are capable of copulating in the water. Delayed implantation is not confined to seals; amongst other mammals it occurs in the armadillo, some deer and the badger, where the period of delay is far more variable than in seals.

The result of the delay is that the total gestation period of a seal is almost a year. In British grey seals, for example, this is made up of a period of about ten days after fertilisation while the blastocyst is being formed, a period of inactivity lasting 100 days, and finally normal foetal development for the next 240 days. The total period thus extends over about 350 days, the remaining 15 representing the interval between the birth of one pup and the conception of the next.

No individual seal has been followed in such detail in the wild and there are good reasons for believing that the length of gestation is to some extent under the female's control. If seals are prevented by disturbance from coming ashore at a breeding beach they will stay at sea. When the disturbance abates there may be a rush of females ashore and a sudden crop of new births. The left-hand side of the normal distribution curve of births against date has been condensed into a peak, and one is driven to the conclusion that the females are able to defer the birth of their pups until they are safely ashore. This would, of course, be a very useful trait for a marine mammal to evolve.

Towards the end of pregnancy the corpus luteum begins to regress. A fibrous core develops and the glandular tissue degenerates. By this time the corpus luteum from the previous pregnancy in the opposite ovary has regressed completely to form a fibrous scar known from its white appearance as a corpus albicans. These corpora albicantia may persist for a long time, even for the life of the seal, and can afford a useful record of its reproductive history. However, other things are happening in the ovary containing the corpus albicans. A new crop of follicles is maturing and by about the time of birth one of these is larger than the others and is destined to be the one that ruptures to produce the next season's egg and to turn into the active corpus luteum.

First and Last Cycles

I have described the reproductive cycle as though it were truly cyclical, with no obvious beginning or end. Yet for all seals there will be a first and a last pregnancy. The last pregnancy in a seal's life is probably a normal one. We know almost nothing about the factors that bring about a 'natural death' in seals. A likely cause will be physiological exhaustion resulting from the efforts of the breeding season. For males this will be the stress associated with competing for mates and defending territory; for females it is most likely to be the strain of lactation, which as we shall see, places truly enormous demands on them. Animals which succumb from these causes will most probably perish at sea; it is rare to find dead seals ashore.

At the other end of the reproductive life of the seal is its first pregnancy. The circumstances of this are almost as obscure as those surrounding death. It is not easy to distinguish virgin seals on breeding beaches, though the lighter build and unscarred appearance of first-time breeders can be recognised by a skilled eye. What does seem remarkable is that virgins do not seem to be seen ashore in the numbers that would represent their abundance in the population. Perhaps some of them mate at sea. So far as is known, there are no physiological peculiarities about these first-time breeders.

Twins

Seals, like sea cows and whales, usually produce only one young at birth. There are, however, many records of twins, perhaps because the event is so unusual that once noticed by a biologist it is almost always recorded. This is particularly true when the twins are born in zoos. Stephen Spotte (1982) has made a study of multiple births in seals. He recorded a pair of grey seals in the Louisville Zoological Garden (in Kentucky) the female of which gave birth to twins in two successive years. In both cases the twins were dizygotic sets consisting of a male and a female. The male pup of the first set was still-born, and the mother refused to suckle the second male after six days; it subsequently died. Even more remarkable, Spotte noted triplets that had been born to a grey seal in the Copenhagen Zoo in 1977 and another set of triplets in 1980. In both cases the triplets were born dead. Multiple still-births may be more common in the wild than is generally supposed but the live birth of twins is certainly rare. Only occasionally is it possible to follow the growth of seal twins and when this does happen it seems inevitable that one or both will die. The seal's reproductive strategy is highly tuned to maximum investment in one offspring over a short period and it seems that it is too much for the mother to cope with two pups.

Lactation

Seals are remarkable for the brevity of their lactation periods. Reducing the time needed ashore for both mother and offspring has obvious selective advantages for an animal as helpless and clumsy ashore as a seal.

Unfortunately not a lot is known about the duration of lactation in the most primitive seals, the monk seals. The better known of the two surviving species, the Hawaiian monk seal, has evolved on Pacific islands in the complete absence of terrestrial predators, so that its recorded lactation period, 5–6 weeks, may not be typical. Rather surprisingly, lactation is said to be even longer in the Mediterranean monk seal, 6–7 weeks, but very little information is available for this species. One author has claimed that the pups are suckled for at least four months but this claim has not been verified.

A more typical species, and one about which there is abundant information, is the grey seal. Sheila Anderson and Mike Fedak (1982) have made a very careful study of lactation in this seal. Lactation lasts between 16 and 21 days, during which period the pup's weight increases by 1.64 kg per day and the mother loses about 3.60 kg per day. The pup is fed every 5–6 hours, most of the milk being transferred in about six minutes, though a hungry pup will go on sucking for much longer. During lactation the average loss of weight by the mother is 65 kg, and she uses about 30,000 kcal/day to maintain herself and produce milk. (As in all seals that have been studied the grey seal mother does not feed herself during lactation.) The pup gains 30 kg during its period of dependence on its mother; it stores 10,500 kcal/day but assimilates 3,500 kcal/day more to provide for its metabolic requirements. If one assumes that the efficiency of transfer of milk into stored or metabolisable energy in the grey seal is the same as in the dairy cow, then the pup must receive about 17,000 kcal/day to assimilate the 14,000 kcal/day already accounted for. From the known energy value of grey seal milk this would be equivalent to nearly three litres of milk a day.

Of the 30,000 kcal/day used by the mother, only 17,000 kcal appear as milk, equivalent to a gross efficiency of 57 per cent. The daily resting metabolism of a non-lactating grey seal is 4,800 kcal/day, so lactating seals increase their energy use by a factor of six when they are secreting milk. Females weigh about 170 kg at the start of lactation, and lose about 65 kg, equivalent to 84 per cent of their stored reserves. As in many other mammals, lactation in the grey seal is the most critical part of the reproductive cycle in energy terms. Seals are remarkable in that this energy loss is concentrated into such a short period during which the mother fasts.

Ice-breeding seals show even more abbreviated lactation periods. The harp seal feeds its pup for only about nine days, during which the pup's weight increases from an average of 10.8 kg at birth at a rate of 2.5 kg/day to reach an average of 34.4 kg at weaning. Such rapid growth obviously demands the secretion of very rich milk. The fat content of harp seal milk increases from about 23 per cent at the start of lactation to more than 40 per cent towards the end. This is associated with a complementary decline in

47

the water content of the milk. Because the females fast while lactating, this increase in fat and decrease in water content may be important in maintaining the water balance of the fasting lactating female. The high water content of the early milk provides the new-born pup with free water at a stage when it is still lacking a proper insulating blubber layer and may be dependent on metabolising carbohydrate and protein to meet its energy demands. Later, when blubber is deposited and the pup loses less heat to the environment, it may switch to a fat-dominated metabolism, with the opportunity of using the metabolic water thus produced to eliminate waste products (Reidman and Ortiz, 1979; Stewart and Lavigne, 1980).

Even more remarkable than the harp seal is another ice-breeding seal, the hooded seal. This has recently been shown by Olaf Oftedal and his colleagues (Bowen *et al.*, 1985) to have the shortest known lactation period of any mammal! A hooded seal pup is weaned between three and five days after birth (most at four days), during which time its weight increases from an average of 22.0 kg at birth to 42.6 kg at weaning. This is an astonishing daily weight gain of around 7.1 kg, which means that the hooded seal mother supports a relative weight gain of her pup that is 2.5–6 times that of other seals (Table 3.1).

Some of the selective significance of these patterns of lactation and breeding strategies will be discussed in the next chapter.

GROWTH RATES AND ACCELERATED DEVELOPMENT

Seals were one of the first groups of wild animals for which accurate information on growth was accumulated. It is easy enough (in most cases) to determine the size of an animal in terms of its length or its weight but to convert this to an expression of growth it is necessary to have a means of determining the age of the specimen. In seals, the young are usually

Table 3.1 Birth weights and weight gain in a series of seals listed in ascending order of maternal weight. (Modified from Bowen *et al.*, 1985)

Species	Maternal weight kg	Birth weight kg	Daily weight gain kg, day^{-1}	Relative weight gain
Harbour seal	70	9.5	0.6	24
Harp seal	130	10.8	2.2	57
Grey seal	170	14.6	1.8	38
Hooded seal	179	22.0	7.1	145
Weddell seal	292*	28.7	2.3	33
Southern elephant seal	680	47.3	5.2	39

* This is lower than other weights recorded for Weddell seals, see p. 61.

relatively immobile and it is possible for observers to note the time of birth and then measure or weigh the pup at intervals, thus establishing a growth curve for the first few days or weeks of life, when growth is at a maximum. Older animals cannot be treated in this way. Marking, by hot iron branding, by cryogenic branding (the application of a brand cooled to about −70°C, which destroys the pigment cells in the skin, and leaves a white mark on the pelt), or by the application of metal or plastic tags (which do not seem to have a very long life in seals), can give information about the ages of animals, but only if a previously marked animal is captured. The discovery that the age of seals could be determined by examining the structure of their teeth changed this and allowed accurate studies of growth to be made over the whole life span.

This technique was discovered simultaneously and independently by two workers, Victor Scheffer, working on northern fur seals in the Pribilof Islands (Scheffer, 1950), and by Dick Laws, working on Southern elephant seals in the Antarctic (Laws, 1952, 1953a). The canines of many seals, such as elephant seals, are open-rooted, with a pulp cavity in which dentine is continuously deposited throughout the life of the seal. Even in those seals where the pulp cavity closes off almost completely as the seal becomes older, such as grey seals or hooded seals, cement is still deposited around the root of the tooth throughout its life. Possibly because of the very strong cyclical nature of the seal's life, imposed on it by its breeding and moulting cycles, these deposits of dentine and cementum are laid down in a series of discrete layers, similar to tree rings. When a thin ground section of a seal tooth is examined, each year of its life is recorded as a complex pattern of rings. These patterns change when sexual maturity is reached and in females the patterns are different in years in which pups are produced from those for years when they are not. Thus, from a study of the teeth, a great deal of information can be gathered. The discovery of Scheffer and Laws has been applied to many species of seals and extended to a wide variety of other mammals; it has probably done more to advance the study of wild mammal populations than any other single technique.

Seal pups are relatively large and active at birth, and are said to be precocious. This is in strong contrast to the young of most other carnivores, which are often born in sheltered dens, blind and relatively helpless; such young are termed altricial. A new born bear (a very altricial species) may weigh only 1/600 of the weight of its mother, and a lion cub 1/160, but a new born elephant seal is about 1/15 and a harbour seal 1/8 of the maternal weight. Because birth and mating are very closely coupled, so that the gestation time is fixed at a little less than a year and this is diminished still further by the period of delayed implantation, it follows that seals must produce larger offspring by accelerating the rate of foetal growth in the larger species (Laws, 1959). An elephant seal has a foetal growth rate in terms of weight nearly ten times that of the small ringed seal.

As we have seen, the growth of the new born pup while it is being suckled by its mother is also very rapid, though of course it does not compare with the foetal growth. But this is a rather specialised kind of growth. The harp seal pup increases its weight from 10.8 kg at birth to 34.4 kg at weaning at a rate of about 2.5 kg/day, but much of this increase is accounted for by a straight transfer of fat from the mother's milk to the pup's blubber. It is difficult to measure the blubber alone but measurements are easily made of the weight of the sculp, the skin of the body together with the subcutaneous blubber. Sculp weights increase from about 30 per cent of the total body weight at birth to 60 per cent at weaning and of the weight gain of 2.5 kg/day, 1.9 kg is added to the sculp, almost all in the form of blubber fat, and only 0.6 kg to the carcase weight (Stewart and Lavigne, 1980).

This fat is the energy store for the newly weaned pup which it draws on in the period before it begins to catch its own food. Seals, once weaned, are entirely deserted by their parents. I should rather say their mothers, for the fathers play no part whatever in their care. This means that the pup has to be entirely independent and its rich fat store serves to bridge the gap between weaning and the development of hunting skills sufficient to bring it into a positive energy balance. A seal pup's hunting techniques are instinctive, but need to be practised before they are perfected. Michael Bryden (1969) has shown that an elephant seal pup fasts for 5–7 weeks before it begins to feed. I have often watched elephant seal weaners swimming in the shallows catching amphipod shrimps and small rock fish. Probably more energy is expended in catching such small prey than can be derived from them, but gradually the hunting excursions take the seals into deeper water and the prey captured becomes larger and more significant in providing energy and nutrients for growth.

A consequence of this is that there is a period of negative growth after weaning, when the seal loses weight. Indeed, there is often very little difference between the weight (or length) of a newly weaned pup and a yearling.

Another peculiarity of the growth of young seals (indeed, of marine mammals generally), is that the order in which the component tissues of the body develop is different from that in terrestrial mammals. The general mammalian order of development is bone, then muscle, then fat. In seals, however, it is fat, then bone, then muscle (Bryden, 1969), and the early development of fat makes possible effective thermal insulation and survival over the post-weaning fast.

LATER GROWTH

The general pattern of growth in mammals is for the sexes to show rather similar growth rates from weaning to puberty, when the male puts on a spurt of faster growth, and then for the rate to decline until the definitive body size is reached. Generally, puberty is earlier in species of smaller body size than in larger ones. Seals only partially follow this general pattern. In the harbour seal sexual maturity is attained between two and five years of age, almost all females being sexually mature by four years, at a mean length of 140 cm and a weight of 50 kg. Males become sexually mature between three and six years, most maturing by five years when they are about 155 cm long and weigh about 75 kg. By five years of age almost all females are fully grown, but males continue to grow until they are nine or ten years old (Bigg, 1969). Ringed seals reach sexual maturity at about seven years in males and six in females. By analogy with most other mammals, one might expect that the huge elephant seals would take much longer to reach sexual maturity. This is not so, however. At South Georgia females reach puberty at about three years of age and a weight of about 250 kg, while the males reach puberty at about five and 1,500 kg (Laws, 1953b).

Interestingly, at Macquarie Island puberty is delayed on average about a year and a half in both sexes and growth rates are slower (Laws, 1984). Both sexes continue to grow after puberty, but the males grow faster, and continue to grow for longer, than the females, resulting in the remarkable difference in size (dimorphism) in this species. A pubertal elephant seal has little opportunity to breed, because of the tightly organised social structure of the species (Chapter 4). Social maturity is not reached (in an undisturbed population) until the age of nine or ten and a weight exceeding 2,500 kg. Bull elephant seals continue to grow throughout their life, which rarely exceeds 20 years, and at the peak of pre-breeding condition can reach the astonishing weight of over 3,000 kg!

LONGEVITY

The inevitable sequel to growth is death. The ability to age seals accurately from incremental layers in the teeth has meant that a good deal of information has accumulated about longevity in this group. Ages recorded in captivity may bear little relationship to those of wild populations and, indeed, neither may the odd record of great age mean much to the population as a whole. Laws (1953b) found two very large elephant seal skeletons at Signy Island in the South Orkneys, one of which was found to be 20 years old at death, the other 18. Yet it is certain that very few elephant seals, even in an undisturbed population will reach an age of much more than 15. The stresses on an active breeding bull elephant seal are extreme and few will survive more than a few breeding seasons as a harem master. Females, on the other hand, are subject to different stresses — those of bearing and feeding a pup. The oldest female elephant seal in a sample of 84 collected by Laws was 17 years old.

Probably most seals have effective life spans (once they have cleared the hurdle of the first few years) of around 20 years. Laws believed that the average expectation of life of a female elephant seal, once she had reached three years old, was a further ten years. Grey seal bulls may reach 26 years, and cows 38 years (Platt *et al.*, 1975), bearded seals 25 and 31 years respectively (Benjaminsen, 1973) and the little Baikal seals 52 and 56! (McLaren, 1984). It is noticeable that in all the determinations (except that for the elephant seal) the female has a slightly greater longevity than the male, a general mammalian characteristic and one which throws some light on the comparative stresses of the different reproductive roles of the sexes.

4 Breeding patterns and social organisation

Seals are not social animals in the sense that a herd of elephants or a pack of wolves are social. For the most part their social interactions are confined to the periods when the individuals must aggregate — to produce their young, to mate or to moult. Outside these periods, when the seals are dispersed at sea feeding, they seem to live solitary lives. Seals may congregate at a concentrated food source, a salmon run, for example, or a fish farm rearing cage, but there are no accounts of co-operative feeding or regular associations between individuals. However, I should introduce a note of caution here. We really know very little of the life of seals away from their breeding sites and it is possible, though not likely, that social relations exist of which we are unaware.

As we noted earlier, seals have not carried their adaptation to the aquatic environment to the point of producing their young at sea; they must return to land (or to ice) to give birth. True seals, together with their cousins the fur seals and sea lions, are the only mammals that show this combination of offshore marine feeding and terrestrial breeding. Those same anatomical and behavioural adaptations that make the seals such elegant and efficient hunters at sea render them clumsy and inefficient on land. Their life has to be a compromise between harvesting the riches of the sea and coping with the problems of a body adapted to water on a solid substratum when they come ashore to breed. True seals exhibit more variable mating habits than do fur seals or sea lions. In part this is due to the wider range of habitats occupied by true seals, but there are also innate differences.

Limited terrestrial mobility makes seals vulnerable to predators when on land. There are, of course, predators in the sea, too (sharks and killer whales or even other seals) but in the water the seal can meet an aquatic predator on equal terms. Because of this, seals are constrained in their choice of areas where they can haul out to produce their pups. Ideally, they need to choose a site that has no terrestrial predators, or provides the means for speedy escape to deep water. It is for this reason that we find seal breeding colonies on offshore islands or rocks, or on sandbanks in estuaries. Drifting floes in the pack ice provide another safe haven and by far the greatest number of seals breed on ice and are said to be pagophilic or 'ice lovers'. I shall consider the ice-breeding seals first.

ICE-BREEDING SEALS

Seals have adopted an ice-breeding way of life at least twice, and probably more often, in their evolutionary history. Life amongst the drifting ice has allowed seals to exploit the rich feeding grounds of high latitudes. Ice floes provide perfect security from terrestrial predators though in the Arctic the polar bear has developed a semi-aquatic way of life which allows it to swim between floes to prey on seals. Ice has many advantages for a breeding seal. It can afford immediate access to deep water; it provides a virtually limitless area for breeding; and a seal's reduced agility out of the water is much less important, since its body slides much more easily over snow or ice than over rock or sand (Stirling, 1975). Favoured areas of ice may attract tens of thousands of seals, but there is no crowding and the surface remains clean and uncontaminated. There are, however, some disadvantages. It offers relatively little shelter in what is inevitably a harsh environment and it acts as a heat sink. We have seen that this is of little consequence to the adults, invested in their insulating layer of blubber, but new-born pups, which have still to acquire their fatty overcoats, have an immediate and pressing need to develop blubber so that they can achieve a proper control of their body temperature and they can grow. Another disadvantage of ice is that it is a mobile, unstable substrate. Strong winds can cause ice floes to break up or raft over each other, crushing pups or throwing them into the water, from which they are unlikely to be able to emerge again.

The disadvantages of ice as a breeding platform can be overcome by accelerating the rate at which fat is transferred from the mother to her pup and radically shortening the period of juvenile dependence. We have already seen (Chapter 3) how the harp seal has reduced its lactation period to about nine days and the hooded seal to only about four days.

The Harp Seal

There are about 2.5 million harp seals in the world divided into three distinct stocks which breed in different areas — in the White Sea, near Jan Mayen Island to the east of Greenland, and around Newfoundland. Here the seals assemble to give birth around the time that the thin ice over the leads between the floes begins to melt in the daytime. This is in late February in the White Sea and Newfoundland and about a month later at Jan Mayen. Adult females form aggregations, known as whelping patches, of several tens of thousands on floes of one-winter ice. Although the seals aggregate, they do not seek out each other's companionship, maintaining a distance of several metres between each seal by snarling displays with the head held vertically.

Within a day or two of arrival on the ice the female gives birth. As in all seals, this is a very rapid process and is not preceded by any obvious straining. Once the pup has been delivered (usually tail first) the female turns quickly, leaving a characteristic trail of blood — the birth spiral — on the ice, so as to bring herself into nose-to-nose contact with her pup. At once she sniffs at her pup, learning its individual odour and establishing a bond with it. The pup soon begins to bleat and its voice is another character that the mother learns to associate with her offspring. Its visual appearance or its location on the ice are probably of little importance in maintaining the link. It is important that this link is established and maintained, for female harp seals will feed only their own offspring. If the bond is not established at this critical period immediately following birth, perhaps because the female is forced to leave the ice, then the pup will starve.

The pup is born in its natal coat, or lanugo, of white fur, from which it derives the name of 'white coat'. At birth it is a skinny creature, measuring some 92 cm in length and weighing 9–10 kg. It lacks any blubber beneath the skin and initially it generates a little heat by shivering. This is not its only way of generating heat, however. Beneath the skin over the shoulders and neck and surrounding the venous plexuses of the kidneys and around the heart there are deposits of a tissue known as brown fat. This has the ability to produce heat by the oxidation of lipid stores. Brown fat is found in the new-born young of many mammals and is also important in hibernating mammals when they awaken. Its role in the ice-breeding seals is an important one, for without it the skinny pup would soon cool below the point of no return.

A pup begins to search for the nipple sometimes within a few minutes of birth but it is usually a couple of hours or so before the female lets down her milk and suckles it. A suckling bout may last 5–10 minutes or up to half an hour. Durations of suckling are difficult to determine, as a pup may continue to suck vigorously after the milk has ceased to flow. As we noted earlier, the milk produced at the beginning of the lactation is less rich in fat than that at the end — some 23 per cent fat compared with 40 per cent (Lavigne *et al.*, 1982). As the growth rate of the pup remains nearly constant it has been suggested that the frequency of suckling may decline, so that the total daily caloric intake remains the same.

Females stay with their pups almost continuously for the first few days after birth, defending the area around them from other females or pups that may approach too closely. Later the mothers spend longer away, resorting to the water by way of a hole in the ice or through a lead between floes. However, they seem to stay fairly close and Dave Lavigne and Kit Kovacs, in their excellent book *Harps and Hoods* (1988), suggest that they stay in visual contact with their pups. When a female does return to suckle her pup she probably identifies it first by the sound of its voice, but then by its smell. The nose-to-nose contacts between a mother seal and her pup are perhaps the most characteristic sight in a breeding colony.

When not feeding, the pup spends its time sleeping, waking only to call to its mother for food. Weaning is an abrupt process. The mother simply fails to return to her pup following a normal period of absence. There appears to be no other change in the pattern of suckling. This abrupt change in behaviour is brought about by hormonal changes in the female, as the follicle that is about to ovulate in her ovary matures. The pup, of course, knows nothing of this and continues to call to its mother for several days, before settling down to a period of quiescence.

Up until this stage the males have played no part in the breeding assembly. Males begin to appear on the ice soon after the females and form small groups around breathing holes or leads. Like the females, the males are aggressive towards each other and the seals in a group are well spaced out. As the females begin to come into heat, the males begin to circulate through the whelping patches. Mating appears to be a fairly promiscuous affair, with little evidence of pair bonding. Males chase females over the ice and snap at their hindquarters but this seems to be the extent of their courtship. Mating almost always takes place in the water, the bull gripping the cow's neck with his teeth while grasping her shoulders with his flippers. It is not known whether each female mates once only, or whether she mates several times with one or more males. Neither is it known how the males compete with each other for the females. During the pre-mating period the males are very vocal under water and it is likely that some sort of dominance hierarchy is established then.

Within a few days of mating the adult harp seals leave the whelping patch to begin a migration that takes them to their feeding grounds. The seals from Newfoundland migrate up along the Labrador coast to the Davis Strait and Baffin Bay, with smaller numbers travelling to Hudson Bay (Figure 4.1). Here they disperse until in the following year their migration takes them in the reverse direction, back to the ice fields where

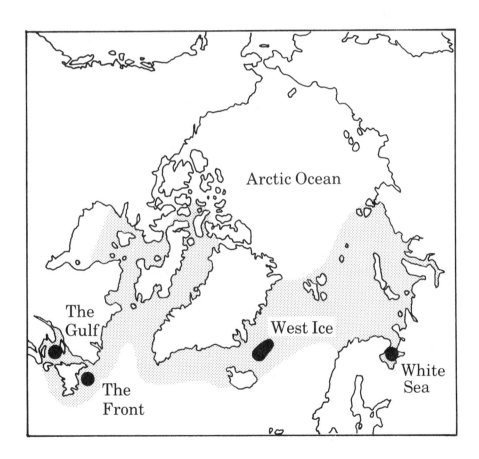

Figure 4.1 Breeding areas and migration routes of harp seals.

the whelping patches are formed. The entire intraspecific association of this species is thus condensed into a period of about two weeks during which the birth of the pups, their suckling and the mating to produce the next generation take place. Pair bonding is the briefest possible to allow mating to take place; the mother-young association lasts only for the lactation period; and there is no paternal association whatsoever.

The Hooded Seal

Hooded seals share much the same distribution as harp seals around the north-west Atlantic and east of Greenland (Figure 4.2). However, outside the breeding season hooded seals are not often found together with harps. They tend to feed further offshore in deeper water than the rather coastal harp seals. When the leads begin to thaw in the ice off Newfoundland and Jan Mayen and the harp seals congregate at their whelping patches, the hooded seals also gather for breeding. Besides the breeding areas which

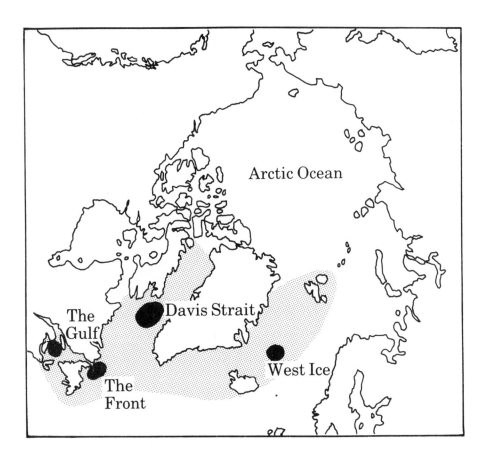

Figure 4.2 Breeding areas of hooded seals.

they share with the harp seals, there is a third breeding patch in the Davis Strait. Although this was known to nineteenth century Scottish sealers it had been overlooked until rediscovered in the 1970s by Canadian biologists.

Hooded seals are not as abundant as harps — there are probably about half a million of them — and their breeding aggregations are neither so large nor so dense as those of harp seals. They are larger than harp seals, males weighing about 300 kg and females about 179 kg (both sexes of harp seals weigh about 130 kg). When the females haul out to give birth it is well away from other females and usually some distance from the water, in the centre of a floe. Lavigne and Kovacs (1988) have pointed out how birth is a more difficult process for the hooded seal mother than for the harp seal. Strong contractions are seen before the appearance of the pup and after the delivery the mother does not turn towards her offspring, but lies motionless, as if exhausted.

This difficulty may be caused by the much larger relative size of the hooded seal neonate. At a birth weight of 22 kg it is one-eighth of its mother's weight, compared with one-thirteenth for the harp seal. The pup is relatively, as well as absolutely, larger because it is even more precocious than the young of the harp seal. It has moulted its natal coat while in the uterus and arrives in the world in a luxurious pelt (which it will wear for the next 14 months), blue-grey on the back and silvery on the flanks and belly. From this it has received the name blueback from the sealers. Besides having a yearling coat, the blueback is born with a thin blubber layer beneath the skin, a feature unique amongst seals which otherwise lack blubber entirely until they lay down fat from their mothers' milk. The pups are capable of much more co-ordinated movements than harp seal pups. Finally, male pups are larger than females at birth and grow faster to result in the marked sexual dimorphism seen in the adults.

The mother hooded seal remains with her pup for the short lactation period, which as we noted earlier, is from three to five days. Almost immediately she is joined by one or more males, towards whom she is extremely aggressive until she comes on heat at the end of her lactation. The males display towards each other, using a pair of remarkable organs which are matched only in the elephant seals. In the adult male hooded seal the nasal cavity is enlarged to form an inflatable hood (from which the species gets its name) on the top of the head. This hood starts just behind the level of the eyes and when not inflated its tip hangs down over the front of the mouth. When the seal is excited, however, the nostrils are closed and the hood is blown up to form a vast sac about twice the size of a soccer ball. The hood is divided into two parts, an anterior and posterior, and air can be passed from one to the other. Seals sometimes inflate their hoods when lying quietly on the ice and have been described as playing with the hood, moving air gently from one part to the other.

Besides the hood, the bulls can extrude an extraordinary pink balloon from one nostril, usually the left. This is the very extensibly membranous part of the internasal septum which divides the right and left nasal passages. It is extruded by closing one nostril and blowing air into the hood. By muscular pressure the hood on the closed nostril side is prevented from expanding upwards and the balloon eventually protrudes through the open nostril (Berland, 1966).

These two display organs, accompanied by roars and a strange sort of pinging noise, made by shaking the balloon from side to side, are used by the bulls to establish dominance. If visual and acoustic displays do not decide the outcome, the bulls will resort to fighting, biting at each other with their large canine teeth and clawing with their fore flippers. Most large males bear wounds resulting from sexual fighting during the breeding season.

The result of such contests is to leave one successful male on the ice with the female and her pup. These triads look like family groups, but the bull is unlikely to have been the father of the pup with the female, since we have no evidence that any long-term bond is set up between male and female in this or any other seal.

Mating takes place at the end of the lactation period, after which the female departs to return to the feeding grounds. The bull, on the other hand, may seek out another cow-pup pair and fight for access to this female. This type of breeding behaviour has been described as 'serially polygamous' and involves a successful male mating with several females in the course of a single breeding season.

The Crabeater Seal

Harps and hoods are seals of the relatively accessible North Atlantic, and have both been the subject of important sealing industries. Not surprisingly, therefore, there has been a good deal of observation and research on these species. It is quite different with the crabeater seal, scattered over the vastness of the ice fields of the Southern Ocean, remote from any centres of civilisation and offering no economic incentives to repay research. To study crabeaters at their breeding season it is necessary to employ an icebreaker, or at least a dedicated vessel with the capability of entering the pack. Not surprisingly then, observations on breeding crabeaters are few and have become available only in recent years (Bengtson and Siniff, 1981; Siniff et al., 1979).

During the breeding season, which starts in September, the austral spring, adult male and female crabeater seals form pairs, often each pair on a separate floe in the pack ice and some 1–2 km apart. Originally it was thought that the northern border of the ice, where the floes were more broken, was the principal habitat, but recent observations suggest that crabeaters may also be found nearer the continental coast. The pups are born in September and October, with most births in early October. Lactation lasts about four weeks, during which the pup's weight increases from about 20 kg to about 113 kg, the mother losing 50 per cent of her weight as a consequence. During this time the male is very active in defending the area around the female for a radius of about 50 m from the attentions of other seals (or human observers!). Despite the wide spacing of pairs there is frequent competition between the males and all breeding males bear wounds that are characteristic of intraspecific encounters. However, the females (which are about the same size as, or slightly larger than, the males) are also very aggressive to the males at first, and some of the males' wounds may result from bites from females.

As the female comes into heat so the male becomes dominant and it has been suggested that weaning takes place when the male drives the female away from her pup. Mating has not been observed, but the great efforts the males make to prevent the females entering the water suggests that it takes place on the ice.

The Ringed Seal

The seals considered so far have been seals of the drifting pack ice. The next example is an Arctic seal which is characteristically found in the fast-ice. The ringed seal is the commonest seal of the Arctic, with a population that may total six or seven million, though the real total is impossible to estimate (Stirling and Calvert, 1979). It has a wide circumpolar distribution though the population density is rarely high. The ringed seal is peculiar in that it is the only seal to construct a shelter, or lair, in which to bear its young. Ringed seals have well-developed claws which they use to scrape away the ice so as to keep breathing holes open. In the spring the pregnant female selects a place at the lee side of a pressure ridge, where movements of the fast-ice have caused the ice to raft up over itself. From a crack, or breathing hole, on the lee side, the female scrapes away at the snowdrift that will have accumulated in the lee of the rafted ice (Figure 4.3) to form the lair. Here she produces her pup (McLaren, 1958).

It has been suggested that the function of the lair is to give the pup some protection from Arctic foxes and polar bears. In this they are not very successful as in some areas predation rates by Arctic foxes may reach 58 per cent of all pups born, the foxes find the lairs by scent and dig down through the snow. A more likely function is to provide protection from the wind for the new-born pup. The ringed seal is small; males weigh between 65 and 95 kg, and females between 45 and 80 kg, and the pup is correspondingly small, weighing only about 5 kg at birth. For such a small animal, thermoregulation could be a serious problem in the open and the warmth generated by its mother in the confines of a small lair could be of considerable benefit to a blubberless pup (Smith and Stirling, 1975). Be this as it may, a closely related subspecies of the ringed seal that lives at Lake Saimaa in Finland, gives birth on the surface of the ice and not in lairs.

The pups are born in a white lanugo between about the middle of March and the middle of April. Lactation lasts for about 42 days (McLaren, 1958) but its length may be affected by the break-out of the fast ice. Pups born on stable ice may have a longer nursing period and wean at a greater weight than those from less stable areas. These differences in the length of lactation may permanently affect the size attained by the seal when it becomes mature. Small ringed seals have often been reported and sometimes have been given distinct specific or subspecific names but it seems likely that these small animals are the consequences of curtailed nursing periods.

Little is known about the circumstances in which ringed seals mate. It has been suggested that mating occurs soon after birth, or alternatively towards the end of the lactation period. (The latter would conform better with what is known of other seals.) Mating has not been observed, but is assumed to take place in the water, beneath the ice. Because the lairs are widely separated it seems unlikely that a male could defend more than one lair at a time. Males, however, often carry wounds which are most likely the result of sexual fighting, so some sexual competition probably

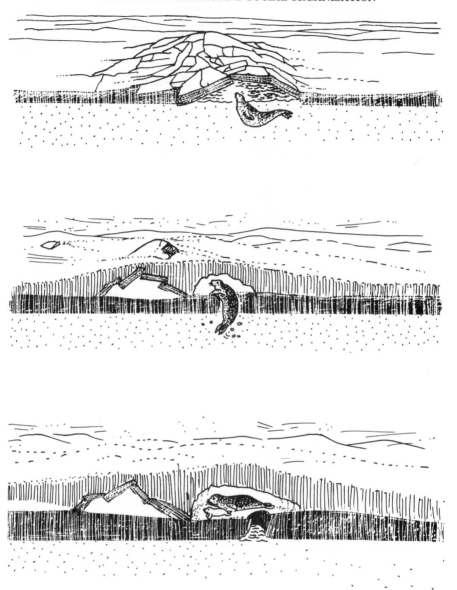

Figure 4.3 The breeding lair of a ringed seal.

does occur. Males become sexually mature at seven years old, while most females mature at five years, and this would imply that there might be fewer sexually active males than females, leading to a limited form of polygamy.

The Weddell Seal

The Weddell seal is another denizen of the fast-ice, but unlike the ringed seal, the Weddell is found in the deep Antarctic. Weddell seals are large animals, both males and females weighing around 400–500 kg. They breed in low-density colonies on the very stable fast-ice around the shores of the Antarctic continent and its offlying islands. During the pupping season, from September to November, Weddell seals form breeding assemblies along pressure cracks and tide cracks in the ice. The seals can keep breathing holes in the ice open by gnawing with their protruding upper canines and incisors, but they seem to prefer to use naturally occurring open water for breeding. The shortage of suitable cracks seems to cause a concentration of seals around them. Several females may share a single breathing hole or length of crack, but they remain well spaced out on the ice. Females with pups are more widely spaced than seals at other times of the year.

Pups weigh about 25–30 kg at birth and by ten days have doubled in size, and are weaned at around 40–50 days (Bertram, 1940), at a weight of around 110–140 kg.

The breeding males spend most of their time in the water beneath the cracks, where they defend what are rather unfortunately called aquatic territories against other bulls. The bulls vocalise, display and fight in order to establish exclusive access to the females using a crack or hole, and in so doing frequently receive wounds. Copulation takes place in the water (Cline *et al.*, 1971), though some preliminary courtship behaviour, consisting of the male orienting head on to the belly of the female as she lies on her side on the ice and emitting a repertoire of vocalisations, has been observed on the ice. The only copulation actually observed was seen through a television monitor located beneath a breathing hole. The copulating pair were at a depth of about 1–3 m below the ice in water some 40 m deep. The male grasped the neck of the female with his teeth and her flanks with his fore flippers, just as harp seals, or harbour seals do. The female was identified by the observers as one which had given birth 43 days previously, and was thus near the end of her lactation period.

Weddell seals are largely sedentary animals, so there is no great dispersion after the breeding season, though as the ice breaks up the concentrations around tide and pressure cracks disappear. In some localities, such as White Island near Ross Island off Victoria Land, the seals are found on permanent ice and make use of permanent tide cracks, resulting in very stable groupings.

LAND-BREEDING SEALS

There are only six species of seals that regularly breed on terra firma: the two surviving species of monk seals, the southern and northern elephant seals, the grey seal and the harbour seal. Some of the ice-breeding seals may occasionally breed on land (for example the hooded seal and the Weddell seal), and occasionally land-breeding seals breed on ice (grey seals do so in the Baltic), but in general there is a clear division between the two groups. The grey seal and the harbour seal are probably rather recently derived from ice-breeding ancestors, but for the others there is no evidence of an ice-breeding ancestry.

The Harbour Seal

Harbour seals are closely related to the ice-breeding spotted seal, or largha seal, which produces its pups on floes near the edge of the pack ice in the Bering, Chuckchi and Po Hai Seas. Spotted seals produce their young, clad in a whitish lanugo, between mid-February and April and feed the pups for 3–4 weeks. Harbour seals, having abandoned the ice-breeding habit, have been able to extend their range southward and are now the commonest seal of the cold temperate waters of the North Atlantic and North Pacific. They show a wide range of habitat, but are usually found as fairly concentrated colonies on sand- and mudbanks in river estuaries, or as more dispersed populations along rocky shores. There are even some freshwater populations in lakes in eastern and northern Canada and everywhere throughout its range the harbour seal has a tendency to wander up rivers.

The birth season varies widely. On the Cedros Islands, off Baja California at latitude 28°N, young are born in early February, while as one goes further north the pupping season becomes later in the year, March and April at the Californian Channel Islands, May along the Washington coast, and late July in southern British Columbia and Puget Sound. In the British Isles and the southern North Sea most pups are born in late June and early July.

Harbour seals are relatively sedentary animals, so there are no marked migratory movements to the pupping areas. In a typical estuarine habitat, such as the Wash in eastern England, harbour seals reguarly haul out on selected tidal sandbanks. These are the banks that are least disturbed by passing boats and the seals choose the scoured side of the bank, where the sand shelves off steeply into deep water. The seals begin to haul out as the crest of the bank emerges from the ebbing water, but usually edge down towards the water as the tide falls further, thus retaining an easy escape route.

There are no obvious changes in haul-out pattern as the pupping season approaches but once pups begin to appear the mothers defend the areas around them from other seals; rarely, a harbour seal mother will remain with her pup to defend it from a human intruder. Birth sites on sandbanks are usually situated near the top of the bank, often at a place where the slope of the bank changes. They are marked by a circle of trampled sand, 2–3 m in diameter, near the edge of which are to be found the expelled placenta and the compacted tufts of foetal hair which is shed before birth. The pup can swim soon after birth, as indeed it must if it has been born on a tidal bank. The pup can swim and dive efficiently from birth but is closely attended by the mother, who will push it beneath the surface if danger threatens or carry it on her shoulders if it is tired (Venables and Venables, 1955; Bonner, 1972).

In the rocky habitats it is less usual for the colonies of seals to be so large and mother-pup pairs are usually more widely separated. Pups are born on a sheltered beach, on an offshore rock or shelf, but almost always between tide lines. There is some evidence (Venables and Venables, 1955; Bonner, 1972) that births occasionally take place in the water. From what has been observed of the behaviour of new-born pups and their mothers it would seem that pups born in this way might well survive, but the practice does not seem to be common.

Cows suckle their pups at the water's edge, usually at ebb tide. Newby (1973) recorded an average duration for feeding of 73 seconds (range 25–160) in Washington State. Feeding intervals were 3–4 hours, which corresponded to local tidal cycles. Lactation lasted 4–6 weeks. In the Dutch Wadden Sea, Van Weiren (1981) found pups were suckled for 40–45 minutes on each low tide throughout the lactation period, which lasted for only 3–4 weeks. Between late July and mid-September weaned pups are rarely seen at haul-out sites and may be spending their time in the water, learning hunting techniques (Thompson, 1987).

Mating occurs around or soon after weaning (Thompson, 1988) and though copulation attempts are sometimes observed at haul-out sites, copulation generally occurs in the water (Allen, 1985). Bull harbour seals show marks of sexual fighting during the breeding season and it seems that fights take place in the water. It is likely that the breeding pattern in this species is similar to that in hooded seal — serial polygamy, where the male mates with several females in the course of one breeding season.

The harbour seal, more than any other species, has come to terms with living in proximity to terrestrial predators, including Man. This it has done by producing highly precocious young and greatly reducing the period that it needs to spend ashore with its offspring. Because of this, there has been no need for the harbour seal to shorten the period of its lactation, which in fact may have lengthened from the ancestral ice-breeding lactation (Bonner, 1984). Harbour seals show considerably more maternal care for their pups than any other seal, and an extended mother-young association may contribute to better survival of the young.

The Grey Seal

The other land-breeding seal with a pagophilic background, the grey seal, shows no such tendency. In one part of its range, the Baltic, the grey seal still breeds on the ice in triads of a cow and her pup together with an accompanying bull. Elsewhere these seals breed in large assemblies on beaches or grassy slopes, often several hundred metres from the sea. The timing of the breeding season varies greatly in this species and it has been noted that there are reports of grey seal pups being born in the United Kingdom in every month of the year. Generally, however, it is in January or February in the western Atlantic and from September to January in the eastern Atlantic, though the Baltic population breeds in February and March and an extinct population that once inhabited the Danish islands bred in January (Bonner, 1979).

Outside the breeding season grey seals are widely dispersed over their feeding grounds but as the breeding season approaches large pre-breeding assemblies, with bulls predominating, form near the breeding grounds. The females are the first to arrive. They do not take up a particular site at first, but move about until the birth of their pups, when they settle down and defend the areas around them. The bulls arrive as soon as the first females are ashore. They do not form territories as such, with recognisable boundaries, but compete for proximity to the females. Terrain has a very important effect on the number of females that a bull can control. In open country, such as the broad sandbanks of Sable Island off Nova Scotia the cows are widely spaced and the ratio may be of the order of one male to two females; where the terrain is broken, or restricted, as in rocky gullies, successful males can exclude others and the ratio may rise to one to ten (Anderson and Harwood, 1985). Where there are only a small number of females in a cove, it is usual for the bulls to station themselves in the sea at the approach to the beach; where the colony extends far inland from the beach, the bulls are ashore (Hewer, 1957; Anderson et al., 1975).

The area dominated by a single bull changes from day to day. Bulls may lie within three or four metres of each other, suggesting that the tolerance they will show to the proximity of other bulls may depend on the density of cows. Boundary displays are absent and fighting minimal (though intense when it does occur), so that dominant males conserve energy for a prolonged stay on the breeding grounds.

The pups are born in the white natal coat (a reminder of the ancestral association with ice), males weighing on average 15.8 kg and females a kilogram less. This difference in weight is maintained and increased throughout life, males reaching 330 kg and females only 170 kg. Immediately after the delivery of the pup, its mother turns round to smell it (Burton et al., 1975), exactly as the harp seal does. In this way the bond is formed between mother and pup and any failure of this process, perhaps caused by disturbance on the breeding ground, will lead to the death of the pup. Cows are very defensive towards their pups, biting savagely at other cows or pups which stray too near. They are even seen to defend the placenta against scavenging birds.

Cows may remain ashore with their pups throughout lactation or, more usually return to the sea between feeds, particularly if they have pupped near the beaches. Susan Fogden (1971) has described mother-young behaviour at crowded and uncrowded beaches. On an undisturbed beach the pup lies where it was last suckled, usually sleeping. A cow returning to feed her pup hauls out near where she left it and calls. The pup responds to its mother's voice and answers, whereupon the cow advances and finally identifies the pup by smell before settling down to feed it. This simple system breaks down on crowded, disturbed beaches where one finds many deserted, starving pups. This is probably the consequence of failure to establish the bond immediately after birth. There are many accounts of grey seals feeding pups not their own, so called 'adoptive feeding' (Smith, 1968; Fogden, 1968, 1971). Some of these adoptive mothers may be cows that have lost (or cannot identify) their own pups; others appear to tolerate additional pups as well as their own. However, this does not appear to be a compensatory mechanism to ensure the survival of the greatest number of pups — those pups that sucked from more than one cow did not thrive as well and spent less total time sucking than those which sucked from one cow only.

Lactation lasts from 16 to 21 days, and the cow comes into oestrus towards the end of this period. She is then mated by the nearest established male (Boness and James, 1979). Each female may be mated about three times, by the same or different males, and mating can take place either on land or in the water. The bulls show little discrimination in approaching cows; once some cows are in oestrus they will attempt to mate with any available female. Females respond aggressively to the male's attentions, though this reaction diminishes as they come into heat. The vocal complaints of a female being approached by a male attract the attention of other bulls and make it more likely that she is mated by a dominant male (Boness *et al.*, 1982).

There are wide differences between the copulation success of different bulls on the breeding grounds. At North Rona in the Hebrides Sheila Anderson and her colleagues (Anderson *et al.*, 1975) found that the three most successful bulls of 31 observed accounted for 35.6 per cent of all copulations. This implies that for some bulls there is a very high degree of reproductive success in the form of pups sired, with the consequent exclusion of others from the stock of breeding animals. The most successful bulls are those that can stay ashore longest, and some show remarkable endurance. This may extend over the full breeding season, a period of eight weeks, during which time the bull does not feed and loses weight at a rate of 2.2 kg per day. In such circumstances there is clearly a premium on being a large animal! The reproductive strategy of the grey seal is known as polygyny (the form of polygamy where one male has many females).

The cows, which have also not fed throughout the breeding season, leave the breeding grounds, having been mated and weaned their pups, for a lengthy period at sea to regain their body condition before hauling out to moult the following spring (Figure 4.4). The bulls drift away at different times through the season, only the largest staying all the time, but smaller bulls haul out towards the end. Eventually all the adult seals leave, and only the weaned pups remain on the breeding grounds, where they stay ashore for a week or two longer before entering the sea and feeding independently.

Monk Seals

Monk seals are the most primitive of the seals alive today and a careful study of their behaviour ought to provide much information on the behaviour patterns that have developed in other seals. Unfortunately it is not possible to carry out such a study. Of the three species that survived into the Recent era, one, the Caribbean monk seal, is extinct, and the other two have minuscule populations of less than a thousand each. No colonies are dense enough to allow intensive observation and much of what is observed may well be abnormal behaviour, forced on the remnants of persecuted populations.

Historical accounts indicate that both Mediterranean and Hawaiian monk seals in the Mediterranean breed generally in caves or grottoes but groups but we know nothing of the social organisation of these. Today monk seal in the Mediterranean breed generally in caves or grottoes but it has been suggested that they have been driven to this strategy by human persecution from the open beaches that they preferred. Pups have been reported from May to November and the lactation period is said to be 6–7 weeks. Hawaiian monk seals give birth between January and August on open beaches. Pups are about 16 kg in weight at birth and are clad in a black natal coat which is moulted to reveal the yearling coat, grey or black above and silvery below, at about 3–6 weeks of age. During the five- or six-week lactation period the female remains with her pup, without feeding. Throughout the breeding season adult males (which outnumber adult females by about three to one!) cruise along the beaches

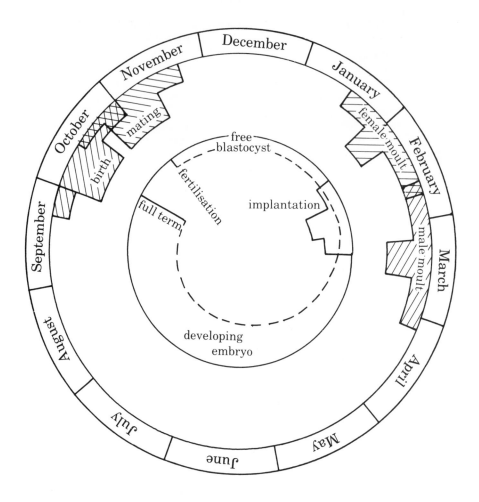

Figure 4.4 The breeding cycle of the grey seal.

searching for receptive females. Mating takes place in the water, and in one observed incident a female was severely wounded by the teeth of several males that attempted to copulate with her (Kenyon, 1981). Females are even known to have been killed by this 'mobbing' from amorous males, and it represents a serious problem in the conservation of this species (Chapter 9).

We can deduce rather little from what we known of monk seals. It appears that they are promiscuous breeders, like harp seals, though it is possible that in denser concentrations they would be serially monogamous. Polygyny appears unlikely. The occurrence of such a great excess of males in the Hawaiian species is puzzling; it may well be the result of disturbance which has led to a higher mortality of females.

Elephant Seals

Without doubt, the most impressive (if not the most visually attractive) of the seals are the elephant seals. Their huge size, with mature bulls of the southern species weighing up to 3,000 kg, is alone sufficient to compel attention, but in addition their breeding aggregations provide a spectacle which has fascinated observers since their discovery. Their study has provided insights not only into seal behaviour but also into mammalian behaviour in general, including that of Man.

There are two species of elephant seal: the southern elephant seal, found breeding on the oceanic islands of the subtemperate regions of the Atlantic, Indian and Pacific Oceans (Figure 4.5), with occasional small

Figure 4.5 Breeding locations of the southern elephant seal.

groups in southern Argentina and Tierra del Fuego; and the northern elephant seal, which breeds on islands off the coast from central California to Baja California (Figure 4.6). These two species are very closely related and their breeding patterns are similar, the main difference being in the time of breeding, which peaks in January in the northern elephant seal, and in October in the southern species. I shall describe events in the southern elephant seal.

Early in the southern spring in September the first of the pregnant female elephant seals begin to arrive ashore. They prefer relatively open sandy or shingle beaches and show no preference for sheltered coasts. The beaches used are traditional, the cows returning again and again to the same site (probably the ones they were born on, or on which they had

Figure 4.6 Breeding locations of the northern elephant seal.

their first pups). Already a few bulls will be present at favoured sites, but with the arrival of the first cows the bulls assemble quickly. The cows are gregarious and form groups, though individuals are aggressive to each other and adjacent animals never lie in actual contact with each other.

As the season advances the groups of females enlarge and coalesce to form crowds of several hundred females, with maximum numbers being present around 25 October (McCann, 1981). In favourable situations there may be thousands on one beach, the largest grouping I have ever seen being about 4,000 cows together. A cow gives birth to her pup about eight days after coming ashore. The pup is born in a black natal coat and weighs around 46 kg, or about one-fifteenth of the mother's weight of around 680 kg. This weight is doubled in eleven days and quadrupled by the end of lactation, which lasts on average for 23 days.

Meanwhile, there has been intense activity among the bulls around the groups of females. Bulls compete very aggressively for proximity to the cows, driving off intruding males. Usually this is achieved by threat alone. The bull elephant seal, like the hooded seal, is equipped with an inflatable proboscis. The development of this starts when the bull is about two years old but it is not fully developed until about eight years of age, when the bull is physically mature. This trunk consists of an enlargement of the nasal cavity, marked by two transverse grooves and with its tip overhanging the mouth. When excited, the proboscis is inflated, partly by muscular action and engorgement with blood, and partly by inflation from the lungs. With its forequarters reared up, its trunk inflated and its mouth wide open, the bull elephant seal produces a deep, throaty roar, audible for more than a mile away. In the northern species, this trunk is much longer and its tip is directed into the mouth cavity when the bull is roaring and this may give rise to the difference in the roar of a northern bull from that of the southern species. However, in the southern seal the role of the trunk seems to be mainly visual; animals with most of the trunk lost through fighting produce roars with the same sound quality as those with intact trunks.

If roaring is not sufficient to deter an intruder the display may continue with the bull rearing up so as to raise the anterior two-thirds of its body 3 m or more vertically in the air. Such a posture is highly conspicuous in the generally horizontal world occupied by the seals. Most seals when displaying aggressively raise their heads and necks — indeed, this is essential to provide the necessary mobility should the jaws be needed to bite an opponent — but only in the elephant seals has this gesture been exaggerated to the point where the fore flippers are raised so far clear of the ground.

The final stage of an aggressive encounter is when the two opposing bulls actually exchange blows and bites. As in most examples of male sexual interactions in animals, this occurs only as a last resort. Seamus McCann, in his careful study of the behaviour of elephant seals in South Georgia (1981b), found bites were delivered in only 1.9 per-cent of all aggressive behaviours. But when bites are delivered, they are serious. The two fighting bulls square up to each other, chest to chest, and deliver massive swipes and slashes with their greatly enlarged canine teeth. Most of the bites are received on the chest and shoulders, which in mature bulls are always covered in a criss-cross web of scar tissue derived from earlier encounters. This dermal shield is developed not only from previous encounters on the breeding grounds, but also from play-fighting as juveniles, an activity that begins in males within four weeks of birth. Bites on the chest or shoulders tear the hide and bleed profusely, but do not seem to cause their recipient much discomfort; however, should one bull overpower the other, bites can be delivered to the head, tearing away the trunk or bursting an eye. Even so, fighting rarely results in the death of an opponent. (In twenty years of observation, Burney LeBoeuf has recorded five deaths from fighting.) A bull that has been vanquished and is lying in a prone position ceases to represent a threat to the dominant animal, which usually allows it to escape with no more than a cursory nip or two to its hindquarters.

By displays and fighting, the bulls sort themselves out into a sort of hierarchy. Dominant bulls maintain their position on the beach, within the crowd of females; generally one bull, the beachmaster, is dominant over all others. He can move around freely within the group of cows without being challenged by other bulls. Other high-ranking bulls stay within the group of cows in fixed areas, but give way to the beachmaster (McCann, 1981b). Less dominant bulls are distributed around the periphery of the females, joining them whenever they get the chance, while the lowest ranking breeding bulls patrol the shallows off shore (Figure 4.7). It should be noted that these seals (like grey seals) do not strictly defend a territory with boundaries at which they display to other males. The groups of females (at least in their early stages) are mobile, and the dominant bulls follow them around, exerting their dominance in the general proximity of the females. For this reason, I have avoided using the term harem in referring to the groups of females, for a harem is strictly speaking a location, rather than the females contained within it. This strategy of the bulls may be termed 'female defence polygyny'.

The elephant seal cow comes on heat at 19 days after giving birth (Laws, 1956), and remains receptive for about four days (McCann, 1980), during which time she will be mated several times. Usually it will be the dominant bull that will be the first to detect and mate with an oestrus cow, since he is constantly moving about the group of cows and testing their willingness to mate. However, matings by other bulls are not infrequent and usually, when the cow finally leaves the beach to return to sea after about 30 days ashore, she will be mated by one of the low-ranking aquatic bulls. We can only suppose (since the pattern of terrestrial breeding dominated by a few males has evolved) that these later matings are not effective in fertilising the cow, which is probably already impregnated by the sperm of the beachmaster. McCann found that in the group of seals he studied the two top-ranking bulls accounted for 57 per cent of observed matings. Because of the strain of fasting (a beachmaster may be ashore without feeding for 90 days), coupled with the exhausting activity of defending a place on the beach, a beachmaster is unlikely to have more than a few seasons of dominance, though in a successful season he may pass on his genes to some 80 females or so. This means, of course, that there is a very uneven spread of reproductive success among male elephant seals.

When a female has finally escaped from the beach, she swims out to sea to enter a feeding period before her return to land once more in the southern autumn, in February, to moult. The cow has to feed voraciously

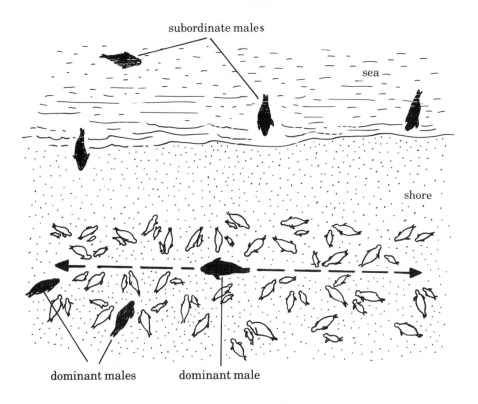

subordinate males

sea

shore

dominant males dominant male

Figure 4.7 The structure of an elephant seal breeding beach. The dominant male moves freely about within the crowd of females; less highly ranked males maintain a station within the females; subordinate males patrol the beaches just off shore.

to replace the body reserves depleted during the feeding of her pup. It is during this period that the suspension of the development of the blastocyst she carries in her uterus is taking place, and there are presumably advantages in not adding further stress to the female's system with a developing embryo during this period.

On Año Nuevo Island, off the Californian coast just south of San Francisco, Burney Le Boeuf has been leading a team of researchers who have made a very intensive study of breeding strategies in the northern elephant seal. Through a long-term programme of marking and recording, these dedicated workers have been able to follow individual animals from one year to the next and make observations on reproductive success.

The reproductive strategy of the male elephant seal is to seize every chance he can to mate with females while at the same time deterring any other bull from doing so. Bulls do not attempt only to mate with females in oestrus. From the time the females first appear on the beach at Año Nuevo, the bulls pursue them relentlessly, seeking to mate. There are no courtship preliminaries; the male approaches a female, throws a flipper over her side, grips her neck in his teeth and attempts to copulate. If a female protests and attempts to move away the male may try to subdue her by slamming his great weight down on her back and biting her more vigorously. As Burney Le Boeuf has pointed out, in these encounters, the outcome is usually bad for the females. Mounting can injure a pregnant female; it can prevent the formation of the mother-pup bond, with the consequent death of the pup; and it can disrupt suckling.

Not only are the attentions of the male potentially harmful. A 2½ ton bull dashing straight through, or over, a crowd of females and their pups to challenge a rival may crush pups to death. Up to 10 per cent of the pups born at Año Nuevo may perish each year in this way. Finally, at the end of her stay ashore, a cow having weaned her pup and been mated by the dominant bull on the beach has to run the gauntlet of the attentions of the low-ranking bulls that lie in wait in the shallows just off shore.

Le Boeuf (1978) has summed this up by saying that 'rape or attempted rape appears to be a predominant strategy among male northern elephant seals'. To be successful in this strategy males must be large, for it is the largest males that are most successful. Associated with this need for size is the strange phenomenon of milk stealing. After feeding on their mothers' milk for an average of 27 days, and increasing their birth weight at least three times, and sometimes as much as seven times, the pups escape from the breeding crowd on the beach to form groups — weaner pods — at the back of the beach. Some male pups risk serious injury by returning to the breeding crowd in an attempt to steal milk from nursing females there (Reiter et al., 1978). If successful, these milk theives may double their weight and obtain additional nutrients at a time when other pups of the same age are losing weight. The pay-off from this may be a permanent size advantage, which will result in higher social rank and hence greater breeding success. Female pups do not attempt to steal milk because for them the risks of injury (which can be fatal) outweigh the advantages — a large female can at best still raise only one pup a year, whereas a large and successful bull may impregnate 100 breeding females in the same time (Le Boeuf, 1974). True, a successful female may produce twelve pups in successive years, while a successful bull is unlikely to dominate breeding for more than three seasons before the strain tells and he dies. Nevertheless, the potential reproductive success of the males is much greater than that of the females.

An observer, standing at the edge of an elephant seal breeding beach, whether in California or South Georgia, and watching the turmoil and violence before him, may wonder why the females do not desert the crowded beaches, and seek out a quiet cove where there is space and their pups are not likely to be trampled to death by the bull lumbering across them. It is obvious that pup mortality is highest in the most crowded beaches, and yet these beaches remain crowded because the females flock to them. Why should this be? The answer to this question was given by another American seal biologist, working on elephant seals in California, George A. Bartholomew.

THE EVOLUTION OF SEAL POLYGYNY

Bartholomew (1970) was struck by the remarkable similarities in the pattern of social breeding structure in polygynous pinnipeds, whether they were true seals or eared seals. At the time he was writing it was generally believed that these two groups shared a common ancestor, though as we shall see in the next chapter they are now believed to have been derived from different branches of the carnivores. However, the eared seals show essentially the same breeding structure as elephant seals or grey seals — dense assemblies of females, with a few males, very much larger than their consorts, nearly monopolising the chance to pass on genes to the next generation.

From this, Bartholomew deduced that the factors that led to the evolution of pinniped polygyny are closely related to the main adaptive features that characterise the pinnipeds. Starting from the two factors that uniquely distinguish these animals from the rest of the mammals — offshore marine feeding and terrestrial birth — Bartholomew devised a schematic model to describe the evolution of pinniped polygyny (Figure 4.8).

The model has firstly to account for the extreme gregariousness shown by the seals when ashore, for without this, polygyny on the scale shown by these animals would be impossible. Gregarious breeding permits large numbers of animals which are widely dispersed at sea when feeding, and whose body plan has been extensively modified to achieve maximum mobility during this phase, to utilise especially advantageous sites, such as oceanic islands or protected beaches where suitable terrain and the absence of terrestrial predators allow them to breed safely despite the aquatic modifications that render them less fitted for locomotion ashore. There would have been particularly strong selective pressure on those species that fed far offshore to develop strong breeding-site fidelity to ensure that the sexes were reunited for breeding.

The limited mobility of seals ashore, combined with their tendency to aggregate, results in breeding in extremely congested circumstances. Female grey or elephant seals lie in close proximity (though not in actual bodily contact), and bulls are so closely spaced that aggressive interactions between adjacent males may be almost continuous. Males are more widely spaced than females because of their aggressive tendencies, mediated by sex hormones, notably testosterone. Aggression is maximal in the breeding season, when testosterone levels in the blood are highest; during the moult in the autumn, elephant seal bulls are so placid towards each other that they lie in heaps without evoking aggressive responses.

If the males are more widely spaced than the females (and if the males occur in near-equal numbers in the population), it follows that many of the males — the marginal males — will be excluded from a position among the breeding females and so will be unable to pass on their genes. Those few males which are most vigorous and can maintain their position longest on the breeding beaches will pass on a disproportionate number of genes to the next generation. There will thus be a very strong selection pressure towards the development of those characters which allow a male successfully to establish himself among the females, and once established, to maintain his position as long as there are females on heat, or still to come into heat, on the beach. The relationship of some of these features is shown on the left side of Figure 4.8.

To establish a place on the beach and defend it in the face of the testosterone-induced aggressiveness of neighbouring males and newly arrived competitors, a bull must be well equipped with a set of characters, known as epigamic characters, such as large size, aggressiveness, big canines, a protective shield of skin over the chest, special structures used in display and vocal challenge, and so on. Males which possess these

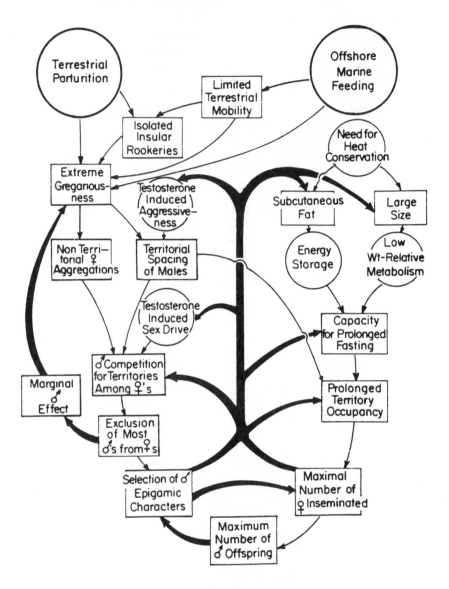

Figure 4.8 A schematic model for the evolution of pinniped polygyny. The large circles represent the two key attributes of pinnipeds; the smaller circles are attributes common to most animals; the rectangles show attributes and functions typical of polygynous pinnipeds. The broad arrows show positive feedback loops. From Bartholomew, 1970.

characters, combined with sexual vigour and fertility, will mate with the most females and produce the most offspring. To the extent that the epigamic characters are genetically determined, there will be a strong positive feedback to reinforce selection for these. Positive feedback loops are shown as broad arrows in Figure 4.8.

The length of time a bull can maintain a position among the breeding females is critical to his genetic success. A bull grey seal or elephant seal does not feed during the whole of the period he is active in the breeding season. To abandon his position on the beach to return to sea to feed would bring the risk of his females coming into oestrus and mating with another male. Additionally, on returning, he would have to expend energy and risk injury in re-establishing himself on the beach. By staying ashore without feeding, a bull improves his genetic efficiency. Prolonged fasting is more possible for a large mammal than for a small one because of the low weight-relative metabolic rate, and hence large size is clearly an advantage here. The blubber layer, which in the water serves as thermal insulation, is a major energy store when the bull is on land. Because of the correlation between the length of time ashore and the number of females fertilised, there is a strong selection pressure for large size and well-developed fat stores (right-hand side of Figure 4.8). But these considerations do not apply in the same way to the females. They need to be large to produce healthy pups, but beyond this there is no special advantage in large size, and hence we see the development of the difference in size, the sexual dimorphism, which is such a characteristic of the polygynous pinnipeds.

Bartholomew's model, however, is not exclusively a male one. Three attributes of the female reproductive pattern which favour a brief, precisely timed breeding season are basic to it. These are a short oestrus, soon after giving birth; a high degree of sexual receptivity in the osetrus female; and delayed implantation. Because oestrus follows birth promptly, it occurs while the females are still aggregated and in contact with the bulls ashore. With the females so receptive during oestrus the bulls need spend little time courting and copulating with each, and can thus devote more time to deterring other bulls, thus facilitating a higher degree of polygyny without the risk of losing his position or having one of his females fertilised by another male. Bartholomew believed that delayed implantation might assist in the synchronisation of the time of pupping, irrespective of the time females were fertilised, thus promoting a more compact breeding season and ensuring that there are more receptive females ashore during the peak of the season.

How can this model help to explain those features, like the mortality of pups on crowded beaches, which we observe in these seals and which, to us, seem so obviously disadvantageous? The extent to which bulls trample and kill pups which may be their own progeny from a previous season obviously reduces their own reproductive efficiency, but because of their high fecundity, this is of much less importance than if a female were to show a behavioural trait which endangered one of her pups. But pups are also killed by aggressive, unrelated, females in the thick of a breeding patch, and disturbance on a crowded beach leads to abandoned and starving pups, so there would seem to be substantial inducements for the female to seek a quieter place in which to give birth. However, what happens to a female that moves away from the crowded beach to produce her pup? In isolation she is likely to wean her pup without disturbance, and because there are so many bulls excluded from the breeding grounds, she is unlikely not to find a mate (or be found by one). But the bull that fertilises her will be a male that has been unsuccessful in establishing his status in competition with other males (McClaren, 1967). To the extent that this marginal male lacks status because of genetic factors, his male progeny would be expected to show a similar tendency to a marginal position and hence impregnate a smaller proportion of the females. Most, of course, would not impregnate any at all, and their gene lines would become extinct. In this way, the tendency of the females to move out of the crowded areas will be self-limiting. The best reproductive strategy for a female is to position herself in an area where she will be mated by a dominant male. This marginal male effect is shown at the extreme left side of Figure 4.8. As long as some males are excluded from the breeding pool, gregariousness in females will be positively reinforced. Of course, all males were marginal at some period of their life; it is only those which remain marginal that contribute to the marginal male effect.

Biological systems are rarely so simple as this model suggests. Carried to its logical conclusion, Bartholomew's model would suggest that all the grey seals, or all the elephant seals, would attempt to breed in one huge colony. This, of course, does not happen. There are limits to the size of group which even the largest bull seal can dominate. Small breeding groups do occur, and new colonies with minimal numbers can be established. Joanne Reiter and her colleagues (1981) have shown that young elephant seal females actually improve their chances of breeding successfully by emigrating from crowded beaches and establishing new colonies. But this may apply only to their first pups. Experienced mothers (who can look after their offspring better) will still be better off breeding in the crowd where they are likely to be mated by the dominant bull.

Can we deduce a common thread in the reproductive patterns of all the seals? This must be bound up with the evolution of the group, the subject of the next chapter.

5 Diversity, classification and origin of seals

There are eighteen species of true seals living today and before attempting to describe their classification and origin, it will be helpful to give brief accounts of each species and their biology.

The Ribbon Seal, *Phoca fasciata*

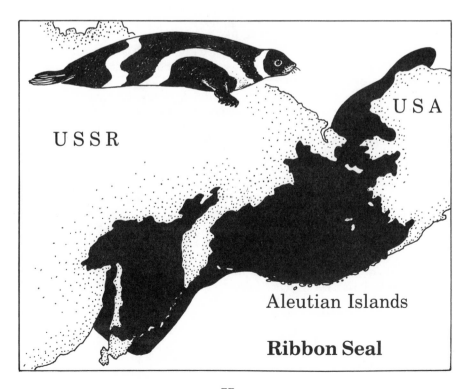

USA

USSR

Aleutian Islands

Ribbon Seal

The ribbon seal is a seal of the Pacific Arctic, breeding on ice in the Bering and Okhotsk Seas, and occasionally straying to the Beaufort and East Siberian Seas, with stragglers very occasionally seen off Hokkaido and even California. It is a smallish seal, reaching a nose–tail length of 160 cm and a weight of 95 kg in both sexes. Ribbon seals have a unique and very distinctively patterned coat. Adult males are dark chocolate brown but have broad white or yellowish white bands around the neck, around the hindquarters and forming a circle around the insertion of each fore flipper. In the female the coat is paler and the bands less distinctly marked. Pups are born in a white lanugo and after the moult they are blue-grey on their backs and silvery beneath. The ribbon pattern is first seen at two years old, but reaches its full intensity only in males a year later. Pups are born on relatively heavy ice floes between the beginning of April and early May and are suckled for 3–4 weeks. The diet is believed to consist of pelagic fish, such as pollack, eelpout, and Arctic cod. Shrimps, crabs, and cephalopods are also taken. The world population, which is probably declining, is about 180,000.

The Ringed Seal, *Phoca hispida*

The ringed seal is found around the whole of the Arctic and subarctic region and in the Baltic Sea, including the Gulfs of Finland and Bothnia. There are two very small populations living in Lake Saimaa in Finland and Lake Ladoga in Russia. Ringed seals have been divided into several subspecies. *P. hispida hispida* is the seal of the Arctic coasts of the USSR, Norway, Greenland, Canada and Alaska, including islands such as Nova Zemlya, Svalbard and Baffin Island. It is seen in Iceland during the winter (and very occasionally in Shetland) and may extend down the Labrador coast as far as Newfoundland. *P. hispida krascheninikovi* is found in the northern parts of the Bering Sea where it is said to merge with *P. hispida ochotensis* in the Sea of Okhotsk. This latter subspecies ranges from Sakhalin as far south as Hokkaido, but does not breed in Japan. The ringed seals in the Baltic are called *P. hispida botnica*, in Lake Saimaa, *P. hispida saimaensis*, and in Lake Ladoga, *P. hispida ladogensis*. Other subspecies, based on differing body size, have been proposed, but as mentioned in the section on breeding patterns, these differences are probably the result of differing suckling periods and have nothing to do with stocks.

Ringed seals are small, males reaching 150 cm nose–tail and 65–95 kg and females 138 cm and 45–80 kg. The coat is basically a light grey spotted with black, the spots often being surrounded with lighter ring markings (hence the name) on the back. On the back the spots are often confluent, giving the appearance of a dark stripe down the back; beneath, the coat is lighter, the belly often being a clear silvery grey. Pups are born in white lanugo on the ice (usually in snow lairs — see p.59) in March and April and lactation is prolonged, lasting up to two and a half months on fast-ice. Their food when in shore consists largely of polar cod (*Boreogadus*) and bottom-dwelling crustaceans such as the shrimp *Mysis*. Off shore, the seals feed on planktonic crustaceans, notably the amphipod shrimp *Parathemisto*. The world population has been variously put at between 3.5 and 6 million, but it is very difficult to estimate.

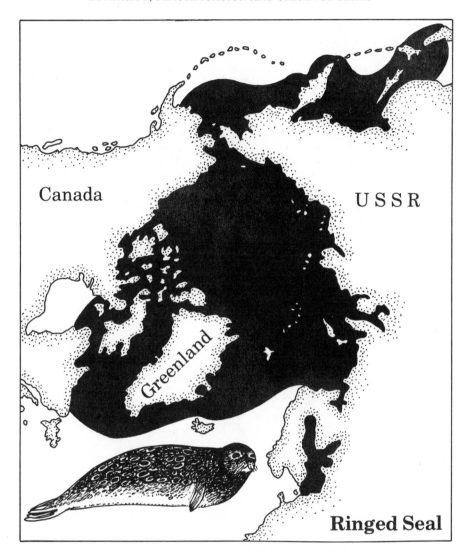

Ringed Seal

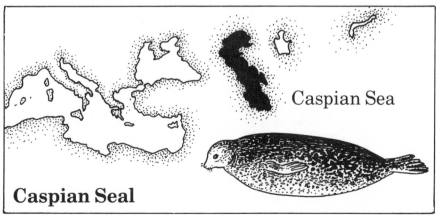

Caspian Seal

The Caspian Seal, *Phoca caspica*

This near relative of the ringed seal is found in the Caspian Sea, where it is the only species. The Caspian seals concentrate in the north-eastern corner of the sea during the breeding season but disperse to the cooler, deeper, central and southern parts during the summer. They are small, males and females both reaching about 125 cm nose–tail length and weighing about 55 kg. The coat is grey, darker on the back and spotted with fine black marks. The males tend to be darker than the females, as in several other species in this group. The pups are born in white lanugo in the jumble of big ice floes thrown up by the winter storms. The pupping season begins in late January and lasts until mid February. The lactation period is about two weeks. Caspian seals feed on a wide range of small fishes and crustaceans. The population numbers about 450,000.

The Baikal Seal, *Phoca sibirica*

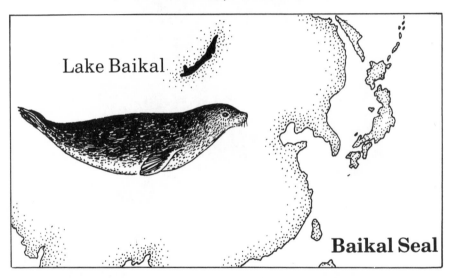

The Baikal seal is confined to Lake Baikal, the huge freshwater lake in Siberia, near the Mongolian border. Lake Baikal is the deepest lake in the world, and the seals are found mainly in the surface waters of the deeper parts. Like the ringed and Caspian seals, the Baikal seal is very small, reaching a length of 122 cm and a weight of 72 kg in both sexes. The coat is dark grey, darker above, and uniform in colour with no discernible spotting. Pups are born in white lanugo from late February to early April on the ice in solitary snow lairs, as with the ringed seal. The lactation lasts 8–10 weeks. The seals live on fish, largely deep-water species. The population numbers about 70,000, representing a marked recovery from a low in the 1930s when the seals were overexploited.

The Harp Seal, *Phoca groenlandica*

There are three populations of harp seals, one breeding off Newfoundland, one off Jan Mayen and one in the White Sea (page 53). These are medium sized seals, both sexes reaching about 170 cm nose–tail length and 130 kg in weight. Their appearance is highly variable as their coat patterns change as the animals mature, and the sexes also differ. An adult male harp seal is light silvery grey over most of its body. From the front of the head to just behind the eyes is black, and there is a blotchy dark patch over the shoulders which extends down both flanks. This has rather fancifully been likened to a harp though it is more like a very badly made horseshoe. In the females the 'harp' is paler and less well defined. The juveniles of both sexes are silvery grey with an irregular pattern of black spots. This pattern gradually changes to the adult coat with successive moults, though some females never develop the 'harp' marking. The pup is born in white lanugo on the ice where the mothers assemble in large whelping patches (page 53). Lactation lasts 9–12 days. Harp seals feed on capelin and other fishes and (particularly in young animals) on planktonic crustacea. The total world population is estimated at 2.6–3.8 million.

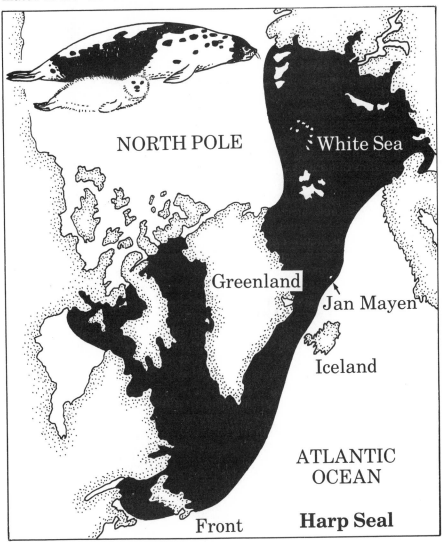

The Spotted Seal, *Phoca largha*

The spotted, or largha (larga) seal is a seal of the pack ice of the North Pacific and the adjacent part of the Arctic Ocean. Its main location is in the Bering and Chukchi Seas. It extends as far west as Chaun Bay and as far east as Herschell Island. It is found in the Sea of Okhotsk, extending southwards as far as Sakhalin and northern Hokkaido in the winter. A separate population occurs in the Po Hai Sea and the northern Yellow Sea. Breeding areas are fairly discrete and there may be some size differences between different stocks (those from Hokkaido and Peter the Great Bay are said to be some 10 cm longer and 15 kg heavier than those from elsewhere).

It is a small seal, males from the Bering and Okhotsk Seas reaching 156 cm and 90 kg, females 150 cm and 80 kg. In appearance, the spotted seal greatly resembles the harbour seal (and has been regarded as a subspecies, though it is clearly distinct). The coat is a pale silver with a darker area on the back; scattered over this are large numbers of small dark irregular spots. Pups are born in a white lanugo on the ice from mid-February to April, on ice-floes towards the margin of the pack. Lactation lasts 3–4 weeks, the female and her pup being accompanied by a male to form a triad. Pups moult direct to the adult coat, though the area around the snout may be paler than in the adult. Spotted seals feed mainly on fish, with some invertebrates. The population may be in the region of 400,000.

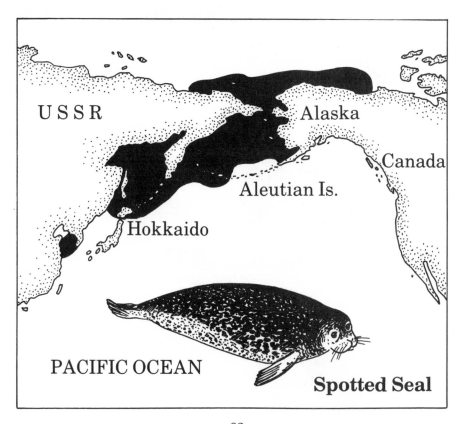

USSR Alaska Canada Aleutian Is. Hokkaido PACIFIC OCEAN **Spotted Seal**

The Harbour (Common) Seal, *Phoca vitulina*

This abundant seal has a similar circumpolar distribution to that of the ringed seal, but at a lower latitude, in cold-temperate and temperate waters. In the North Atlantic region (in the widest sense), harbour seals are found from Murmansk along the Norwegian coast, around the North Sea and in the southern Baltic; around British coasts, with particularly large populations in East Anglia and the west of Scotland; Svalbard, Iceland, south-east and west Greenland; and the Canadian Arctic south to Cape Cod. In the North Pacific they are found from Bristol Bay down the west coast of North America as far as Baja California in Mexico, in the Pribilof, Aleutian and Commander Islands, and in the Kuril Islands to northern Hokkaido.

As with the ringed seal, several subspecies have been named. While the Atlantic and Pacific stocks are clearly isolated the status of the named subspecies is doubtful. *P. vitulina vitulina* is the harbour seal of Europe and Iceland. *P. vitulina concolor* is the seal of Greenland and eastern North America, but Doutt (1942), after examining skulls of both, was unable to say how they differed. A separate subspecies, *P. vitulina mellonae* was described from a population living in some freshwater lakes in the Ungava Peninsula, Hudson Bay, but there is no good reason to regard these seals as anything other than the same as the rest of the

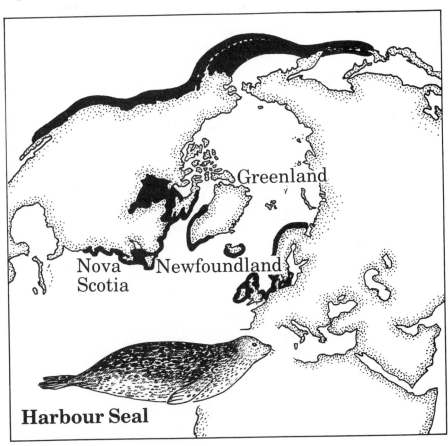

Harbour Seal

83

harbour seals of Hudson Bay. North Pacific harbour seals are probably distinct from those of the North Atlantic. The seal of the American coast is *P. vitulina richardsi* (often erroneously spelt *'richardi'*). Seals at the south of this range are somtimes referred to as *P. vitulina geronimensis*. In the west, another form, *P. vitulina stejnegeri*, has been described from the Kuril Islands and northern Hokkaido. This perhaps really is a separate subspecies. There is some evidence that the Kuril seal is larger and more sexually dimorphic (males about 200 cm, 185 kg, females 170 cm, 120 kg) than the rest of the species (males to 170 cm, 120 kg, females 156 cm, 90 kg).

There is considerable variation in coat colour and pattern in the harbour seal. Basically, there is a mottle of dark spots on a light ground. On the back the spots may coalesce to give a pale interrupted reticulation on a dark ground, and there may be a black dorsal stripe. Occasionally, the spots take the form of ring markings, though smaller than those of the ringed seal. Some seals are very much darker than others, so that the general impression is of animals varying from pale to dark grey. It has been noted in both *P. vitulina vitulina* in the United Kingdom and *P. vitulina richardsi* in British Columbia that seals from sandy estuaries tend to have duller and more uniform coat patterns than those from rocky habitats. Pups are precocious, shedding the white lanugo before birth. They are born from early February to September in different parts of the range on isolated rocks and skerries or on sandbanks and can swim from a few moments after birth (see page 62). Lactation lasts 3–6 weeks, and there is considerable contact between mother and pup. The diet consists of fish, both bottom-dwelling and free-swimming, and some invertebrates. The world population numbers between 300,000 and 400,000.

The Grey Seal, *Halichoerus grypus*

There are three populations of grey seals: one in the north-east Atlantic, one in the Baltic and one in the north-west Atlantic. In the northeast Atlantic grey seals are found rather sparsely around the west and south-west coasts of Iceland; around the Faroe Islands, where they are the only breeding species; on the Norway coast from Møre to North Cape; in small numbers on the Murman coast of Russia; and very sparsely on the Brittany coast near the Ile d'Ouessant and Archipel de Molene. By far the greatest part of this population is found around the British Isles, with concentrations in the Hebrides, North Rona, the Orkneys and the Farne Islands off the Northumberland coast. The Baltic population is greatly reduced. Those seals that remain range widely, but are scarcer in the Gulf of Bothnia. The north-west Atlantic population is spread from Cape Chidley on the Labrador coast by the eastern arm of Ungava Bay, southwards to Cape Cod and Nantucket. The headquarters of the species in this region is around the islands of the Gulf of St Lawrence. There is an important population on Sable Island, a large sandspit some 180 km from the coast of Nova Scotia.

Grey seals are medium to large showing considerable dimorphism, males reaching 230 cm and 330 kg and females 195 cm and 170 kg. Coat colour is very variable; there is a generally darker tone on the back which

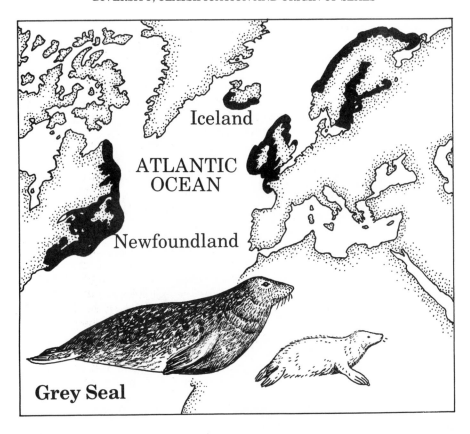

Iceland

ATLANTIC
OCEAN

Newfoundland

Grey Seal

shades into a lighter belly (particularly noticeable in females). In males the darker tone is more extensive, forming a continuous background with lighter patches; in females the lighter tone is the continuous one, with darker spots. Some females may be a pale silvery grey with only a few dark patches, while some males may be nearly black all over. The pup is born in a white lanugo on land in September to December in the north-east Atlantic group; on ice in February and March in the Baltic; and on land or ice in January and February in the north-west Atlantic (page 63). Lactation lasts 2–3 weeks. Grey seals feed on a wide variety of fish with some invertebrates. The world population numbers between 120,000 and 135,000.

The Hooded Seal, *Cystophora cristata*

The hooded seal is found in the north-west Atlantic in much the same region as the harp seal, with breeding colonies in the Gulf of St Lawrence and to the north-east of Newfoundland; there is also a breeding area in the Davis Strait. Another group breeds north-west of Jan Mayen Island, between Iceland and Svalbard. Outside the breeding season, hooded seals are widely distributed from Svalbard, around the Greenland coasts, to Davis Strait, Baffin Bay and Newfoundland. It is an animal of deep water and heavy ice floes. Hooded seals are large, males reaching 250 cm nose–tail length and a weight of about 300–400 kg. Females are smaller,

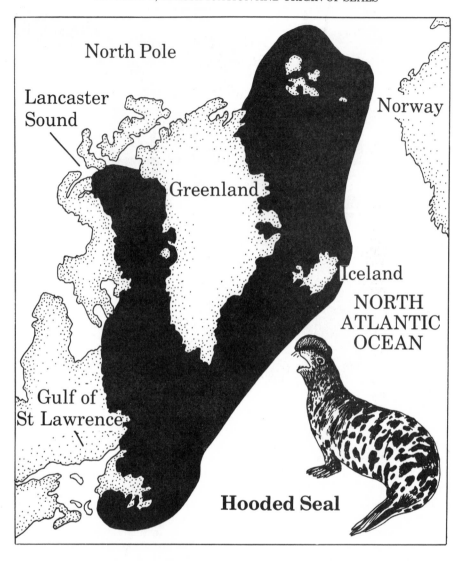

North Pole

Lancaster Sound

Norway

Greenland

Iceland

NORTH ATLANTIC OCEAN

Gulf of St Lawrence

Hooded Seal

about 220 cm and about 180 kg. Both sexes are pale grey with large black blotches and spots and darker heads and hind flippers. The remarkable 'hood' of the adult male has been described on page 57. The pups are born in a silvery coat with a darker back, the light grey lanugo having been shed before birth. Births occur from mid-March to early April and lactation lasts from three to five days. Hooded seals feed on deepwater fishes, such as redfish and Greenland halibut, and squid. The world population is estimated at between 250,000 and 400,000.

The Bearded Seal, *Erignathus barbatus*

The bearded seal has a circumpolar distribution that corresponds closely to that of the ringed seal, being found all along the European, Asiatic and American Arctic coasts and their associated islands. It is essentially an Arctic and subarctic seal of relatively shallow waters. It is a large seal

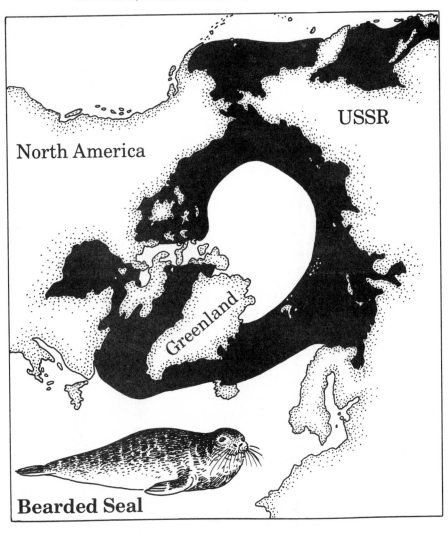

Bearded Seal

with both sexes reaching about 230 cm nose–tail length and a weight of about 260 kg. They are greyish, darker on the back, with a scattering of rather small dark spots. As the name suggests, bearded seals have long, conspicuous and very abundant whiskers. Each whisker is smooth along its length, and not beaded, as in other seals (except monk seals, which also have smooth whiskers). Another characteristic that bearded seals share with monk seals is the presence of four nipples, other seals having only two. The pups are born in a greyish brown lanugo, with scattered patches of white on the back and crown. Births take place on pack ice between mid-March and early May. The lactation period lasts for about 12–18 days. Bearded seals feed on shallow water benthic organisms, bottom-dwelling molluscs, crustaceans, sea cucumbers and fishes. The world population has been estimated to be between 600,000 and a million.

The Mediterranean Monk Seal, *Monachus monachus*

The Mediterranean monk seal is found, as its name suggests, in the Mediterranean, though there are colonies off the west coast of North Africa as well. These seals were once widely distributed and abundant in these areas, but they are now reduced to a series of small relic populations. The most abundant of these is found around the Greek islands and the Turkish coast. A few are found in the south-western Black Sea, some in the eastern Mediterranean, a very few in the Adriatic, and some around the Algerian and Tunisian coasts and the Balearic Islands. In the Atlantic there is a very small population around the Desertas Islands, near Madeira, and another larger one off Cap Blanc in the Western Sahara.

Females are slightly larger than males, reaching 270 cm and 300 kg, males 250 cm and 260 kg. The coat is similar in the sexes, dark chocolate brown above, paler beneath, often with a large very pale or white patch over the belly. There are four teats. Pups are born in a black lanugo, mostly in caves (though there is evidence that they were born on open beaches until recently). The length of lactation is uncertain. The diet is not known for certain, but they take fishes, some large, and octopus. The total population probably numbers less than 500 animals.

Until quite recently another monk seal, the Caribbean monk seal, *M. tropicalis*, was to be found on remote sandy beaches on islands around the Bahamas, the Greater and Lesser Antilles and the Yucatan Peninsula. The last individual was seen in 1952 on the Serranilla Bank, between Nicaragua and Jamaica, and the species is now extinct. (It is the only seal to have become extinct in recent times.)

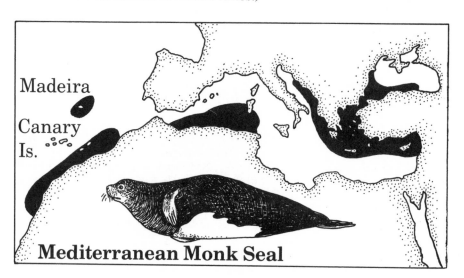

Madeira

Canary
Is.

Mediterranean Monk Seal

The Hawaiian Monk Seal, *Monachus schauinslandi*

The Hawaiian monk seal now breeds only on atolls of the north-west Hawaiian Islands, from Pearl and Hermes Reef to the French Frigate Shoals. Until very recently it used to breed also on Kure and Midway Island, but these areas are now abandoned. Like the Mediterranean monk seal, the Hawaiian species has been greatly reduced in recent years by human activities. Females grow to 230 cm and 250 kg, males to 210 cm and 170 kg. The coat is dark yellowish brown or grey above, and buff or pale grey beneath. Pups are born in black lanugo between January and mid-August on open beaches. Lactation lasts 5–6 weeks. Hawaiian monk seals feed on fish and cephalopods, but few studies have been made. The total population is between 500 and 1000.

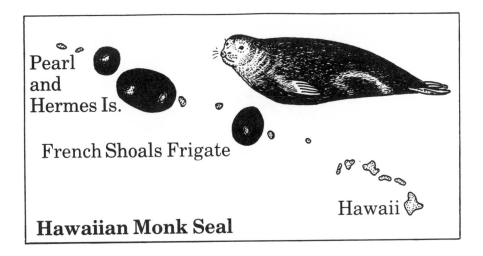

Pearl
and
Hermes Is.

French Shoals Frigate

Hawaii

Hawaiian Monk Seal

The Crabeater Seal, *Lobodon carcinophagus*

Crabeater seals are found around Antarctica in the pack ice. They are rarely seen ashore. They breed on floes near the broken periphery of the pack and retreat to the residual pack, nearer the continent, in the summer. Crabeater seals are great wanderers and isolated individuals have been found in New Zealand, Tasmania, South Africa and Rio de la Plata.

They are large seals, females measuring up to 235 cm and about 220 kg; males are slightly smaller. The coat in both sexes is mainly dark brown above and fawn below. The pattern is generally blotched, particularly in young animals, with patches of darker colour on a light ground. The pattern is strongest on the flanks and towards the posterior end of the body. Older animals have more uniform coats, and old males in particular may fade almost to white. The pups are born in a pale coffee-coloured lanugo on ice floes in September to October (see page 58). The female and pup are joined by a male to form a triad. Lactation lasts around four weeks. The crabeater seal is a specialist feeder (page 23), taking about 90 per cent Antarctic krill, though small quantities of fish

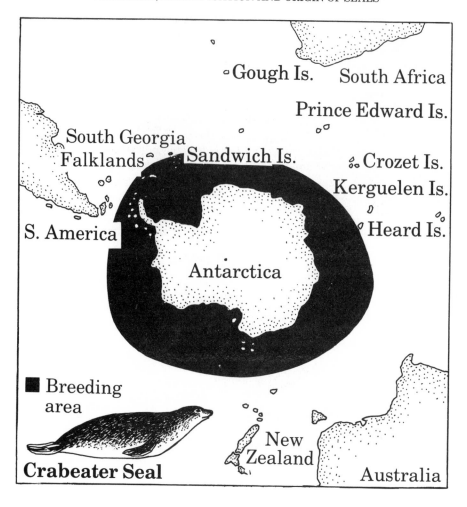

Gough Is.   South Africa

Prince Edward Is.

South Georgia
Falklands   Sandwich Is.

Crozet Is.

Kerguelen Is.

S. America

Heard Is.

Antarctica

Breeding
area

Crabeater Seal

New
Zealand

Australia

and squid may also be taken. The population has been estimated at about 35 million, though recent calculations suggest that it may be less than half this. In either case, it is still by far the most abundant seal.

The Leopard Seal, *Hydrurga leptonyx*

Leopard seals have the same general distribution as crabeaters, i.e. circumpolar in the pack-ice, but they extend further to the north, and are regularly found at subantarctic islands such as South Georgia and Macquarie Island. Also like crabeater seals, there are a number of records of leopard seals being found far north of their range, as for instance at Raratonga in the Cook Islands, South Africa and Tristan da Cunha.

The leopard seal is a large animal, adult females reaching 358 cm with an estimated weight of 500 kg. Average lengths and weights are 291 cm and 367 kg for females and 279 cm and 324 kg for males. The coloration on the back is dark grey to black, which changes at the flanks to steely grey while the underparts are silver. On the belly there is a scattering of

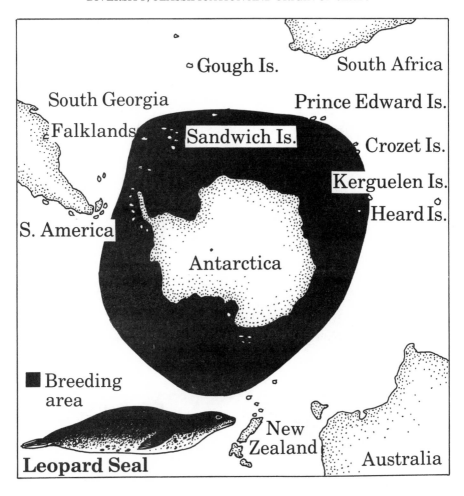

South Africa
Gough Is.
South Georgia
Prince Edward Is.
Falklands
Sandwich Is.
Crozet Is.
Kerguelen Is.
Heard Is.
S. America
Antarctica
Breeding area
New Zealand
Australia
Leopard Seal

dark spots while on the back the pattern is reversed and the spots are light on a dark ground. Its silhouette is unmistakable; it has a large heavy head and a very well-developed thoracic region, giving a characteristic humped outline. The new-born pup has a lanugo resembling the adult pattern. Leopard seals breed in the pack ice, probably between October and November. The length of lactation is not known, but has been estimated at four weeks. Leopard seals are opportunistic predators. They feed on krill, but also take young crabeater seals and penguins, as well as fish (page 23). The world population is estimated at 220,000.

The Weddell Seal, *Leptonychotes weddellii*

Weddell seals are found in the fast-ice region round the shores of the Antarctic Continent and on a number of island groups surrounding it. The most northerly breeding colony is at South Georgia. Weddell seals are bulky animals, both males and females reaching around 400–500 kg in the early spring when the seals are fat. Females are slightly larger

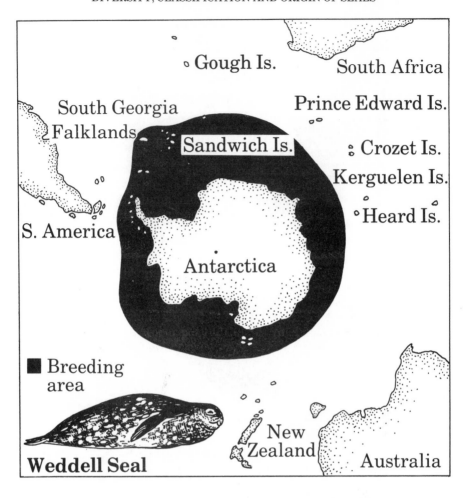

Weddell Seal

than the males, reaching 329 cm nose–tail, while the males reach only 297 cm. In contrast to the leopard seal, the head of the Weddell seal seems small for its body, with a short snout. The coat is strongly spotted with irregularly shaped patches. The background colour is bluish grey, lighter beneath. There are darker spots on the belly and flanks which, as in the leopard seal, are reversed to give pale spots on a dark ground on the shoulders and back. Pups are born in a silvery grey lanugo. Pupping occurs from September to November on the fast ice (page 61). In the more northern parts of its range when sea ice does not form Weddell seals will breed on the beach, but always seek out a patch of snow on which to lie. Lactation lasts 40–50 days. Weddell seals feed mainly on fish, taking both small and large specimens. They also take some crustacea and a small quantity of squid. The population is estimated at 730,000.

The Ross Seal, *Ommatophoca rossii*

Because of their remoteness, Ross seals are the least well known of the Antarctic species. They are found chiefly in areas of heavy pack, with a concentration in the Haakon VII Sea. Of the few that have been measured, the largest female was 236 cm long and weighed 204 kg, the largest male 208 cm and 216 kg. The profile of the Ross seal is instantly recognisable; it has a very short snout set on a wide head. The rear flippers, which may reach 22 per cent of the body length, are proportionately the longest for any seal. The body is brownish grey on the back, becoming paler on the flanks, where there may be considerable spotting, and becoming nearly white on the belly. Around the throat and on the sides of the head the dark colour is extended backwards as a series of streaks. This type of longitudinal streaking is found in no other seal. The lanugo of the new born pup, like that of the leopard seal, is similar to the adult coat pattern. Births occur in November on floes in the pack. The lactation period is unknown. The diet is believed to consist mainly of squid, with some fish and occasional bottom-dwelling invertebrates. The Ross seal gives the appearance of being a deep diver, but there are no records of the depth at which it feeds. The population is estimated at 220,000.

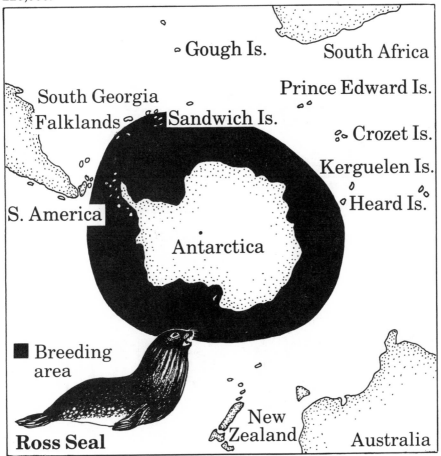

The Southern Elephant Seal, *Mirounga leonina*

Southern elephant seals have a circumpolar distribution, but there are three breeding stocks. One is centered on South Georgia and includes smaller breeding populations in South America (Punta Norte and Tierra del Fuego), the Falkland Islands and the South Orkneys and South Shetlands. A second group breeds at Iles Kerguelen, Iles Crozet and Heard Island. The third is found at Macquarie Island and the New Zealand subantarctic islands. These have been described as subspecies, but there is no evidence of genetic isolation.

The southern elephant seal is the largest of all seals and one of the largest of all mammals, excluding the whales and their kin. Fully grown males reach a length of 490 cm and a mean weight of 3,200 kg. Such a bull at the beginning of the breeding season with its blubber reserves at a maximum might well weigh up to 4,000 kg. Females are very much smaller, reaching around 280 cm and 900 kg. Elephant seals are a uniform brownish colour, though there is considerable variation (particularly in the males) from very dark chocolate to sandy. Some males show a dark vertebral stripe. Old cows have a conspicuous pale mask. The

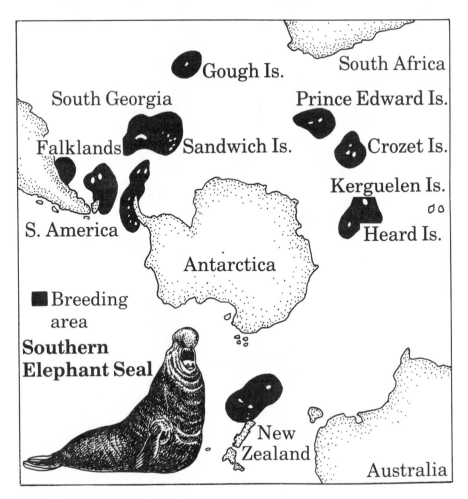

remarkable trunk of the adult bull elephant seal has been described on page 69. Females aggregate in large herds to breed on open sand or shingle beaches from September to November. Pups are born in a black lanugo (very similar to that of the monk seals) which is moulted to a steely grey yearling coat, which is pale cream beneath. Lactation lasts on average 23 days. Elephant seals feed largely on squid, which is probably obtained at depth. They also take fish, particularly the younger seals. The world population is estimated at about 600,000.

The Northern Elephant Seal, *Mirounga angustirostris*

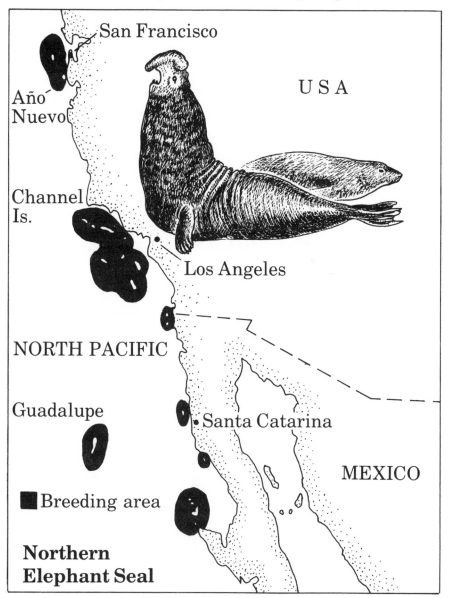

San Francisco

Año Nuevo

USA

Channel Is.

Los Angeles

NORTH PACIFIC

Guadalupe

Santa Catarina

MEXICO

■ Breeding area

Northern Elephant Seal

Northern elephant seals breed off the west coast of North America at the Fallaron Islands, just off San Francisco, Año Nuevo Island, the Channel Islands, Los Coronadas, Guadalupe Island, with a southern limit at the Cedros Islands off Baja California in Mexico. Outside the breeding season the seals are dispersed widely at sea, adult bulls being found as far north as Prince of Wales Island, Alaska. Cows do not enter such cold waters. The northern elephant seal is not so large as the southern species, males reaching about 420 cm and 2,300 kg, females 310 cm and 900 kg. They are similar in colour to the southern species, but the adult bulls have a distinct pinkish hue to their chests in the breeding season. The trunk of the northern species is much longer than in the southern seal. Pups are born in January on beaches and lactation lasts 27 days. Like the southern species, northern elephant seals feed on squid and fish. The population numbers about 55,000.

CLASSIFICATION

The eighteen species of living seals described above can be placed in several groups of different rank, intended to represent common ancestry at different levels of remoteness. The zoological taxonomist commonly uses three levels: that of the species, which, however it is defined, has a biological validity that is not always to be found in the other categories; the genus, which groups together similar species; and the family, which is a larger and far less definite grouping of similar genera. However, other intermediate rankings have been used to show affinities between the seals as they are understood at any one time. These are the subfamily, the tribe, and the subgenus.

There are conventions about the use and orthography of these terms. The family name, spelt with a capital letter, always ends in -idae, the subfamily in -inae, and the tribe in -ini. These suffixes are added to a root derived from the senior or most characteristic genus. The name of the species is made up of two elements — it is a binomial — and is always printed in italics. The first element is the generic name, always spelt with a capital letter, and the second, which is never spelt with a capital, is strictly called the trivial name. It is often referred to as the specific name, however, though the specific is properly the whole binomial. The generic and trivial names do not have to have particular endings, though they are Latinised and the two names must agree in gender. Their use is rigorously controlled by the Commission for International Zoological Nomenclature, and the overriding consideration is that the rule of priority must be applied. This requires that, starting from the tenth edition of Linnaeus's *Systema Natura* (1758), the name first applied to a particular species, provided it was accompanied by a proper description, is the valid name.

In practice, the concept of a species is a rather arbitrary one, though there seems to have been little confusion amongst the true seals. What constitutes a genus is even more arbitary and various specialists have differing ideas on which genus a particular species should be assigned to.

With seals this has chiefly affected the genus *Phoca*, with differing generic names being applied to some of the seals in this genus. These will be referred to later.

A further convention that should be mentioned here concerns the addition of a person's name, and perhaps a date, following the scientific name of the animal. This allows a reference to the original describer of the species. If we write '*Phoca vitulina* Linnaeus, 1758', we know that the common seal was described by Linnaeus in 1758. Sometimes the name of the describer is written in parentheses — '*Halichoerus grypus* (Fabricius, 1791)'. This tells us that the grey seal was described by Fabricius in 1791, but under a different generic name, in this case '*Phoca*'. These 'authors' names', as they are called, are important in some groups where the taxonomy is confused, but they are of little practical use in referring to seals. They are particularly annoying when authors, to show their erudition rather than to avoid confusion, include them in the titles of papers, thus adding considerably and unnecessarily to the bibliographer's task.

All the true seals together form the family Phocidae and this is divided into two subfamilies, the Phocinae, the northern phocids, and the Monachinae, the monk seals, elephant seals and Antarctic seals. These are distinguished mainly by skeletal characteristics, and by the fact that all the Phocinae have 32 chromosomes (except the bearded seal, which has 34, Árnason, 1972) while all the Monachinae have 34 chromosomes. A feature that is diagnostic and easily observable in the living seal is that in the Phocinae the claws on the hind flippers are large and well developed, while they are rudimentary in the Monachinae.

The Phocinae themselves are divided into three tribes. The Phocini include the grey seal, the harbour seal, the spotted seal, the ringed seal and its close relatives, the Caspian seal and the Baikal seal, the harp seal and the ribbon seal. In all these species (and in no others) the least interorbital width in the adult skull is in the anterior half of the interorbital septum. Another character which unites this group is the possession of white lanugo (though this is shed before birth in the case of the harbour seal). Within this tribe the grey seal, *Halichoerus*, is most distinct in the shape of the snout and the anterior part of the skull. The remaining Phocini were at one time divided into four genera, *Phoca*, the harbour seal and spotted seal; *Pusa*, the ringed seal, the Caspian seal and the Baikal seal; *Pagophilus*, the harp seal; and *Histriophoca*, the ribbon seal. A very detailed comparison of a large series of skulls from these seals by two American workers, John Burns and Francis Fay (1970) led them to conclude that while the skulls were distinct and recognisable, the differences between them did not quite attain the 'generic level'. Current practice is to use only *Phoca* as a generic name, and to employ the others as subgeneric names. However, the distinguished American palaeontologist Charles Repenning has pointed out to me that he prefers to use besides *Phoca*, the generic names *Pusa*, *Pagophilus* and *Histriophoca*, because *Pagophilus*, *Phoca* and *Pusa* have respectable separate histories about as long as the history of the Phocidae themselves. (*Histriophoca* does not have much of a fossil history.) However, this point tends to be lost on zoologists (like myself) not much concerned with fossil history.

The bearded seal, *Erignathus*, is placed in its own tribe, Erignathini,

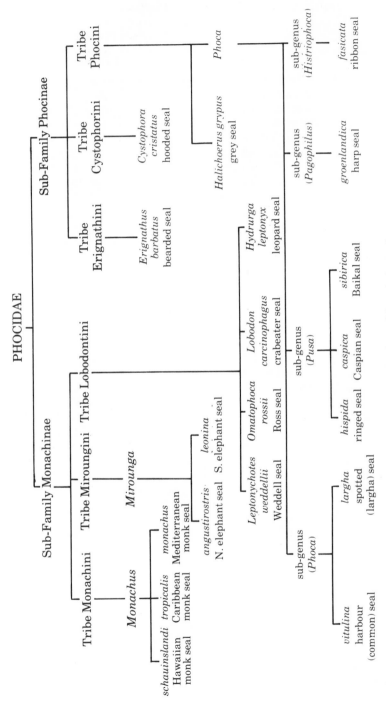

Figure 5.1 The relationships of the existing seals.

and the hooded seal, *Cystophora*, also has its own tribe, Cystophorini. These two seals are very different from the Phocini and from each other. The diagnostic tribal characters are complicated but the hooded seal can be distinguished from the others by having only two upper and one lower pairs of incisor teeth (all other Phocinae have three upper and two lower pairs of incisors), while the bearded seal has four nipples and smooth, not beaded, whiskers. Unlike all the other Phocinae, it has 34 chromosomes, rather than 32 (Árnason, 1972).

The subfamily Monachinae is more difficult. At one time the elephant seals and the hooded seal were combined in one subfamily, the Cystophorinae. This left only the monk seals and the Antarctic seals in the Monachinae. The monk seals are all very similar and form the tribe Monachini (with four nipples and pups born in black lanugo) while the Antarctic seals were lumped together in the Lobodontini. The Lobodontini, however, were not a very similar group, being chiefly united by having only two nipples and pups not born in black lanugo. However, it is now accepted that the hooded seal is properly placed with the other northern phocids, and the elephant seals with the monachines. The erection of a separate tribe for the elephant seals, the Miroungini, (having two nipples and pups born in black lanugo) makes for a tidy arrangement but at least one authoritative source (Hendey and Repenning, 1972) has said that 'recognition of any tribal subdivision of the Monachinae now seems pointless'. Subfamilies, tribes and even subgenera are all very much matters of personal opinion. Where they are useful in drawing attention to relationships, or in grouping common characteristics, they may be used. For the most part, however, we can ignore them.

A scheme for the classification of the existing seals is given in Figure 5.1. Although I have tried to put nearly related forms close to each other in the diagram, too much should not be read into this. Nor should it be supposed that what is called a subfamily or tribe in this diagram has the same status as similar terms used in the classification of other animal groups. The true seals are a remarkably similar group but have been the object of attention of a great many scientists and even small differences can assume great significance in such circumstances.

THE ORIGIN OF SEALS

Our knowledge of the ancestry of animals is based on the study of fossils, the analogies we can make between the group in question and similar groups which we think may be related, and some minor factors, such as numbers and arrangements of chromosomes (karyology) or the structure of structural proteins and enzymes. All these techniques have been used in trying to place seals in their rightful position in the history of mammals, and in arranging their subfamilies and genera within their own group.

Fossils, because they can be accurately located and rather less accurately dated, provide some of the firmest evidence. Until quite recently there was something of a dearth of phocid seal fossils but recently more have come to light and the record, while still scrappy, leaves us with some certainties. We know that phocid seals evolved early in the Miocene, perhaps 20 million years ago, in the North Atlantic region. The ancestors of the fur seals and walruses arose a little earlier, but in the North Pacific area. Both groups arose from carnivore ancestors but the otariids were derived from a bear-like ancestor, whereas the phocids arose from an otter-like ancestor in Europe or western Asia. 'Bear-like' and 'otter-like' refer to appearance and not to direct ancestry, as both bears and otters, as we know them today, were just beginning to evolve at this same time.

Let us look a little more closely at the Carnivora. If for the moment we neglect the seals and their cousins, the fur seals and walruses, the order is primarily divided into two suborders, the Aeluroidea (cat-like carnivores) and the Arctoidea (dog-like carnivores). The latter can be further divided into the Canidae (dogs, foxes, etc.) and the Ursidae (bears), Procyonidae (raccoons), and the Mustelidae (weasels, etc.). The weasel

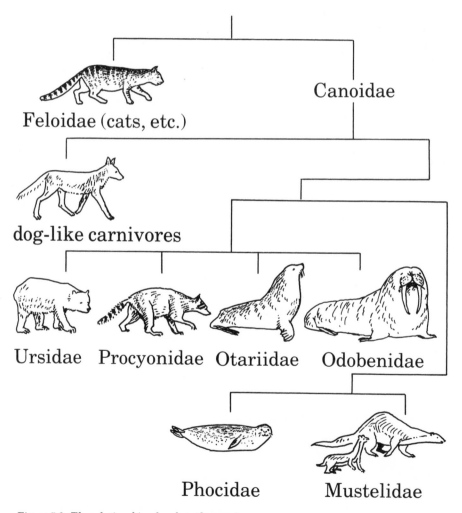

Feloidae (cats, etc.)

Canoidae

dog-like carnivores

Ursidae   Procyonidae   Otariidae   Odobenidae

Phocidae   Mustelidae

Figure 5.2 The relationship of seals to the carnivores.

family — the Mustelidae — include besides weasels, such forms as badgers, skunks and otters. In the early Miocene in both Europe and North America there existed an arctoid carnivore, *Potamotherium* ('lake-mammal') which shows a mixture of mustelid and phocid characters (Savage, 1957). Reconstructions suggest that *Potamotherium* inhabited the shore and swam rather like a phocid and may indicate a possible intermediate structural position. The definitive features that link the Phocidae with the Mustelidae (and the Otariidae with the Ursidae) are fine details of the ear region of the skull and some other osteological features (Tedford, 1976, McLaren, 1960). Figure 5.2 attempts to show (in a simplified way) the relationships of the seals to the rest of the carnivores.

This clear distinction in the origins of the phocids and otariids is not accepted by all palaeontologists. In 1988 a paper was published that drew attention to several close similarities in some of the bones of the flippers of pinnipeds of all three groups — the sea lions, seals and walruses (Wyss, 1988). These comprised the marked elongation and enlargement of both major elements of the first digit of the hand of the foreflipper; the progressive decrease in emphasis of the digits 1–5 of the hand; the reduction of the fifth intermediate finger-bone of the hand; the strong development and elongation of the first metacarpal and proximal finger (and toe) bones in hand and foot; and the elongation and development of the fifth toe. There were some other, less clear, features also. Wyss pointed out that this suite of characteristics does not resemble that seen in other aquatic mammals, nor is it found elsewhere among vertebrates, though several other forms, living and extinct, have flippers. On these grounds Wyss feels that evolutionary convergence resulting from the adoption of an aquatic existence is unlikely.

This view was reinforced when a nearly complete fossil skeleton of an early seal-like animal, *Enaliarctos mealsi*, which lived about 23 million years ago in California, was discovered (Berta *et al.*, 1989). *Enaliarctos* represents a stage in the transition from land to water from a terrestrial carnivoran (bear-like) ancestor and has features that suggest it swam using both undulations of the axial skeleton together with thrusts from its hind flippers (like a phocid seal) and by strokes of its fore flippers (like an otariid).

I have not had the opportunity to examine this material and, not being a palaeontologist, might not benefit much if I did, but I am not convinced by these arguments. Although phocids and otariids usually swim by very different methods it seems to me very likely that in their earlier stages there was less distinction (as was clearly the case in *Enaliarctos*) and hence the opportunity for the acquisition of the common characters Wyss noted. For the moment I shall continue to regard phocids and otariids as having separate origins, though like many others I shall await further work on this subject with interest.

The earliest phocid fossils are from the mid– to late Miocene (12–15 million years ago) and even as early as that are assignable to the modern groups of phocines and monachines. This clear distinction between the two groups raises the intriguing possibility that phocine and monachine seals are not really very closely related and might even have had separate origins from the arctoid ancestors.

Leptophoca is the earliest known phocine and *Monotherium* the earliest monachine. From the early records, it is obvious that the monachine seals had a more southerly preference than did the phocine seals (Repenning, 1980). At that time the northern part of the North Atlantic was inhabited by phocine seals only, their most southerly record being from Virginia, where they lived together with monachines which had probably spread north from a large Caribbean population. A million years later the monachines had moved northwards in the Atlantic and remained widely dispersed until about five million years ago.

This period, from 15 to 5 million years ago, was one of progressive cooling, and the northward movement of the warmth-loving monachines may have been associated with the development of that warm current sweeping out of the Gulf of Mexico which is now known as the Gulf Stream. From micro-organism fossils we can tell that 15 million years ago, the Caribbean was an area of high organic productivity. At that time the Isthmus of Panama had not yet appeared and the Atlantic North Equatorial Current would have been able to sweep through the gap between the two Americas — the Central American Seaway — bringing nutrients to sustain the food web that supported the seal population. Via the Central American Seaway the monk seals were able to spread out into the Pacific to colonise the seas around Hawaii. This must have been a very early movement, for paradoxically the existing Hawaiian monk seal is more primitive in its adaptation to underwater directional hearing and in the structure of its hind flippers than the 15 million-year-old monk seal from Virginia.

Continued cooling of the sea and tectonic movements which shifted the Hawaiian Islands further north, towards the edge of the Pacific North Equatorial Current, increasingly isolated the seals in Hawaii. This combination of cooling and less productive waters with no avenue of escape long ago dictated the eventual extinction of the Hawaiian monk seals, according to Charles Repenning (1980), who has made a special study of the evolution of seals. The seals were doomed because they did not have the necessary genetic plasticity to adapt to changing circumstances. Why this was so we do not know, but the last remnants of the Hawaiian monk seals are as veritable living fossils as any coelacanth or tuatara.

But other monachines did adapt. The remaining monk seals in the Caribbean, and their near relatives that had spread to the eastern side of the Atlantic and eventually into the Mediterranean, evolved more efficient hearing and better adapted flippers. They remained, however, close to the ancestral stock. This was not the case with some other monachines that had followed the Hawaiian monk seal through the Central American Seaway into the Pacific. These seals found themselves at the northern end of the highly productive Peru Current, a cold-water current which is an extension of the circumpolar current — the West Wind Drift — that encircles the Antarctic continent. This monachine stock eschewed the energetic benefits of warm water for the food resources of the cold water and migrated down along the west coast of South America to give rise to the southern elephant seal. A remnant that remained in the Northern Hemisphere (or perhaps reinvaded following a period of cooling) developed as the more primitive northern elephant seal. The great similarity in appearance between the cow and pup of the

Hawaiian monk seal and those of the northern elephant seal is striking today.

The primitive monachine ancestors of the Antarctic seals almost certainly followed a similar route through the Central American Seaway and down the west coast of South America, following areas of high oceanic productivity. Fossil remains from Peru (*Piscophoca* and *Acrophoca*) and South Africa (*Homiphoca*) (Muizon and Hendey, 1980; Muizon, 1981) are clearly related to the Antarctic seals, *Homiphoca* showing a possible relationship to the crabeater seal, and *Acrophoca* to the leopard seal. However, none of these fossils can be regarded as a 'missing link'.

Meanwhile, phocine seals had been exploiting the opportunities offered by the cold waters of the north. Phocines early showed a tendency to enter fresh waters (none of the monachines seem to have done this) and about the middle of the Miocene phocines from the North Atlantic migrated up an ancient forerunner of the River Rhine to gain access to a vast inland sea — the Paratethys — that stretched across the area where the Black, Caspian and Aral Seas are now. It is likely that the ancestors of the subgenus *Pusa* (the Caspian, Baikal and ringed seals) originated here. The ancestors of the Caspian seal remained where they were when the Paratethys Sea contracted but about 3 million years ago some seals escaped from Paratethys into the Arctic Ocean, presumably via a river at a time when the Arctic Ocean stretched southwards towards Paratethys west of the Ural Mountains, and became the modern ringed seals. About 300,000 years ago some of these obtained access to the Baikal sea via large lakes at the southern margin of the Siberian ice sheet (King, 1983) and the population which was isolated when Lake Baikal was formed gave rise to the present Baikal seal.

The Bering Strait, which connects the Arctic Ocean with the North Pacific, did not open until about 3 million years ago. This allowed ancestral phocines into the North Pacific and the evolution of the spotted and ribbon seals. The ice-breeding spotted seal is a likely candidate as ancestor of the land-breeding harbour seal (it was until recently considered to be a subspecies of the harbour seal). Harbour seals could have returned to the North Atlantic during a warm period. The grey seal has no Pacific counterpart and must have arisen in the North Atlantic/Arctic Ocean area, perhaps from an early phocine close to the ancestor of the *Pusa* group, or perhaps from a ringed seal ancestor. The ancestors of the bearded seal and the hooded seal probably arose from the early stock of phocine seals in the North Atlantic, prior to the separation of the ringed seal group, but fossil forms relating to these tribes are lacking.

6 Interactions with man: 1. Seals as prey

SEALS AND EARLY MAN

Early Man was a subsistence hunter, an occupation that would have set limits on the density of early populations. It was probably this factor that led small groups of humans in the Stone Age to move from the tropical grasslands, where the species had evolved, up across the Eurasian land mass to the coasts. Colder climates, and particularly harsher winters, must have imposed severe stresses on these early peoples; the driving force for them would have been living space and food.

The people who first penetrated into those regions where seals are abundant — the coasts of west and north Europe, the coast of Asia from Japan northwards, and arctic North America and Greenland — found waiting for them a group of mammals which were almost ideally suited to their needs (Bonner, 1982). Seals were sufficiently large for the pursuit and killing of a single animal to provide an ample reward, yet they were not so big or so fierce that there were serious risks associated in hunting them. Once captured, a seal provided three products vital to survival in the north: food, in the form of good meat and fat; furry skins from which warm and waterproof clothing could be fashioned; and, again, fat — blubber — which could be burned in a primitive stone lamp to provide warmth and light during the long winter nights.

The dates at which human hunters first arrived in areas where they might have made use of seals as prey varied in different regions, dating from about 400,000 years ago for north-western Europe to perhaps 40,000 years ago for North America and even later than that for Greenland. We cannot tell how long it would have taken for hunters to develop the means of taking these marine mammals, but I suspect the required technologies were quickly developed. The rewards for using the resource provided by seals were great and the penalties for not doing so might well have been final.

We cannot be certain of the extent to which early Man in these regions relied on seal hunting as our knowledge of these times is incomplete. Obviously, cultures which exploited seals would be located in coastal regions and because of coastline changes since the Ice Age only very

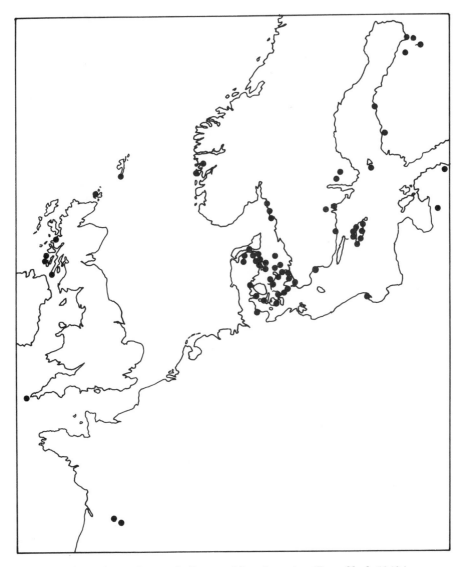

Figure 6.1 Stone Age settlements in Europe with seal remains. (From Clark, 1946.)

limited stretches of Stone Age coast are available for study above modern
sea level. The melting of the Pleistocene ice sheet, with resulting rises in
sea level, has progessively flooded much of the Stone Age coast; only in
some places has the rise of the land, relieved of the weight of the ice sheet,
preserved ancient coastal settlements. In western Europe, for example,
an area very well worked over by archaeologists, Clark (1946) showed
that Stone Age settlements with remains of seals or other evidence of seal
hunting, were clustered in the Kattegat region and the islands between
Denmark and Sweden, with only sporadic sites in Norway, the Baltic, the
Hebrides and Orkneys and the Dordogne of France (Figure 6.1).
(Interestingly, many of the seal remains from the Kattegat and Baltic are

of harp seals, a species which has since become extinct in these areas.) This clustering of seal remains does not mean that seal hunting was concentrated in this region and that it was an unimportant activity elsewhere. Rather, it reflects the fact that coastal sites from the appropriate period happen to be much more abundant around Denmark and that conditions for the preservation of bone are exceptionally favourable there.

The earliest evidence for seal hunting in northern Europe consists of a pair of seal jaws from an Aurignacian level in the rock shelter at Castanet in the valley of the Vezère, a tributary of the Dordogne, and a single jaw from a late Magdalenian level in a cave on the Isle, another tributary of the Dordogne. These sites are now some 200 km from the coast, and would probably have been even further from the sea at that time. However, it seems that the inhabitants of that region were familiar with seals, for they left some remarkable pictures of them, and one of these suggests that the seals were taken from the rivers, where they had come in pursuit of salmon.

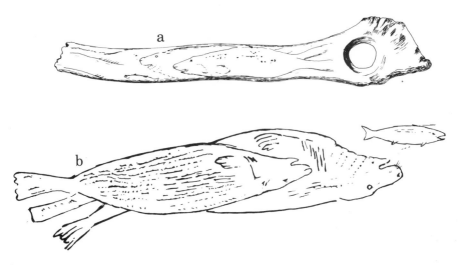

Figure 6.2 The 'Montgaudier baton': above, as usually depicted; below, detail of the inverted grey seals pursuing the fish.

Two beautiful little engravings of seals survive from the Upper Palaeolithic in the Dordogne. Both are so detailed that it is possible to say without doubt that they are grey seals. One drawing found at Duruthy and engraved on a bear's tooth which has been perforated near the root so that it might have been worn as an amulet, shows a grey seal, recognisable from the heavy muzzle. The other drawing, from Mont-gaudier, is much more detailed and amazingly lifelike. It is engraved on a piece of reindeer antler, and this too has been perforated. The engraving covers both sides of the bone and is usually shown 'opened out', so that both sides are visible (Figure 6.2). Two easily recognisable grey seals are swimming in pursuit of a fish (either a salmon or a salmon trout). In almost all reproductions of this remarkable artefact (e.g. Capitan *et al.*,

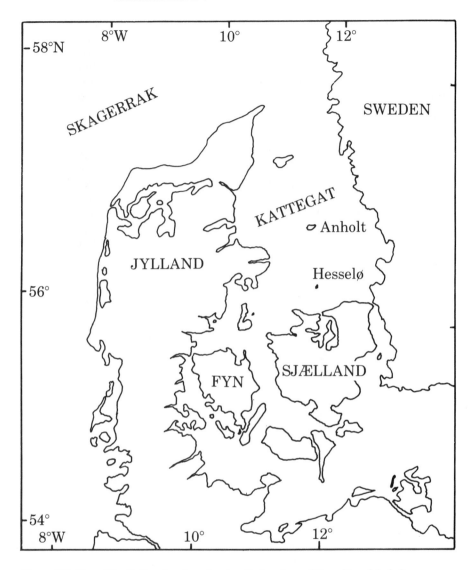

Figure 6.3 Map of the Kattegat region showing the locations of Hesselø and Anholt.

1906), the seals are shown with their backs uppermost, which makes the fish, from the position of its pectoral and pelvic fins, appear to be swimming upside down. In fact, the Stone Age artist was faithfully representing the common habit of seals when swimming in relatively shallow waters, of swimming on their backs. It was many centuries before European artists were able to depict seals so naturally again.

It seems likely to me that seals must have been an important quarry to the primitive peoples of the Dordogne for them to have observed them so carefully and reproduced them so faithfully. However, there is no evidence of hunting techniques from the Dordogne. There is such evidence in the Kattegat, however. At the tiny island of Hesselø, about 25 km to the north of Zealand (Figure 6.3), there was an important sealing station in Stone Age times. More than 90 per cent of the bone material there is derived from grey seals, of which a very great number are from young pups. In a bog at Hesselø were found six wooden clubs, which might have been used to kill grey seals. Hesselø is too small an island to support terrestrial game (it is about 1.6 km across), so it is reasonable to assume that the hunters visited the island during the breeding season to provide themselves with skins, meat and blubber (Møhl, 1970).

Wood does not usually preserve well at archaeological sites except, as at Hesselø, in bogs. A more enduring artefact is the harpoon point, and some of these have actually been found with seal bones. At Norrekøping in southern Sweden in 1907, when the foundations for a new city hall were being dug, the bones of a fairly young ringed seal together with a bone harpoon head, were found in the clay. The sea level at the time the seal was killed would have been some 60 m higher than at present, so one can visualise the wounded seal breaking the harpoon line and sinking to the bottom of the sea to be slowly covered by silt. Another harpoon head was found embedded in the ribs of a harp seal skeleton, found when draining a fen at Närpes in Østerbotten, Finland (Clark, 1946).

Harpoon heads are often found without the accompanying evidence of seal bones of course, but it seems likely that they were used mostly, if not exclusively, for hunting seals, rather than other kinds of game. The essence of a harpoon is that it (or its point) can be attached to the hunter by a line, so that wounded quarry can be retrieved. There is little advantage in using harpoons to hunt game on land, since a wounded animal can be followed and dispatched. The sorts of harpoon points found at these Danish and Baltic sites might have been used also to capture porpoises, but it is likely that seals were the main quarry pursued in this way.

Harpoons were probably used from boats. We know that primitive peoples at these times had considerable boating skills. The existence of cultural remains at offshore islands like Hesselø testify to this, as do finds of bones of cod, which could only be taken from a boat, at Stone Age shelters. Some remarkable rock engravings at Rødøy in Nordland, Norway (Figure 6.4), show a hunter in a canoe, together with a porpoise and a seal-like creature (Gjessing, 1936). No harpoon can be distinguished, but we may suppose that a technique similar to that of the Eskimo kayak hunter, to which I shall refer later, might have been employed.

Stone Age hunters might have used other methods to take seals. They could have been caught in nets or traps, as they still were until very recently in the Baltic (page 115), but these would have left no recognisable remains. Probably hunters would have used a variety of methods, varying them seasonally and in accordance with the species of seal pursued. It is easy to suppose that men in prehistoric times had access only to a very low level of technology. That the contrary is true in relation to seal hunting is shown by a people — the Eskimo, or Inuit — whose Stone Age culture persisted in some groups virtually unchanged up to the present century.

Figure 6.4 Stone Age rock engravings from Rødøy, Nordland, Norway. The porpoise, strange horned seal and figure in boat suggest a hunting scene.

ESKIMOS AND SEALS

Prior to the arrival of modern civilisation, Eskimos owed their survival to their skill at hunting. Coastal Eskimos made use of all the game that they could catch, but their staple prey was the ringed seal. The importance of this animal in their culture is shown by the many carvings of seals (long before these ivory minatures became articles of trade) and the occurrence of seal spirits, like the Angiut of the Greenlanders, in their religious beliefs. Men like Franz Boas, who made a notable field expedition to Baffin Island in 1883–4, were able to record accounts of Eskimo hunting that had changed little, if at all, from the time before the first contacts with the Arctic whalers at the beginning of the eighteenth century.

The basis of seal hunting was the harpoon. Many different types of harpoons were in use, but all had a similar fundamental design. Boas (1888) described one of the types from Baffin Island. This consisted of a shaft, or *unang*, fashioned from driftwood found on the shore, and tipped at each end with stout walrus ivory points, or made entirely from the tusk of a narwhal. The upper end of the shaft was shaped to receive the *naulang*, the harpoon head, also made of ivory. The *naulang* was about 2.5–5 cm long; its base was hollowed out or mortised so that it sat securely on a spigot fashioned on the end of the *ulang*. If available, a piece of metal, or failing that a flake of stone, was mounted transversely across the tip of the *naulang* to provide a cutting edge. The harpoon line, or *iparang*, was made of sealskin. This was fastened through a hole in the *naulang* made parallel to the point and terminated in a loop that the hunter could hold in his left hand. Any strain coming on the *iparang* as the wounded seal struggled to get away would have caused the point to come free from its seating, turn at right angles, and act as a toggle, fastened securely beneath the skin. Such a weapon would not have killed a seal, but it would have allowed the hunter to draw it in with the *iparang*, so that it could be killed.

This type of harpoon was used to hunt ringed seals at their breathing holes. Even as late as 1965, Netsilik Eskimos were hunting in this way. A hunter would go out onto the ice to a breathing hole, build a small shelter of snow blocks, and stand there, motionless, his feet slightly insulated from the cold by standing on a folded sealskin. With such sparse protection, a hunter might wait for hours without a seal coming to the breathing hole, but if he were lucky, a seal would surface and, on hearing it breathing, the hunter would stab down with his harpoon. If the strike were successful, the seal could be dragged to the surface and dispatched by a blow from the side of the hand to the head. The Canadian Government Film Unit, in a remarkable film archive of a vanishing culture, recorded a hunt of this sort, with the hunters eating the raw liver of the animal, and bringing the seal home and dividing it among the whole community.

Eskimos also used their dogs to sniff out ringed seal birth lairs, hoping to break down the roofs and catch the mothers before they could escape into the water. This was not often successful, but a pup could usually be secured. This could then be used as bait, by attaching a line to its hind flippers and letting it down through the breathing hole. When the mother returned to her pup she could be harpooned in the usual way.

Seals were also hunted at sea in the summer from boats. Kayaks were single seater canoes of a pattern now thoroughly familiar; *umiaks* were larger and could carry several hunters and a quantity of game. Both kayaks and *umiaks* were made of a wooden frame over which were stretched sealskins, from ringed seals in the case of the kayak and from the larger bearded seals in the case of the umiak. A kayak is a very unstable craft and, were a hunter to harpoon a seal in the water and retain hold of the end of the line, it would almost certainly capsise. the Eskimos got around this problem by attaching a float, an *avautang*, to the end of the line. The *avautang* could then be thrown over the side when the seal had been struck, and followed to be retrieved later when the seal had tired or been killed by thrusts from a lance. By using multiple floats, and a lot of patience, Eskimos could tackle walruses and even whales.

The kayak harpoon (Figure 6.5) was different from that used at breathing holes. It was designed to be thrown and consisted of a shaft with a bone or ivory hand support at the point of balance and near this an ivory peg for fastening the line. At the top of the shaft was a walrus tusk, held by sinew bindings to a mortised ivory socket, the *qatirn*. At the end of the tusk is the ivory point, the *tokang*, armed with a metal or stone cutting edge. The seal skin line was fastened to the *tokang* which is held in place on the tusk by the tension of the line attached to the ivory peg near the hand support.

When the harpoon was thrown and penetrated the hide of the seal any sideways strain on the walrus tusk would cause it to bend sideways in its

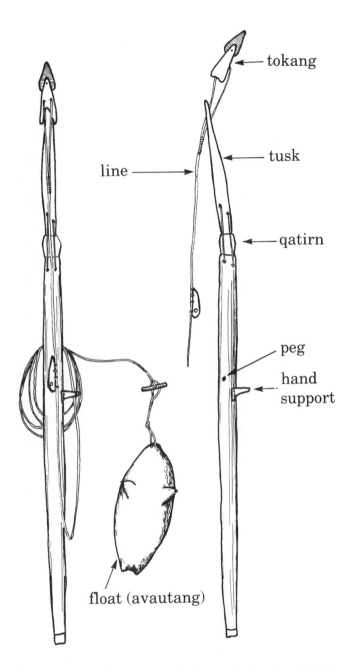

Figure 6.5 Eskimo kayak harpoon. The harpoon is shown ready to throw. The tokang *is held in place by the tension of the line hooked over the peg by the hand support. After the* tokang *is fast in the seal, the tusk swivels in the* qatirn, *allowing the line to slip free of the peg.*

socket on the *qatirn*, shortening the distance between the *tokang* and the peg where the line was fastened, thus allowing the *tokang* to slip off the tusk and turn sideways in the wound, forming the toggle anchor. A kayak harpoon was thus a sophisticated implement and a far cry from the simple barbed harpoons used by the Stone Age hunters in the Baltic. It was only the development of such sophisticated hunting technologies that allowed the Eskimos to survive in the almost incredibly harsh environment that they inhabited.

I have dealt at length with Eskimo seal hunting because it can fairly be said that the coastal Eskimos were the one people that was entirely dependent on seals. Seals dominated their economy. All parts of the seal were used, but nothing was more important than blubber. Blubber was eaten as it was but its most important function was as fuel in stone blubber lamps. Eskimos in their underground stone huts or snow houses might just have survived without the heat from their blubber lamps but the light they provided was essential if they were to manufacture and maintain their clothing, weapons and implements.

The coming of modern cilivisation has changed almost everything for Eskimo peoples. Hunting continues as an important way of life, but the techniques have, of course, changed. Rifles have entirely supplanted harpoons for killing seals. At Wainwright in Alaska in 1965 each Eskimo household owned an average of 2 high-powered rifles, 1.1 .22 calibre rifles and 1.3 shotguns (Nelson, 1969). Rifles, which kill from a distance, alter the balance between hunter and quarry. A seal which is shot but not killed outright will almost certainly escape and many seals killed in the water sink and are lost to the hunter. During a summer hunt at Wainwright only 12 of 22 seals shot in the water were retrieved, and the average loss rate was believed by Nelson to be higher.

Eskimos no longer have the same need for seals for their daily needs. Seal meat and blubber is still eaten in many Eskimo communities, but 'Western' foods are fast becoming the normal fare. The importance of seals is now mainly to provide skins which can be sold in western markets for cash. Cash is essential to buy fuel for motor sledges and outboard motors, guns, ammunition and other items. In recent years, however, changes in Western markets brought about largely by public protest at the killing of harp seals in the north-west Atlantic (Chapter 9) has made it more difficult for Eskimo hunters to sell their skins. This is bringing about a radical change in the way of life for many of these peoples and may be the final factor which wrenches them from their traditional way of life to force them to adopt Western values and culture.

SEALS AND THE EUROPEAN SEAL HUNTER

No peoples in Europe were as dependent on seals as the Eskimos. The way of life soon changed from subsistence hunting to farming and Clark (1946) has pointed out that by the end of the Stone Age the Norwegian seal hunters were basically farmers who supplemented their food supply by seasonal hunting. Even within the last hundred years this practice has continued where small coastal farmers and seals occur together. Martin Martin, in his *Description of the Western Islands of Scotland*

(1703) tells us how the crofters of North Uist used to make a yearly expedition to the islet of Causamul at the end of October, to club the grey seals there, a practice which had been going on since time immemorial. Martin's account is cursory, but a much fuller account of sealing comes from the island of Anholt in the Kattegat. This was published by Bynch in 1801 and quoted by Ulrik Møhl in a fascinating account of the history of marine mammal hunting on Danish coasts (1970). Grey seals no longer occur at Anholt, having been exterminated when bounty payments were introduced for them in 1889, but in the time of which Bynch was writing, they arrived in their hundreds to breed early in January on the sandy beaches at the north of the island. Bynch describes how on Christmas Day the whole north coast of the island was declared a forbidden area and all dogs had to be shut up. On Candlemas Day (2 February), the three aldermen and the sheriff of the island visited the seal breeding beaches to see what the hunt might yield and whether the young seals were big enough to be killed. When the time was judged right, hunters stealthily crept down the beach and killed the weaned pups with a blow to the head from a wooden club fitted with an iron spike, taking care to disturb the adults as little as possible. The dead pups were then dragged up the beach and concealed in the sand dunes. Killing took place every four or five days. Only the pups were killed at this stage; the mothers were never disturbed.

Hunting continued in this way through February and early March till it ended in an assault termed the *store slag*, the killing of some of the old bulls. In what was described by Bynch as 'a difficult, dangerous and blood-dripping spectacle' all the available hunters gathered together, each armed with a pike, to try to kill as many of the old bulls as possible before they escaped to the sea. In fact, only a few of the bulls could be killed in this way; the majority escaped. At the end of the season the blubber, which was the main object of the hunt, was distributed according to definite rules among the inhabitants of the island, who used it in their lamps. Møhl points out that this use can be traced right from the Stone Age to as recently as 1917.

It seems likely to me that the sort of activity at Anholt might have been very similar to what was going on at Hesselø in the Stone Age. It is all too easy to exterminate a breeding colony of grey seals by uncontrolled cropping. If hunting was to continue over many years and even centuries, then there must have been some regulations to control what was killed and how. The Anholters restricted killing to the weaned pups and the old bulls, while leaving the producing part of the stock, the breeding females, unharmed. This would form the basis for a rational and sustainable exploitation policy for a seal stock. The absolute protection between Christmas and Candlemas allowed the seals to assemble and bear their pups without disturbance, while the spacing of the hunts at four- or five-day intervals would allow some seals to escape to provide the future breeding stock. Without such restrictions, no seal hunt of this kind could have continued for very long. Sealing at Anholt, which according to Bynch had been going on since time immemorial, continued until the end of the nineteenth century. At Causamul, grey seals were hunted yearly (but for one day a year only) from long before Martin's account of it to the beginning of the present century.

Harbour seals, with their much more mobile young, could not be caught in this way, but were susceptible to netting and other means of trapping. Linnaeus, in the diary of his journey to Oland and Gothland in 1741 (Linnaeus 1745), describes two types of nets used to catch seals, which from his description appear to be harbour seals. Both net types depended on the seal's habit of hauling out to rest on chosen offshore stones. The first sort were laid in a square around a seal rock, their outer and inner ends held open by transverse rods, and with a rope fastened to the innermost rod and carried ashore. The frame of netting was allowed to lie on the bottom until a seal, or seals, had climbed up on the rock. By pulling on the rope, the frame was allowed to float to the surface whereupon the seal, alarmed by the movement, would slither off the rock and become entangled in the net where the hunters could kill it. The other sort of nets were simpler. They formed a half-circle on the seaward side of the rock. The seals would climb up the rock ignoring the nets, but when frightened would always rush down the seaward side and enter the nets. Seal rocks were so valuable to farmers that if there were no naturally occurring ones along the coast, then artificial ones might be set up. Staffen Söderberg (1972) says that fire-blackened pieces of wood might be used.

Seal traps were made by preparing a wooden platform with hinged doors that floated in the sea. Seals would try to haul out on the platform, fall through the doors and be captured in a net set underneath. Snag hooks were also employed to take seals hauled out on rocks, particularly those clothed in seaweed. Stout three-pointed hooks were attached to a rope which girdled the rock below high water mark. As the tide fell, seals would haul out on the rock. At low water the rope with its hooks would be exposed and, the seals being scared off the rock, some of them might get snagged by the hooks.

The products from seals caught in these various ways would mostly have been consumed locally. Blubber oil, as we have seen, was used in lamps in Denmark until well into this century, and in the Hebrides and Orkney to the end of the previous century. Seal skins were used for leather harness and the skin of the harbour seal is a traditional covering for the Scottish sporran. Seal meat was said by Martin Martin to have medicinal qualities. It is certainly palatable, and must have been a welcome addition to the diet of poor crofters. In a more religious time, seal meat was welcomed as red meat which might be consumed in Lent (seals, living in the sea, could be classed as fish). Grace Hickling (1962) has noted that in 1372–3 the Master of Farne received six shillings and eight pence for four flagons of oil extracted from seals and porpoises, and in 1378–9 four shillings and sixpence were paid for a 'celys calfe'. These are perhaps the earliest records of cash trading for seal products.

Subsistence seal hunting, and even minor market hunting, probably had relatively little effect on stocks. The Eskimos lived in balance with their prey, at least until the advent of guns and snow scooters, but even now the dispersed habit of the ringed seal means that it seems to be but little affected by hunting pressures. In northern Europe, many colonies of grey and harbour seals held their own. Where seals disappeared, it was often for reasons other than hunting (Chapter 8).

COMMERCIAL SEALING

Major industries directed against seals, with the intention of maximising the catch for purely commercial purposes, were another matter. These could, and did, have potent effects on the stocks. Two such industries dominated the last two hundred years, the North-west Atlantic harp seal hunt, and the southern elephant seal fishery. There were others. Seals have long been a hunter's quarry in Russia and Siberia and with the coming of a central economy, operations against harp seals in the White Sea, Caspian and Baikal seals in their respective homes, and spotted and ribbon seals in the Bering Sea and Arctic Ocean, intensified. In all these areas, stocks were reduced by overexploitation, but following stock assessment, catches have been reduced and the industries continue generally on a scale that is commensurate with the existing stocks.

The Northwest Atlantic Harp Seal Hunt

Early in the sixteenth century, fishermen from the Basque country bordering the Bay of Biscay were visiting the banks off Newfoundland to catch the cod that were so abundant there. They also found that they could catch harp seals by setting nets in the Strait of Belle Isle, between Quebec and Newfoundland. The seals were travelling on their migrations to their breeding grounds, and were therefore concentrated. (Chapter 4.) The development of the industry that arose in the eighteenth century and which at its height so greatly exceeded any other northern seal hunt depended entirely on the presence of these concentrations.

When this region was settled, seasonal net fishing was begun by the inhabitants of the Labrador coast. Nets, which might be up to 183 m long and 3–4 m deep, were set for preference in a 'tickle', a narrow channel between the shore and an island, or between two rocks. Seals might either entangle themselves passively in the nets, or be driven into them by men in boats. If no 'tickle' were available, nets might be set out parallel to the shore, with 'stopper' nets which could be raised at the appropriate moment at their ends. Or a fixed net might be run back to the shore at an angle, where the seals could be penned and caught (Busch, 1985). The whole system depended on the predictable presence of large concentrations of seals moving in a given direction.

By the 1740s, the settlers were shipping substantial quantities of seal oil back to England. In 1742 the two small communities of Fogo and Twillingate exported seal oil to the value of £12,550 and based on the available figures for oil exports the settlers in Newfoundland made annual catches of seals between 7,000 and 128,000 between 1723 and 1795 (Lavigne and Kovacs, 1988). Exceptionally large catches were possible in years when the ice with the pupping seals on it was carried close to shore and the seals became accessible to the people on shore. Seal oil was used for lighting, for lubrication, and for the dressing of cloth and jute. To all intents and purposes it was identical to whale oil and was used for the same purposes.

By the latter half of the eighteenth century, small boats or shallops about 10 m long, decked fore and aft but open between, were being used to reach the seals on the ice. The men in these shallops hunted for a day or two near their homes and were, and still are, known as 'landsmen'. The advantage of using larger boats to get more safely to the seals on the ice was soon appreciated and by 1800 the Newfoundland schooner fleet was under construction. These were substantial vessels of around 30–40 tons, crewed by eight or ten and working up to 100 miles off shore in the spring. As David Lavigne and Kit Kovacs pointed out (1988), the winter and spring seal hunting provided a perfect complement for the summer and autumn cod fishing. Sealing increased rapidly to become second only to cod fishing in the Newfoundland economy. By the second quarter of the eighteenth century as many as 300 schooners were sailing to the sealing grounds with 12,000 men, taking more than half a million seals yearly. Catches of 680,000, 740,000 and 686,000 seals (these figures include an unknown quantity of hooded seals) were reported in 1831, 1832 and 1844 respectively (Colman, 1937). During the period 1818–62 over 18.3 million seals, or more than 400,000 a year, were taken. These are minimum figures, for many seals were killed and skinned and their pelts never collected.

The schooners seriously reduced the numbers of seals and profits fell as the seals became more difficult to take. However, in 1863 a new technology was introduced to the industry — steam power. The schooners, powered by wind alone, were limited in their ability to enter the ice, but the new ships, heavy vessels of 200–300 tons built in Dundee and with steam auxiliary engines, could push into thick ice and had wooden hulls strong enough to withstand all but the worst ice pressure. The 'wooden walled steamers' were, of course, more expensive to operate than schooners, but after a faltering start, they justified their expense with better cargoes.

Early in this century, the 'wooden walls' were themselves superseded by larger steel ships with ice-breaker bows and much more powerful engines. Just before the First World War there were nine steel ships and about a dozen of the old 'wooden walls' left (Colman, 1949). The years between the wars, and in particular the Depression, were bad ones for the Newfoundland sealing industry. The expansion of the Antarctic whaling industry and the gross overproduction of whale oil in 1930–1 depressed the market for seal oil. By 1932, the fleet had been reduced to only four vessels.

Sealing recovered rapidly after the Second World War, but this was due largely to the involvement of foreign-registered vessels. Superior technology in the late 1940s, when the Newfoundland steamers were competing with modern Norwegian diesel-powered vessels, effectively killed off the Newfoundland industry, though the Norwegians established companies in Canada to operate the sealing enterprises. The Norwegians had first appeared at the north-west Atlantic hunt in 1937, when one ship arrived. There were two in 1938 and five in 1939 and 1940. These last ships, following the German invasion of Norway, did not return home, but stayed in Canada. The Russians made two trips to the Front Ice in 1961 and 1963, but then withdrew, and have not subsequently returned.

Post-war catches averaged 316,000 yearly between 1951 and 1960, reaching over 456,000 in 1951 (Capstick et al., 1976) but have fallen radically since then, averaging only 36,000 in the five years to 1987. The reason for this is not connected with the abundance of the seals, or the ability of the industry to crop them, but with the activities of conservation groups, which will be discussed in Chapter 9.

The basic technology of sealing was simple. Adult seals were killed by shooting with high-powered rifles, pups by clubbing. The Canadian sealers used a wooden club, shaped like a baseball bat, but the Norwegians used an instrument like a small pickaxe on a long shaft called a *hakapik*, or a *slagkrok*, a heavy iron hook on a long handle. After shooting or clubbing, the seal was turned over and slit down the middle, turning the skin back to cut the major arteries to the flippers, and thus allowing it to bleed. After bleeding, they were pelted and the sculp, the skin with the blubber on it, brought back to the ship where it was stored in chilled brine or treated with anti-oxidants to prevent the oil staining the fur yellow. Carcasses were left on the ice. Landsmen would take some of the flippers, together with the muscles of the shoulders, to use for food and a limited trade in seal flippers developed outside the immediate sealing area, but in general the carcass was not used.

Light aircraft had been introduced to the seal hunt in 1922 to locate the whelping patches on the ice and in 1962 their use, together with helicopters, was extended to ferry sealers and skins between the shore and the ice. Six years later, in response to a decline in seal numbers, the use of aircraft at the Front was restricted to spotting only.

Initially, the products of the sealing had been blubber oil and some leather. In the late 1940s, however, the Norwegians developed storage and tanning methods, including anti-oxidants, that allowed the pelts to be used in the furrier's trade. Seal-skin coats became relatively cheap and very popular, particularly in Germany. This development put particular pressure on the hooded seals, whose pups produced the beautiful bluebacks, the most prized of all seal skins.

It was not until 1950 and 1951 that Canadian fisheries scientists made the first scientific attempts to assess the seal stocks and came up with a figure for pup production of 645,000. This led to immediate concern, since the catch in 1951 had been 456,000, leaving only a very small potential escapement (Fisher, 1952; Lavigne, 1979; Sergeant, 1973). In 1966 control of the sealing was entrusted to the International Commission on North-west Atlantic Fisheries (ICNAF), which appointed a Seals Assessment Group. This reported that the harp seal stock at the Front had sustained a marked decline over the previous fifteen years, though the group was unable to quantify this. To arrest this decline the duration of the hunt was shortened and the killing of adults in the whelping patches was prohibited.

Quota management was introduced in 1971, with a total allowable catch (TAC) of 245,000 for both the Gulf and the Front, distributed as 100,000 each for the Canadians and the Norwegians and 45,000 for the landsmen. Even though the landsmen exceed their allocation, the quota was not reached, perhaps indicating the scarcity of seals (Lavigne, 1979).

In 1971 the Canadian Minister of the Environment set up a Special Advisory Committee on Seals and Sealing (COSS) to review all aspects of seals and sealing. The following year COSS recommended that the harp seal hunt should be phased out by 1974 and should be followed by a six-year moratorium on sealing. These recommendations were not taken up, but in 1972 the TAC was reduced to 150,000, a level which was maintained until 1976, and commercial sealing in the Gulf was banned. The Canadian assessment in 1975 concluded that the seal population was in poor shape and the 1976 TAC was reduced to 127,000. The following year this view was refuted and the quota advanced to 160,000 and 170,000 in 1978. Following the declaration of a 200 mile Exclusive Economic Zone (EEZ) by Canada in January 1977, the entire control of the sealing grounds off Newfoundland and in the Gulf became Canada's responsibility. Because, however, the seals spent some time within the Greenland EEZ, the responsibility for management of the herds was shared by Canada and Denmark, representing Greenland (Lavigne and Kovacs, 1988). Norway's involvement was maintained through a bilateral agreement and responsibility for setting the quota transferred from ICNAF to the North-west Atlantic Fisheries Organization (NAFO). In 1982 the quota settled at 175,000 seals, though catches never reached this level (Table 6.1).

Table 6.1 Quotas for harp seals and catches, Newfoundland and the Gulf of St Lawrence. (After Lavigne and Kovacs, 1988.)

Year	Quota	Catch
1971	245,000	230,966
1972	150,000	129,883
1973	150,000	123,832
1974	150,000	147,635
1975	150,000	174,363
1976	127,000	165,002
1977	160,000	155,143
1978	170,000	161,723
1979	170,000	160,541
1980	170,000	171,929
1981	168,200	200,162
1982	175,000	166,739
1983	175,000	57,889
1984	175,000	30,900
1985	175,000	18,225
1986	175,000	24,532
1987	175,000	49,000

By the 1980s, the activities of anti-sealing groups had mobilised public opinion to the extent that the importation of products from harp and hood seal pups into countries of the European Economic Community was prohibited in 1983. This effectively destroyed the market for seal skins and resulted in an immediate lessening of hunting pressure. Following a report from the Royal Commission on Seals and the Sealing Industry, appointed by the Canadian government in 1984, which concluded that the commercial hunting of the pups of harp and hooded seals was widely unacceptable, the Canadian goverment in December 1987 announced that the killing of pups was to end. The hunt for moulting or moulted pups ('ragged jackets' and 'beaters') and for adults is unaffected by this ruling, and the seal hunt continues, though on a vastly reduced scale. The part played by conservation groups, particularly Greenpeace, in these developments is dealt with in more detail in Chapter 9.

The Elephant Oilers

Elephant seals, the largest and most lethargic members of the seal family, who are also extremely gregarious were an obvious attraction to commercial sealers. Sealing started in the Southern Hemisphere with the pursuit of the fur seals of South America and the Falklands but the obvious oil resource of the elephant seals was apparent to the fur sealers from the start. Elephant seal oil was only marginally different from whale oil and the techniques for extracting it from the blubber were the same, so it is not surprising that whaling and elephant sealing were often conducted from the same vessel. Elephant sealing was also a profitable sideline for fur sealers when the stocks of the more valuable fur seals began to run low.

South Georgia, an island lying below the Antarctic Convergence in the South Atlantic Ocean at latitude 54° S, was the first major elephant sealing ground. From October to April, some elephant seals were always to be found ashore, though the greatest rewards were to be had by harvesting the huge crowds of fat breeding animals in the early spring. Having no experience of terrestrial predators, elephant seals had no tendency to flee when the sealers arrived. The almost incredible indifference of the animals to disturbance impressed all the sealers:

> The loudest noise will not awaken these animals when sleeping, as it is not unusual, though it may appear singular, for the hunter to go on and shoot one without awakening those alongside of it, and in this way proceed through the whole rookery, shooting and lancing as many as are wanted. (Fanning, 1832)

Cows and pups were stunned with a blow on the head from a heavy club and then lanced, while the largest bulls were killed by a musket ball fired up through the roof of the mouth when the animal reared up to roar, being finished off with the lance.

Once killed, the animals were skinned and the blubber removed separately as a series of 'blanket pieces' or 'horse pieces', usually about 45–60 cm long and 40 cm wide. These were then either strung on poles, to be carried by two men, or loaded into barrows, and taken off to the try works, if these had been set up on shore. If the blubber was to be tried out on ship, the blanket pieces would be strung on a line and rafted out to the vessel. Shore try works were the rule where seals were plentiful. A party could be set ashore from the parent vessel with stores and the necessary gear. A rough shelter was prepared from a sod hut, or a sail over an upturned boat, and the try works erected nearby. These consisted essentially of the blubber-cooking apparatus of a whaler, brought ashore. Two huge cast-iron cauldrons, of about 100 gallons (455 litres) capacity each, would be mounted side by side in a brick fireplace. This was usually built by a stream, for it was the custom to soak the blubber in water for 24–48 hours before mincing and boiling. Such ruined try works can still be found at many sheltered anchorages around South Georgia and on other subantarctic islands.

The blubber of elephant seals was said to be harder to boil than that of whales, and so was minced more finely. The sealers claimed that a barrel of blubber would yield a barrel of oil. Clark (1877) stated that a try works

119

of 100 gallon capacity could produce about 900 gallons of oil a day. Barrel sizes varied, of course, but it was generally reckoned that a barrel was 31 gallons (about 125 litres, the gallon not being standard, either). After extraction, the oil was baled out of the try pots into a cooler before being poured into casks for storage and then rafted out to the ship. The scraps left after boiling were used to fuel the fire beneath the try pots, sometimes first being put through a press to extract more oil.

Elephant sealing at South Georgia was carried on by both British and American sealers. The American industry is better documented, for many of their log books have survived, while few of those from the British ships are now available. Certainly, the Americans dominated the last stages of elephant (and fur) sealing at South Georgia. At Desolation Land (as the Kerguelen Archipelago was known to the sealers), the Prince Edward Islands and the Crozet Islands, British elephant sealers seem to have started the early sealing, between 1800 and 1810, but the Americans soon turned up to dominate the industry (Busch, 1985). Heard Island, 420 km to the south of Kerguelen, was a very rich source of elephant seals and was exploited almost exclusively by American sealers, beginning in 1855. Macquarie Island, on the other hand, was worked predominantly by sealers from the newly established colony at Port Jackson (Sydney).

Old-fashioned elephant sealing died out with the demise of open-boat whaling and the era of sailing ships. The last of the old sealers was probably Captain Benjamin Cleveland, who sealed at South Georgia in 1913 and at Desolation Land in 1916 in the famous whaling barque *Charles W. Morgan* (Busch, 1985). Elephant sealing was heavy, dangerous work and the rewards were comparatively slight. These factors combined to lessen the pressure on elephant seals, in comparison with more valuable species such as fur seals or right whales. The total harvest of elephant seals from the South Seas will never be known, though some extravagant claims have been made. Briton Busch (1985) calculated that the harvest to 1900 was of the order of 800,000, but this was a conservative estimate and covered only Kerguelen and Heard Islands, Macquarie, and South Georgia. Elephant seals were also taken in large numbers at the Crozet Islands, St Paul and Amsterdam Islands, the Prince Edwards, the Falklands, the South Shetland Islands, and the islands of the Bass Strait, to mention only some of the places where this trade was carried on. Perhaps the real total was nearer a million.

Whatever the depredations of the nineteenth century, a flourishing stock of elephant seals survived into the present century at South Georgia and formed the basis of an industry that provided one of the best examples of rational and sustainable use of a wild animal population (Bonner, 1982). Most of the islands where elephant sealing had been carried on were uninhabited save for the sealers themselves. South Georgia, however, had a resident British administration installed in 1908 after the setting up there of the Antarctic whaling industry by the Norwegian, C. A. Larsen, in 1904. The administration, centred in the Falkland Islands, was aware of the damage that uncontrolled whaling or sealing could cause and there was already legislation in the Falklands (of which South Georgia was a dependency) which provided protection for the seals. In 1909 this was extended to cover South Georgia, and the whaling company set up by Larsen was licensed to take elephant seals.

Initially the regulations were on an *ad hoc* basis but fortunately the local administrator drew up a set of rules which provided a basis for sustainable exploitation.

The coast of South Georgia was divided into four sealing divisions, of which only three were to be worked in any one year. No more than 2,000 elephant seals were to be taken from any division in one year and the killing was to be restricted to adult males. The maximum number that could be taken in any year was thus 6,000, but this figure was not approached for the first twenty years of sealing and not attained until 1937. In the early years of controlled sealing at South Georgia there was a closed season from 1 October to the last day of February which protected the seals for almost the whole of their breeding season. This made taking seals very difficult, except during the autumn moult in March and April, and by 1921 the start of the closed season had been put back to 1 November and extensions to permit sealing into November were regularly approved.

Techniques differed markedly from those of the nineteenth century sealers, for the modern industry was based on the shore installations of Larsen's whaling station. Obsolete whale catchers were used to take the sealing crews to the beaches and bring back the blubber for cooking out. When I first visited South Georgia in 1953 there were three sealing vessels; the most modern had been built in 1921 and had a gross tonnage of 210, and the oldest had been built in 1884 and was 77.5 tons gross (Bonner 1982).

Sealing was a rough life. Harrison Matthews has given a vivid account of what it was like in his book *Sea Elephant* (1952). Some of the techniques had changed by the time I arrived there, thirty years after the period Matthews wrote about, but the basics were the same. On reaching a suitable beach, the sealing crew would be sent ashore through the surf in a heavy pram dinghy. The crew consisted of nine men, the gunner (who was the mate of the sealer), a beater, three flensers, three hookers and the pram man. The master, the engineer, one seaman and the cook remained on board the sealer to receive and load the catch as it came out.

The gunner was in charge ashore and had to decide which seals to take, in what order and how to handle them. It was important always to take the dominant bulls first, to prevent the movement of the beachmasters from driving the lower status bulls into the sea. The beater, equipped with a metal tube, about 18 mm in diameter and some 2 m long (a discarded condenser tube from the engine room of the sealing vessel), would approach the first bull and strike it sharply over the head with the tube. This would, of course, cause the bull to rear up and challenge his assailant. But the beater could continue to strike the seal about the head, while remaining safely outside the range of its lunges. In this way, without using undue force, the bull could be driven backwards down the beach to the water's edge. Just as its hindquarters entered the water, the beater would move to one side, so that the bull, still facing its tormentor, would be at a slight angle to the slope of the beach. At this stage it would be shot in the head by the gunner, using a heavy cartridge with a soft-nosed bullet. In these circumstances, death was instantaneous and rarely was a second shot required. In contrast to the nineteenth century sealers, shots were never fired through the palate and lances were never employed. Much of the efficiency of modern sealing depended on driving the bull to exactly the right spot where it could most easily be flensed and its blubber floated out.

The gunner and beater would then go off to take the next bull while the flensers took over. The first task was to stab the seal in the heart with a long-bladed knife. This was not to kill it, as it was already dead, but to arrest the action of the heart, which would still be pumping vigorously despite the destruction of the brain. Without stopping the heart, the flensers would be sprayed with blood from every vessel they cut as they stripped the blubber from the seal.

The early practice of removing the blubber in blanket pieces (Matthews 1929) was abandoned at South Georgia in the 1930s and the skin and blubber taken off together in one almost circular sheet. This saved a lot of labour and prevented the loss of oil that would otherwise have occurred from the cut blubber. The first cuts were made around the flippers, followed by cuts just behind the eyes and above the tail, and finally a longitudinal cut down the centre of the back (Figure 6.6). Once these cuts had been completed, the flaps of skin and blubber were freed from the sides of the body, using small hooks to pull the slippery blubber away. The fore flipper on one side (the side facing down the slope of the beach) was then pulled through the slit cut in the skin, and dissected away together with its associated shoulder-blade. The other, uphill, flipper was seized with long hooks by the hookers and pulled over the back of the carcass. In this way the carcass could be rolled off the skin while the flensers cut away at the tissue. If the seal had been properly positioned on the slope of the beach, this was an easy task. If not, or if pieces of ice or heavy seas impeded the work, it could be exceedingly difficult.

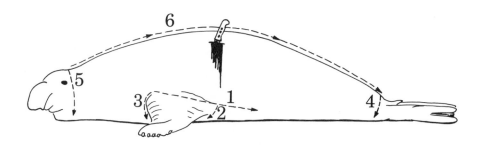

Figure 6.6 Cuts made in flensing an elephant seal.

The carcass was left to rot or be eaten by the birds which flocked to the sealing beaches. The skin, which might weigh half a tonne or more, had a long rope strop threaded through one of the flipper holes and was then doubled over itself, the upper half sliding easily over the blubber of the lower half, to float off into the sea. The waiting pram would pick up the skins and, perhaps with the help of the sealer's motorised lifeboat, tow them out to the vessel. Here they would be stowed in the hold or on deck until the vessel had little freeboard. A full cargo might be from 70 to 230 skins, depending on the size of the sealer and the fatness of the seals. A good day's work would be the blubber of 40 seals, though I have seen 70 taken in one day. The sealer then returned to the whaling station where the skins were offloaded, put through blubber-mincers and cooked out in steam digesters at a pressure of 60 psi (0.4MNm^{-2}) for six hours. The oil was then blown off and stored in tanks. Seal oil prepared in this way was of a high grade, equivalent to No. 1 whale oil, despite the inclusion of large amounts of skin and muscle with the blubber.

This sealing was highly profitable for the whaling company, since it took place at a time in the season when whales were not generally very abundant. Inevitably, there were attempts to increase the profits still further and in 1948 it was decided to raise the quota to 7,500 and to 9,000 in 1949. This quota was never achieved, the higest take being 7,877 seals in 1951. However, this was sufficient seriously to damage the stock. Help was at hand, however, when Dick Laws, who had been studying the biology of the southern elephant seal at the South Orkneys, came to South Georgia to continue his work. Laws noticed the signs of deterioration of the herd which had occurred progressively since the 1930s, when he went out with the sealers (Laws, 1960). Laws quantified the efficiency of the operations in terms of the number of seals taken per 'catcher's day's work' (CDW), a term borrowed from the whaling industry. This had declined from 38.3 seals per CDW in the 1930s to 29.4 seals per CDW in 1951–54, a decline of 23 per cent.

Laws's most useful tool in his study was his discovery that the age of elephant seals could be determined from the structure of their canine teeth. This enabled him to show that in 1951 the average age of bulls killed by the sealers was 6.6 years, and not one of 100 bulls killed was older than ten years, whereas at the South Orkneys the average age of breeding bulls was ten years and some were as old as 20 (Laws, 1953c). As a result of his research, Laws was able to make recommendations for management measures that would restore the South Georgia stock of elephant seals. These included setting quotas for the various sealing divisions that were proportionate to the stock present in those divisions, restricting the kill to bulls exceeding 3.5 m in nose–tail length, and ensuring that 10 per cent of bulls above this size were left on the beaches to impregnate the females. Additionally, a canine tooth was to be collected from every twentieth seal killed, so that a check could be kept on the trend of the age of the catch.

These measures were adopted in 1952 and over the next decade proved extremely successful. I was employed as a biologist to monitor the sealing and regulate the distribution of the quota over the sealing divisions according to the age distribution of catches. The yield of seals per CDW rose in response to increased stocks, as did the average age of the catch and the oil production per seal, this last being affected not only by the fact that older, larger bulls were being taken, but also by an advance of the date of the midpoint of the sealing season — a consequence of more abundant seals — since the earlier in the season a bull is taken, the more oil it yields.

Laws had been able to plot age/biomass curves for elephant seals calculated from length/age relationships. These showed that for males the biomass of a year class increases from birth to age 1 as a result of growth, then decreases to age 3 as a result of mortality, before reaching a

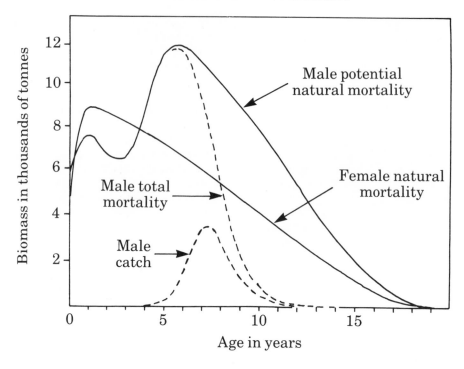

Figure 6.7 Biomass of elephant seals at various ages in the South Georgia stock. (From Laws, 1960).

peak at age 6 with the rapid growth to sexual maturity, and then declining steadily as mortality takes its toll (Figure 6.7). If the estimated biomass of the catch of 6,000 seals is plotted on the same graph, it can be seen that this is equivalent to taking no animals less than eight years old, and then taking the entire eight-year age class, leaving no escapement. A catch about 17 per cent heavier should theoretically result if it were possible to take the entire six-year age class, but this would involve a large increase in effort, as instead of 5,457 eight-year-olds it would be necessary to take 7,922 six-year-olds (Laws, 1960). These are very theoretical figures, of course, but it seemed that the most efficient strategy would be to hold the average age of the catch around 7.5–8 years for maximum sustainable yield exploitation. In fact, by the time the South Georgia sealing industry ended in 1964, the average age of the catch had levelled off at 7.7 years (Laws, 1979), a value fitting exactly the requirements postulated by Dick Laws's model.

Exploitation at this level, which was about 6 per cent of the standing crop per year, had an effect on the stock, but it was not the effect expected in the normal fisheries models for maximum sustainable yield exploitation, where the stock size is reduced to about half its original value. The reason for this was that the elephant seal catch was confined exclusively to males, and because of the very polygynous nature of the species (Chapter 4), this had little effect on the reproductive potential. Indeed, what effect it may have had could have been a beneficial one, for the removal of some of the males may have reduced competition for food, thus benefiting the smaller females.

One aspect of the sealing at South Georgia that did not conform well to a rational management plan was the waste of the raw materials in the 6,000 carcasses that were discarded every year. Both oil and a protein-rich meat meal could have been obtained from these and experiments were carried out to see if they could not be recovered. These all failed because of the difficulties in transporting the bulky and highly perishable caracases from the beaches to the reduction plant. The available transport was not adequate to do this and deal with the blubber at the optimum time in the season, and to have purchased extra shipping would not have been economic. A possible solution would have been a small floating factory that could have travelled round the coast, taking entire seals on board and wasting nothing, but the South Georgia quota alone could not have justified such an investment.

Twelve years after the ending of sealing at South Georgia, sufficient time for a new bull class unaffected by sealing to appear, a study was made of the changes that had occurred. Seamus McCann (1980) found that there were at least three times as many bulls aged six and over in the population as in the days of sealing, and that most harem bulls were aged ten or eleven years, compared with an average of eight in 1951. Although the cow–bull ratio had declined, the average harem size had increased, because the larger, more experienced bulls were better able to exclude others from larger groups of cows.

Whatever views one may hold on the ethics of exploiting wild animal populations, it is surely better to do so in a sustainable manner. The South Georgia elephant seal industry provided an oustanding example of successful scientific management of a natural resource. Elephant seals seemed almost pre-adapted to this role. Their gregariousness meant that operations could be economically concentrated; their polygynous habit meant that the natural ratio of males to females could safely be reduced without risking a drop in the impregnation rate; the eagerness of the cruising bulls in the sea to get ashore ensured that even a beach completely cleared of adult bulls would soon be repopulated; while finally, the extreme sexual dimorphism meant that there was no difficulty in picking out the bulls, and their huge absolute size meant the sealers were handling economically sized packages (Bonner, 1982).

Elephant sealing ended, not because of any shortage of seals, but because the whaling industry, to which it was inextricably linked through its logistic support, collapsed from gross overexploitation of the whales. Whaling, for a variety of reasons, could never have been managed so successfully and its collapse dragged the rationally managed elephant sealing industry down with it.

7 Interactions with man: 2. Seals as competitors

SEALS AND FISHERIES

Today the number of people who make their living hunting seals is very small; many more are engaged in catching fish and in many areas this involves interactions with seals. Where seals are abundant and conspicuous the usual view of the fishermen is that the seals are serious competitors for the fish stocks which they both exploit and that reduction, or better, elimination of the seals would benefit the fishery.

This is an oversimplistic view of what is, in fact, a very complicated relationship. Seals do, indeed, eat fish, but it does not necessarily follow that the stocks the seals feed on are the same as those that the fishermen catch. Seals have large appetites, but quantifying them is not easy and exaggerating the amount consumed by seals is a natural response from aggrieved fishermen. If seal stocks are reduced the remainder will certainly eat less fish, but it does not follow from this that the local fishermen will therefore catch more and make bigger profits. Sorting out the various parts of this puzzle in its many settings in different parts of the world has employed a large number of scientists. Not all their conclusions have been as dispassionately scientific as one might have hoped. Some fisheries scientists have chosen their evidence selectively to show seals as ravening monsters with epicurean dietary tastes, while some from the other side are equally anxious to understate the damage caused by seals.

Seals can certainly cause damage to fisheries, but it is important to put this damage in its proper context. Let us start by considering what the damage consists of. First, and most conspicuous, is the damage to fishing gear and to fish already caught. Second, and generally assumed to be more serious by fishermen, is the toll taken of fish in the sea, which they say reduces their own potential harvest. Thirdly, and of local importance only, is the role played by seals as hosts for parasites which may infest food fishes and reduce their commercial value.

Damage to Gear and Captured Fish

'But when the fishermen have unwittingly enclosed a seal among the fishes in their well-woven nets, then there is swift labour and haste to pull the nets ashore. For no nets, even if there are very many at hand, would stay the raging seal, but with its violence and sharp claws it will easily break them and rush away and prove a succour to the pent-up fishes but a great grief to the hearts of the fishermen. But if betimes they bring it near the land, there with trident and mighty clubs and stout spears they smite it on the temples and kill it: since destruction comes most swiftly upon seals when they are smitten on the head.' (Oppian, *Halieutica*, vol. 1)

The Mediterranean monk seals which caused such distress to Oppian's fishermen in Roman times are still persecuted because of the damage they are believed to cause, though they are now so rare that encounters between them and the fishermen must be very infrequent. Where seals are more abundant the story may be different.

Damage to nets occurs most frequently and most severely where the nets are set regularly in one place which fish are known to frequent — what the Scottish salmon fishery terms 'fixed engines'. Salmon nets are particularly vulnerable, possibly because salmon fisheries are frequently situated in places where seals are abundant, possibly because seals have a liking for salmon. A common form of net used for catching salmon on the Scottish coast and elsewhere in Europe is the bag net (Figure 7.1). The bag consists of a series of netting enclosures, protected by narrow openings called doors, which gradually decrease in size until the smallest enclosure, the fish court, is reached. The net is set with the fish court nearest the shore and a long netting wall called the leader extending out seawards from the bag. The whole apparatus is fixed to anchors or stout stakes driven into the sea bed. When salmon are swimming down the coast on their spawning migration, they encounter the leader and turn along it until they are directed into the bag. Here they can enter quite easily through the door, but can not find their way out again past the backwardly sloping sides by the doors. Eventually the fish pass through the narrowest door into the fish court, where they are trapped.

Seals damage such nets in two ways (Rae, 1960). A seal may follow the fish through the doors into the bag. Here it finds it difficult to escape and in its struggles tears the netting, thus allowing what fish the seal has not already eaten to escape. A net damaged in this way will fail to catch any more fish until it is repaired and, if the hole is not speedily detected, a significant loss can result. Alternatively, a seal outside the net may see the fish in the bag, and tear the netting in an attempt to get at them. The resulting hole again allows the loss of the existing, and potential future, catch. Where seals are numerous, as on the Kincardineshire coast north of Montrose in Scotland, it is usual to set these nets where a watch can be kept from the cliff tops by a net skipper armed with a rifle to shoot at seals. Not many seals are killed in this way, however.

When synthetic fibres were introduced to replace the tarred hemp that had previously been used to manufacture such nets, the incidence of damage was markedly reduced. Seals can, of course, still get into the nets, but they are usually unable to tear their way out again and drown inside the net. This reduces the loss to the fisherman but there are still complaints that a net which has had a seal in it catches less well than a 'clean' net. This belief may be well founded. Seals are notably smelly animals, even to a human nose, and salmon and other fish are known to

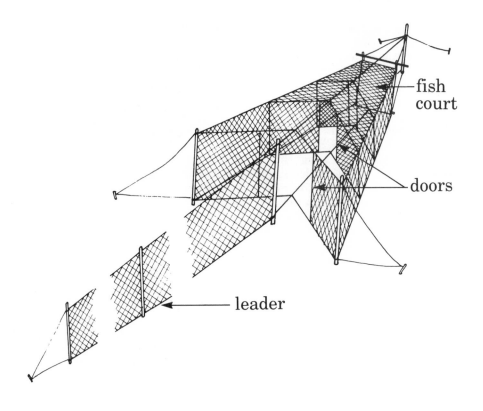

Figure 7.1 A salmon bag net of a type used in the Scottish fishery.

have an exceedingly well-developed sense of smell. Alderdice and his colleagues (1954) found that rinses of mammalian skin, particularly from harbour seals and sea lions, produced alarm reactions in Pacific salmon, so it seems likely that the presence of a dead seal in a net, or even the aroma left after one has been removed, might well deter salmon from entering it.

In the Maritime Provinces of Canada trap nets are set for shoaling fish such as herring and mackerel. These are suspended from floats at the surface and seals enter the traps by sliding over the float lines at the top of the nets. A seal, or seals, swimming about inside may drive captured fish back out of the mouth of the net and away to sea. Because of this, in areas where seals are abundant, a net with fish in it must be guarded by men with guns (Mansfield and Beck, 1977).

Nets and traps of the sort described contain fish only from time to time. Potentially much more attractive to a seal are those nets which are continually stocked with fish. The explosive expansion of the fish-farming industry has led to the appearance of such netting cages, stocked usually with salmon, in many sheltered lochs and bays. These are vulnerable to

1. In the foreground, a leopard seal rests on an ice floe, while behind, a group of crabeater seals occupy another floe. Coronation Island, South Orkney Islands. (Photo: Nigel Bonner)

2. A Hawaiian monk seal shelters from the sun under bushes at the top of the beach. Hawaiian monk seals are the most primitive of all the seals. (Photo: Bryan L. Sage)

3. A Weddell seal floats gracefully in an icy sea. The blubber layer beneath the skin reduces heat loss to the environment. (Photo: Nigel Bonner)

4. A Ross seal. This is the least commonly seen Antarctic seal, since its preferred habitat is dense pack ice, where ships rarely penetrate. The streaky markings at the side of the neck are unique to Ross seals. (Photo: British Antarctic Survey)

5. Old male crabeater seal. This animal shows the typical parallel scars on its flank. These are the result of an attack by a leopard seal when the crabeater was an adolescent. (Photo: Nigel Bonner)

6. *A young southern elephant seal flexes its body to scratch its hind flippers. Seals swim by lateral flexion of the hinder part of the trunk combined with movements of the flippers and this results in their having very limber bodies.* (Photo: Nigel Bonner)

7. *Mating in the northern elephant seal. The male grasps the female by the neck and clasps her with his flipper. The female responds by bawling, which alerts the dominant male should he not be the one mating with her.* (Photo: Nigel Bonner)

8. *An immense herd of northern elephant seals on the beach at San Miguel Island, California. The elephant seals share these beaches with California sea lions and occasional fur seals.* (Photo: Nigel Bonner)

9. *A dominant bull northern elephant seal amongst his cows on Año Nuevo Island, California. The size difference between males and females is greater in elephant seals than in any other mammals.* (Photo: Nigel Bonner)

10. *Two southern elephant seal bulls battle it out for the privilege to pass to their genes to the next generation. Sexual fighting between males has resulted in the great sexual dimorphism shown by elephant seals. South Georgia.* (Photo: Nigel Bonner)

11. A hunter drives a massive southern elephant seal bull to the shore in South Georgia. The abundant blubber of this, the largest of all the seals, was sought after by sealers in the nineteenth century. The industry continued into the present century but finally ended in 1964. (Photo: Nigel Bonner)

12. A newly weaned southern elephant seal pup. The well-developed whiskers on the muzzle, nose and above the eyes are characteristic of seals. (Photo: Nigel Bonner)

13. *Male spotted seal. This ice-inhabiting species is a close relative of the more familiar harbour seal.* (Photo: Lloyd Lowry)

14. *A female northern elephant seal and her newly-born pup. The placenta lies on the sand beside the pup. Año Nuevo Island, California.* (Photo: Nigel Bonner)

15. *A ringed seal pup in its lair in the fast ice off Nome, Alaska. Ringed seals are unique in giving birth to their pups in a prepared shelter.* (Photo: Lloyd Lowry)

16. *A leopard seal shows its impressive teeth. These seals are versatile predators, taking about a third of their diet in the form of red meat, mainly young crabeater seals and penguins. Bird Island, South Georgia.* (Photo: Nigel Bonner)

17. *Male ribbon seal. The pattern on the coat of these seals is perhaps the most striking of all the pinnipeds.* (Photo: Kathy Frost)

18. *A young male harp seal in the breeding habitat on sea ice.* (Photo: Planet Earth Pictures)

19. *A yearling harbour seal on a sand-bank in the Wash, East Anglia. These abundant seals have recently suffered severely from a viral disease, phocine distemper.* (Photo: Nigel Bonner)

20. *The 'roman nose' of the grey seal is characteristic of the species and has given rise to its being called the 'horse head' in eastern Canada.* (Photo: Nigel Bonner)

seal attack and damage to a rearing net can result in the escape and loss of fish valued at several thousand pounds.

It is rare for drift nets to be damaged by seals, but seals can remove fish gilled in a drift net, and in doing so may shake others loose, thus reducing the catch. Furthermore, fish may be damaged so as to be less marketable. Rae and Shearer (1965) reported how in one sample of 286 salmon caught in Scottish drift nets 24.4 per cent bore marks which they attributed to seal damage. Potter and Swain (1979) estimated that 5 per cent of salmon caught in drift nets on the north-east coast of England had been removed by seals and a further 1.4 per cent damaged.

Losses of salmon, for which the fishery is usually restricted, are especially serious for the fishermen, but other more abundant species are also vulnerable to seals. In eastern Canada drift nets set for mackerel, pollack and cod are subject to damage by seals (Mansfield and Beck, 1977) as are herring and mackerel nets off East Anglia (Bonner, 1972). I have watched an exasperated fisherman tugging at his herring net to get it inboard while a harbour seal in the water was tugging in the opposite direction. Long-lining, too, may be adversely affected by seals. Bennet Rae (1960) gives an account of a grey seal caught on a line that had stripped the fish, codling, haddock and whiting, from each hook up to that on which it had caught itself and drowned.

Removing baits from hooks or traps may be another way in which seals affect fisheries. Seals are reported in eastern Canada to break into lobster pots to steal baits, releasing lobsters already caught and, of course, making it unlikely that the trap will catch further lobsters (Mansfield and Beck, 1977).

Another complaint by the fishermen concerns the 'marking' of salmon. Salmon are not infrequently taken which when landed are seen to bear a series of rips in the skin, sometimes single but usually several together, about 2.5–15 cm long and 2.5–4 cm deep. They can occur on any part of the fish and while most are freshly inflicted, some show healing. These marks could be caused by the claws or, less likely, by the teeth of seals. Quality fish like salmon depend at least partly on their good appearance when they reach market, and marked salmon fetch a considerably lower price than intact fish. How the marks are caused is not known. Grey seals and harbour seals (and probably other species) use their fore flippers when eating fish, but there are no reports of them using their claws to catch them. The occasional occurrence of tooth marks or deep bites which correspond to the jaws of a seal, together with the putative claw marks, suggests that they are indeed caused by seals and it would be difficult to suggest any other animal which might inflict such wounds.

Depletion of Fish Stocks by Seals

It seems self-evident that if seals eat fish, and there are a lot of seals, there will be fewer fish. In fact, it is exceedingly difficult to find convincing examples that fish-eating marine mammals have affected the abundance of a fish stock (IUCN, 1981). Ray Beverton (1985) noted that the only really convincing case of which he was aware was the rather unusual one of a population of freshwater harbour seals living in the Lower Seal Lake on the Ungava Peninsula in Quebec which had depleted the lake trout, *Salvelinus namaycush*, living in the lake. The fish population showed all the signs of sustained severe depletion, i.e. high mortality, reduced age at maturity, fast growth rate and high specific fecundity, in comparison with other populations living in lakes where the seals did not occur.

The seemingly self-evident proposition that more seals mean fewer fish is not actually soundly based. One should ask: Fewer than what? In an undisturbed system seals and their prey will have evolved together to form a complicated web of feeding relationships. Seals that feed on fish usually take a variety, some of which may themselves be fish predators. If one species becomes scarce, the seals may switch to another, allowing a recovery of the depleted species. Such relationships will have been built up over thousands of generations and are not easily susceptible to the simple modelling that is implied by the fishermen's argument. Nevertheless, we must recognise that today we are not dealing with undisturbed systems, but with systems that have in many cases been stressed to their limits. Most commercially exploitable fish stocks are now fished at levels near the maximum possible; fishermen look at other fish consumers, seals, cetaceans and birds, and wonder what part of the available quota is being taken by them, and fisheries scientists work hard to provide an answer.

Beverton (1985) devised a series of very simple models to illustrate the possible interactions of marine mammals and fisheries. In the simplest case (Figure 7.2a) the seal and the fishery both exploit a stock of a single prey species. This is an unlikely situation, for both the fishery and the seals are likely to exploit several species. Combining simple models for each species is difficult to do, for the relative importance of each component in the fishery and the seals' diet may vary independently. Furthermore, the prey species are likely to have other predators, such as seabirds or porpoises (Figure 7.2b). Fish eat other fish, and these fish predators may themselves be eaten by seals and fished commercially (Figure 7.2c). Sometimes, the fish predator will be preyed on by the seals, but not fished commercially (Figure 7.2d). Here the seals may actually benefit the fishery, if they consume large quantities of predatory fishes. A limiting case for this would be if the seals were to feed exclusively on the predator, while the fishery concentrated exclusively on the prey (Figure 7.2e). The converse of this, where the fishery takes the predatory fish, and the predator and the seals both eat the same prey stock, is shown in Figure 7.2f.

In all these cases the effect of the seals on the fishery will be different, ranging from adverse to beneficial. It is certainly easier to think of examples where the seals are competing against the fishermen than where they are helping them, but in only very few cases are sufficient data available to attempt even the simplest models of seal/fishery interactions.

To assess the effect of seals feeding on fish stocks in our simplest example (Figure 7.2) it is necessary to assemble four sets of data: the size and composition of the stock of seals concerned; the qualitative and quantitative composition of their diet; their daily food requirements with appropriate adjustments for age class, season, etc.; and their feeding locations and how these correspond with the fishery that is believed to be impacted. We have seen in Chapter 2 that it is difficult to determine the diet and daily food requirements of seals. Equally, it can be difficult to

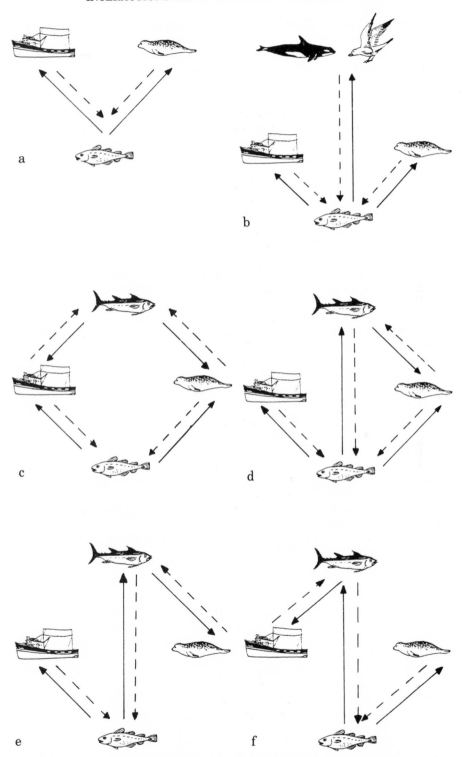

Figure 7.2 Possible interactions between seals, fish and fisheries. (After Beverton, 1985.)

determine seal populations. The efforts that have been made in this direction for one seal stock, the United Kingdom grey seals, will be described later (pp 141). Information on the precise location of the feeding grounds of seals are often ignored by fisheries scientists, largely because it is very difficult to obtain. Where very large scale interactions are being considered this is perhaps less important, but it is unwise to assume that seals and fishermen are both exploiting the same stock of fish without some evidence.

However, given adequate data on the fish stocks, the fisheries, the seals and their feeding patterns, it is not difficult in theory to estimate the impact of seals on commercial catches. The approach used is similar to that involved in assessing the interactions between the impact of two fisheries on the same stock of fish; the removal of fish by the seals is regarded as constituting a special kind of fishery.

The data required are complex and it is impossible to achieve precise results. The problem is usually approached by fisheries biologists in terms of the possible increase in commercial catches should predation by seals on the stock that is fished be reduced (probably by removing the seals). The Report of the Royal Commission on Seals and Sealing in Canada (Anon., 1986) gave a simple model to show that if, as a result of a change in the seal predation rate, the numbers consumed by seals and the numbers caught by fishermen both change, the ratio of the change of catch to change in seal consumption, R, depends only on the relative magnitudes of the fishing mortality, F, and the natural mortality (excluding seal predation) of the fish stock, M, and is not affected by their absolute values or by the rate of predation by the seals.

$$R = F/(F+M)$$

This simple model does not allow for the fact that if a fish is not eaten by a seal it may continue to grow before it is caught by the fishery, an error which tends to underestimate the impact of the seal predation. Terms can be introduced into the model to correct for this and for the differences in the age at which fishing mortality and seal predation begin in the stock.

In general terms it appears that the relative gain to the fishery from a reduction in seal predation changes so that:

1. the relative gain increases as the fishing intensity (F) increases;
2. the relative gain increases as predation intensity increases, particularly when fishing intensity is high;
3. the relative gain is greater when the seal predation starts earlier in the life of the fish than does the fishing mortality, i.e. the seals are eating fish smaller than the commercial catch.

The theoretical gain to the fishery may be either greater or less than the quantity of fish taken by the seals if the seals are removed. This depends on the relative mortality rates due to the fishery, seal predation and natural causes, and on the ages at which the fish become susceptible to fishing and seal predation.

In applying such models, a number of assumptions have to be made. These include:

1. that a change in the rate of seal predation would not change the natural mortality of the fish from other causes;

2.   that the seal predation is spread evenly over the whole population;
3.   that the seal predation rate (i.e. the proportion of the fish stock taken by the seals) is independent of the fish density;
4.   that fish growth and recruitment rate are not density dependent.
                                                              (Anon., 1986)

These are fairly broad assumptions and, coupled with the imprecision of the data on both the fish stock and the feeding pattern of the seals, make the application of such theoretical exercises to actual situations exceedingly difficult.

Consider an example of grey seals at the Farne Islands and the Isle of May on the east coast of Great Britain. These feed extensively on cod, which makes up about 50 per cent of their diet. The mean size of cod taken by the seals is less than the mean size in the commercial catches, which might indicate that the impact of the seals is greater than the amount of fish actually consumed. However, there are no certain data on density effects nor on whether the stock exploited by the seals and the fishery is the same. (In other words, it is not known exactly where the seals from the Farnes and the Isle of May are feeding.) The impact of the seals on the fishery would be overestimated if the seals confined their predation to relatively lightly fished local concentrations of cod, between which and the main fishery stock there is relatively little interchange. This possibility is clearly of some importance when considering seals which may frequent coastal areas for feeding. In these circumstances, it is scarcely possible to say more than that the seals have a likely impact on the catch, without being able to qualify that impact.

Furthermore, changes in catch are not simply related to changes in landed value, the statistic which most directly affects the fisherman. The effect of an increase in catch, whether caused by a reduction in seal numbers or any other factor, will depend on the relationship between supply and demand for fish at that moment. Williams (1981) has even argued that not only might the price per tonne fall as landings increase, but so too might the gross return to the fishery, leaving the fishermen worse off. Most fishermen would probably regard this as another forecast by an economist, doomed forever to get it wrong, and cheerfully accept the risk of getting less money for greater catches, but it represents another factor in the complexity of assessing the impact of seals on fisheries.

Seals as Parasite Hosts

Seals, like most wild carnivores, harbour a large and varied array of parasites. In general this parasite burden seems to have little effect on their hosts. I have seen grey seals in excellent condition and with ample blubber reserves whose stomachs contained more than two litres of large nematodes. The great majority of these are an anisakine nematode *Contracaecum osculatum*, the larvae of which develop in cephalopods and are ingested by the seals when they eat squid. Less frequent, but of greater significance in the context of fisheries, are two other anisakines, *Pseudoterranova* (=*Porrocaecum*, =*Terranova*, =*Phocanema* — the taxonomy of these worms is confused) *decipiens* and *anisakis simples*.

These three nematodes are found in a wide variety of seals, sea lions and walruses and are probably best regarded as universal in the pinnipeds though there are important differences in the frequency of infestation.

Pseudoterranova is the adult form of a nematode whose larva is the codworm. The life cycle of these nematodes is complicated and, in the case of *Pseudoterranova*, still not completely understood. Adult and pre-adult worms are found in a number of marine mammals, but seem to be particularly prevalent in grey seals (Scott and Fisher, 1955; Young, 1972; Mansfield and Beck, 1977). The mature worms produce huge quantities of eggs which are shed into the water in the faeces of the seal and hatch within 10–60 days, depending on water temperature. The resulting first-stage larvae are believed to be eaten by benthic crustacea, perhaps cyclopoid or harpacticoid copepods. These in turn are eaten by a second intermediate host, which may be a crustacean (an amphipod, cumacean, decapod, isopod or mysid), or a polychaete worm or nudibranch mollusc. If infected organisms are eaten by demersal fish, the liberated larvae bore their way through the gut wall and migrate to the mesenteries or to the muscles, where they encyst. Here the larvae remain until their host is eaten by a suitable final host, whereupon the larvae emerge from their cysts in the host's stomach and finally mature to produce eggs and begin the cycle again (Figure 7.3).

Pseudoterranova would remain of academic interest only were it not for the occurrence of its larvae in the flesh of cod. Most larvae are found in the mesenteries, which are discarded when the fish is gutted, but some

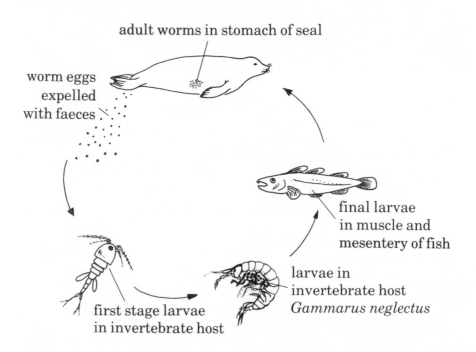

adult worms in stomach of seal

worm eggs
expelled
with faeces

final larvae
in muscle and
mesentery of fish

larvae in
invertebrate host
Gammarus neglectus

first stage larvae
in invertebrate host

Figure 7.3 The life cycle of 'cod-worm', the parasitic nematode Pseudoterranova decipiens.

migrate into the muscles of the body wall, the flaps, and even more conspicuously, into the thicker muscles of the back, the fillets. Codworm are coloured yellowish or rose, which stands out well against the white flesh of cod fillets. They are also capable of movement (if the fish has been iced and not frozen), and the sight of a small pink worm gently undulating on the cod fillet does not improve its appeal to the housewife. Codworm are of little danger to humans as they are killed by the gentlest cooking or by freezing. Margolis (1977) reported 46 cases of confirmed or presumed infection from codworm, of which 37 were in Japan, where eating raw fish is a common practice. However, the presence of codworm in fish not only renders it less marketable but also prejudices the consumer against future purchases. In consequence, fillets of cod suspected of being wormy must be examined individually over an illuminated plate, a process known as candling, and the worms removed by hand, or the most heavily parasitised fish discarded. This adds greatly to the cost of processing the fish and results in lower profits for the fishing industry.

Codworm has proved a serious pest in Canadian, United Kingdom and Norwegian fisheries. Both Canada and the United Kingdom have large and increasing populations of grey seals. The incidence of codworm infestation in cod from the North Sea increased substantially throughout the 1950s and early 1960s at the same time that the stock of British grey seals was increasing rapidly (Rae, 1972). However, while the seal population has continued to increase, since 1977 there has been no evidence of an increase in the infestation rate around the United Kingdom (Parrish and Shearer, 1977). In Canada there has been a recent dramatic increase in codworm infestation, to much higher levels than those reported in the United Kingdom, and a serious problem exists there, with estimates of losses (additional costs plus reduced income) in 1987 amounting to C$25–30 million (Gulland 1987).

The relationship between seals, particularly grey seals, and codworm is undoubted, but it is not a simple relationship. In both Canada and Norway the parasite load increases near seal colonies (Bjorge, 1985; McClelland et al., 1983), but the relation between numbers of seals and numbers of parasites, or between parasites and fisheries losses, is not simply proportional. Gulland (1987) has suggested that both relations are S-shaped, increasing slowly at low numbers or density, then faster, and then flattening out when factors other than seal numbers become more important in controlling parasite abundance, or when the numbers of parasites become so high that it is no longer worth processing the fish.

Anisakis simplex is the herring worm. Athough potentially dangerous to Man (there have been cases of worms developing in humans after eating lightly salted raw herring) seals are less involved in the transmission of this parasite, whose principal definitive hosts appear to be small cetaceans.

Control Measures

Fishermen naturally want to reduce or eliminate the damage caused by seals. Their options are, however, limited. Damage to gear can in some cases be reduced by modifying the gear. The introduction of synthetic fibres in the construction of salmon nets had this effect, though this was a happy by-product of a technology change introduced for other reasons. Some salmon fishermen tried introducing steel bars 7.5 cm apart in the door to the fish court in an attempt to keep seals out (Lockley, 1966), but it is possible that a door as narrow as this also kept out some salmon. Salmon rearing cages can be protected by erecting seal-proof netting around them so that the seals cannot get at the fish within, but this is a heavy extra expense. Mansfield and Beck (1977) noted that bait-stealing from lobster traps by seals was much reduced if the baits were salted for at least a week before use.

Modifications of gear or fishing techniques are not usually sufficient to satisfy the fishermen. Direct reduction of the seal population is seen as a more effective response. The shooting of seals at nets has already been referred to. This is more or less effective, depending of the intensity of seal attacks, the accuracy of the marksman and the extent to which the net can be guarded, bearing in mind that many seal attacks can take place in darkness. Shooting certainly can be effective. Rae (1960) recounts an episode where the catch at a salmon netting station in Scotland rose from two to 767 salmon over five seasons, during which period 624 seals had been shot at the nets. Laying baits poisoned with strychnine in salmon nets was a common practice in Scotland until legislation in 1970 made it illegal. A kelt (a spawned-out salmon) was taken and a small packet of strychnine sewn into its body which was then hung on the side of the bag net. It was generally believed by the salmon fishermen that the troublesome seals were regular visitors and that the use of poison in this way reduced their damage. A more humane way of deterring seals at salmon nets has been the use of recorded sounds, such as killer whale vocalisations, which it was hoped would keep the seals away. Unfortunately, this technique has proved ineffective, as the seals quickly became accustomed to the sounds and stopped responding to them (Anderson and Hawkins, 1978). This result might have been foreseen in view of the adaptability of the behavioural repertoire of seals.

Wholesale reductions of seal populations has been tried on several occasions. Often this has been done through bounty schemes organised by government departments or local fishery authorities. Rewards are paid to hunters in return for proof of killing a seal. Canada introduced a bounty scheme for harbour seals in 1927 (Mclaren, 1977) which lasted until 1976 (Anon., 1986). This scheme greatly reduced local seal populations in the Maritimes and, strangely, was instrumental in bringing the Canadian grey seals to the attention of biologists. Up to 1949 the bounty had been paid on the production of the snouts of the seals, but these were not very readily identifiable and various other biological materials (including, it is said, the occasional porcupine scrotum) were put forward to claim the reward. To circumvent this, the authorities asked for the production of seal jaws, which could easily be identified. It was the presence of large numbers of grey seal jaws in the material produced for bounty claims that provided the first firm evidence of the abundance of this species in the Canadian Maritimes. In 1976 the bounty was paid for grey seals, and from 1976 to 1983 the number claimed was 5,751, an average of 720 a year, though it is believed that the number of grey seals actually killed by the bounty hunters may have been twice this (Anon., 1986). The amount of the bounty was substantial, C$50 for an adult and C$25 for a juvenile. However, this should be set against an estimated average annual cost to the fishing industry of C$900–C$1600 per adult grey seal. Such costs, derived from estimates of damage to gear, transmission of parasites and competition for fish, are highly speculative, but are claimed to give at least a useful indication of the magnitude of the average impact per seal on the fishery (Table 7.1)

Table 7.1 Calculated impact of seals on commercial fisheries in Canada. (From Gulland, 1987.)

Species	Total impact (C$1,000)	Impact per seal (C$ per year)
Grey seals	30,000–84,000	430–1,200
Harbour seals	1,600–3,700	120–285
Harp seals	23,000–75,000	11–37

European countries which have paid bounties for seal killing have included Sweden, Denmark, Ireland and the United Kingdom. Bounty payments in Sweden resulted in a marked reduction of seal populations, particularly the grey seal, in the Baltic though since 1974 grey seals have been protected except in the vicinity of salmon nets (Söderberg, 1975). In Denmark the payment of bounties led to the extinction of the January-pupping grey seals at Anholt and elsewhere. In the United Kingdom harbour seal bounties were paid by the Eastern Sea Fisheries Board, a practice which ceased when commercial hunting of the pups of this species began in the 1960s. Official bounty schemes for seals no longer operate in Europe, though some Scottish salmon fishing interests employ men to shoot seals, and pay them by results.

Bounty schemes are generally most effective where there is already some hunting activity. They are, however, a very imprecise way of achieving a population reduction and are often more effective against very young animals than against the breeding stock.

Officially organised killing of seals (a practice now almost universally termed culling) has been employed in several places as a means of reducing populations. In Canada between 1967 and 1983 rather more than 17,000 grey seals were killed by government hunters in the southern part of the Gulf of St Lawrence. Killing was done on the breeding grounds, and 80 per cent of the animals killed were pups (Anon., 1986). Culls of grey seals have also occurred in the United Kingdom, but in circumstances sufficiently interesting to be considered separately.

Grey Seals and Fisheries in the United Kingdom

Grey seals around Great Britain were comparatively scarce and little known at the beginning of this century (Chapter 9). By the 1920s, however, the seals were becoming more numerous and inevitably complaints about their effects on fisheries began to be heard. By 1934, feeling against the seals was running sufficiently high among fishermen for the South-western Sea-fisheries Board to organise a seal control operation on the Cornish coast in which 177 seals, most if not all grey seals, were shot.

It was salmon fishermen who were most vocal in their complaints against seals, and more importantly, were better organised and better represented than the other parts of the industry. In 1959 the Nature Conservancy, the principal adviser to the government on wildlife matters, set up a Consultative Committee on Grey Seals and Fisheries. This gathered evidence from the fishermen, the two fisheries departments (the Ministry of Agriculture, Fisheries and Food in England and Wales and the Department of Agriculture and Fisheries in Scotland), and its own research staff, and in 1963 produced its report (Nature Conservancy, 1963).

The report noted that grey seals had increased substantially around British coasts since their supposed scarcity had resulted in the passing of the Grey Seals Protection Act, 1914. Using counts of pups which were then multiplied by a factor derived from actuarial life tables for grey seals drawn up by H.R. Hewer, the population of grey seals in Scotland was estimated to be then 29,500, or 64 per cent of the calculated world population at that time. Another 6,400 grey seals were believed to occur in England, Wales and Ireland. The Committee was not able to quantify the amount or type of fish consumed by the seals, but concluded that the total 'has to be scaled in thousands of tons', most of which would be of potential commercial value. The effects of seals on fishing gear, chiefly salmon set nets, and the role of grey seals as hosts of codworm, were reviewed. The conclusions of the Committee were that the case against the seals had been established and that control measures should be instituted to alleviate damage to fisheries.

The control measures proposed were to reduce the stock of grey seals by 25 per cent of its 1961 value in two localities — the Orkneys, off the north coast of Scotland, where some 10,500 seals were believed to occur, and the Farne Islands, off the Northumberland coast of north-east England, with a grey seal population of 3,500 (Figure 7.4).

In Orkney it was proposed to achieve the necessary reduction by allowing private hunters to take an annual quota of weaned grey seal pups, whose skins could then be sold by the hunters to defray the costs of their operations. The annual quota was set at 750 pups, though when the Consultative Committee recommended this level it was done in the knowledge that this number would be insufficient to achieve the desired reduction; however, it was believed that it would be easy to increase the quota subsequently.

At the Farne Islands, the proposal was for a cull consisting partly of adult females and partly of female pups. In fact, the recommendation for a cull at the Farne Islands had been anticipated and the first fisheries-related seal control operations there began in 1958, though only ten pups were killed then. Between 1963 and 1965, 996 grey seals were killed at the Farne Islands. These small rocky islands were owned by the National Trust, a charitable body concerned with preserving the nation's heritage, which operated them as a nature reserve. Following the 1965 kill of seals, and a good deal of adverse publicity, the National Trust declined to allow further seal killing on its property, though it was sympathetic to the position of the salmon netsmen.

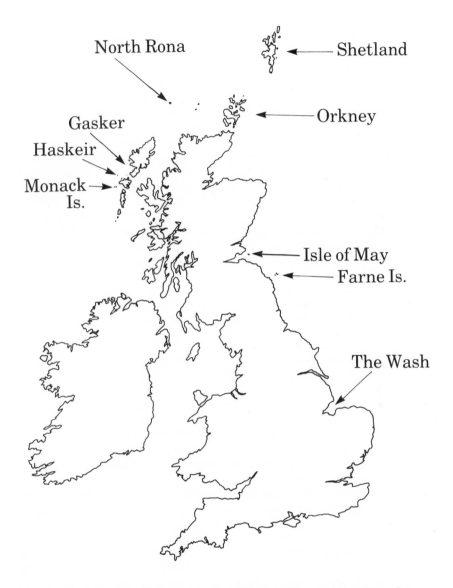

Figure 7.4 Location of some important seal breeding localities in the United Kingdom.

In Orkney the killing of grey seal pups became something of a local industry. Most of the sealing was done by a pair of hunters who moved to Orkney and purchased two of the smallest islands for their potential as seal breeding sites. The moulted pups were shot with a .22 calibre rifle, and skinned. The salted skins were sold to a Norwegian firm of skin dressers whose main products were harp and hooded seal skins. Grey seal skins, which were attractively marked, fetched good prices, and the small industry soon established itself.

An interesting consequence of this was the extension of sealing to harbour seals. There had been no particular complaints about harbour seals (except in connection with their activities in salmon river estuaries) but they were unprotected and their pups, while less easy to hunt than those of grey seals, were produced in the summer when conditions for boat work were generally good. There had been a small local harbour sealing industry in Shetland, which also took a few adult and pup grey seals, but elsewhere harbour seals were undisturbed. Orkney seal hunters, however, moved to the west coast of Scotland and to the Wash in East Anglia, to hunt harbour seal pups. Operations on the largely deserted and deeply indented west coast of Scotland were conducted discreetly and attracted little public attention. The same was not true at the Wash, however, where the sealers were obliged to use an established harbour and could not easily avoid public scrutiny. Animal welfare organisations became involved, and the Wash sealing was a principal factor in the eventual passage of the Conservation of Seals Act (Chapter 9).

Meanwhile, further research continued on grey seals. A group of scientists, the Sea Mammal Research Unit, working under the auspices of the Natural Environment Research Council, had been developing sensitive methods of determining grey seal populations. An improved life table was prepared (Harwood and Prime, 1978) and counting of pups extended, chiefly through the use of aerial surveys conducted at weekly intervals throughout the breeding season. The newly born seal pups in their white lanugo show up clearly against most backgrounds in photographs, and refinements in interpretation, such as the use of stereoscopic pairs of photographs, which introduce an impression of relief into the picture, allowed accurate counts to be made, which were confirmed by simultaneous ground counts. Serial counts at several breeding sites (Summers, 1978; Summers *et al.*, 1975; Anderson and Curry, 1976) provided factors which related the number of pups ashore at any one time (the figure that could be derived from aerial photographs) to the cumulative total of births at the end of the season. The ratio of the peak number of pups ashore to the total born varies from place to place, producing a range of factors (e.g. 1.45 at Auskerry in the Orkneys, 1.6 at Stockay in the Outer Hebrides, 1.8 at North Rona) which must be applied (Ward *et al.*, 1987). The multiplier used to convert pup counts to total population values was set at 3.5 by Hewer, but this was for a stable population. Harwood and Prime (1978) showed that the multiplier would vary from colony to colony, depending on local rates of increase. A population expanding at 7 per cent a year would need a multiplier of 4.4; values between 3.5 and 4.5 are appropriate for most populations.

The results obtained from these more accurate counting methods were startling. Charles Summers (1978a) calculated that in Scottish waters grey seals had increased from about 35,000 in the mid-1960s to about 60,000 in 1978. This represented an average annual increase of about 7 per cent, though of course different groups of seals were increasing at different rates. The most startling increases had occurred at the Outer Hebrides and North Rona, where few seals had been killed. At Orkney, grey seals had continued to increase despite the pup cull, while at the Farne Islands there had been some decrease (Figure 7.9).

The Department of Agriculture and Fisheries for Scotland (DAFS) estimated the annual fish consumption by grey and harbour seals in Scottish waters to be around 195,000 tonnes, of which it was suposed that 130,000 tonnes would consist of commercially exploitable fish (Parrish and Shearer, 1977). Using a value of 0.5 for the exploitation rate of the stocks by the fishery, they assumed that this consumption represented a loss to the fishery of 65,000 tons, which was 5–10 per cent of the total catch of all species taken within the UK's extended fishery limits. It was calculated that this amount of fish had an estimated market value of £15–£20 million.

These calculations were reasonably soundly based on the data then available, though as Harwood and Greenwood have pointed out (1985), they ignored the more subtle effects of competition. The fisheries department regarded this loss as intolerable and a decision was made to reduce seal stocks to their level in the mid-1960s. This was to be done by killing 900 cows and their pups together with 4,000 moulted pups in each of the six years 1977–82 (Table 7.2). Culling operations were to take place at the Orkneys, the islands of Gasker, Coppay and Shillay and the Monach Isles in the Outer Hebrides, and at North Rona. Pup culling alone was rejected, because it had been shown that a population equilibrium obtained by killing only pups was unstable and that the six-year lag between control operations and their observable effects (the time taken for surviving female pups to mature and produce pups of their own which could be counted) could leave the stock vulnerable to unforeseen environmental hazards, as well as to the control (Harwood, 1978). Killing adult seals alone would have a direct effect, but was technically difficult, so a compromise of a combined adult/pup kill was adopted.

In 1977 the management policy was introduced. A Norwegian sealing vessel was chartered at a cost believed to be between £10,000 and £20,000, depending on the number of seals taken (Lister-Kaye, 1979), and started work in the Hebrides at the Monach Isles. Bad weather hampered the operation, which the Norwegians, more used to clubbing harp seals on the ice, found difficult and dangerous, and only 394 pups and 286 cows were eventually taken.

These figures may not represent the total effect of the operation (Harwood and Greenwood, 1985). Disturbance at breeding sites may deter some cows, perhaps around 15 per cent, from coming ashore to breed (what becomes of their pups is not known), and some of those which are ashore desert their pups. Furthermore, there is evidence that some cows at disturbed colonies fail to return in subsequent years. At the colonies culled in 1977, pup production in 1978 was up to 40 per cent lower.

Table 7.2 Culling programme for grey seals in Scotland, 1977–82.

Location	1977, 1979, 1981		1978, 1980, 1982	
	Pups	Cows	Pups	Cows
Orkney	1,000	0	1,000	450
Gasker, Coppay, Shillay	1,750	450	1,500	0
Monach Isles	1,250	450	1,000	0
North Rona	0	0	500	450

The 1977 culling operation had attracted a great deal of adverse comment from the general public and when it was announced that the plan was to continue in Orkney in 1978 active opposition was organised. John Lister-Kaye has summarised these events in his admirably balanced account, *Seal Cull* (1979). The Greenpeace Foundation was contacted and their trawler *Rainbow Warrior* arrived in Orkney at the beginning of October. A week later a petition of 42,000 signatures was presented to the Scottish Office. Two days after this, during a debate in the European Parliament, the Commissioner for Agriculture promised a neutral study on seals and their effects on fisheries. This was followed by an emergency motion calling for a halt to the culling of seals until a scientific study had been carried out! Few if any of the members of the European Parliament seemed aware of the twenty years of research that had preceded the proposed management operation.

A week later, the International Union for the Conservation of Nature and Natural Resources (IUCN) passed a resolution calling for the United Kingdom to suspend the cull until adequate data on the impact of grey seals on fish stocks and their role in the ecosystem had been obtained. These pressures proved too much for the Scottish Office and the Secretary of State, Mr Bruce Millan, issued a statement saying that it had been decided to reduce the cull (this meant abandoning the management plan and returning to the previously existing pup cull which had proved to be ineffective) 'so that everyone will have the chance to study the scientific evidence'.

Pup culling continued in Scotland for some years (Table 7.3), but this was the end of attempts to control seals for the benefit of fisheries in Scotland. The evidence was indeed examined in the succeeding years. No one doubted that the estimates of the numbers of seals and their rates of increase were reliable, but there was considerable debate about the feeding habits of seals and the effect that they might have on fisheries (Council for Nature, 1979). There was little real argument that a lot of seals would eat a lot of fish. As Charles Summers, the head of the Sea Mammal Research Unit, put it:

'Some of the parameters involved are very difficult to investigate by direct observation but in the absence of more rigorous data it is reassuring that several independently determined evaluations of the impact of seals on fish stocks by workers in different countries are in such close agreement.' (Summers, 1978b).

Table 7.3 Grey seals killed in the management operation and subsequently taken in the same area, 1977–81. (From Harwood and Greenwood, 1985)

		Orkney	Outer Hebrides	North Rona
1977	Pups	841	394	0
	Cows	0	286	0
1978	Pups	1067	85	0
	Cows	0	0	0
1979	Pups	1015	0	0
	Cows	0	0	0
1980	Pups	1195	200	0
	Cows	0	0	0
1981	Pups	1200	0	0
	Cows	0	0	0

The difficulties came in deciding whether, if the seals eating all the fish were reduced in number, the fishing industry would be better off, and these difficulties proved insoluble.

An important aspect of this matter was that the seals were, and are still, increasing. Hence any impact they may have on fisheries will also increase. The introduction of arguments that the problems of fishermen relate to chronic overexploitation of the fish stocks for a long period is not relevant to the question of damage. Of course overfishing should be rigorously controlled (and regulations have been tightened up in recent years), but whatever the state of the stocks, an increasing seal population will take more fish and most of the scientists who have examined this question believe that this will be at the expense of the fishing industry. In the virtual absence of natural predators or of hunting activity by Man (who for several millenia has probably been the chief predator on grey seals in the British Isles), some form of management is required to regulate grey seal populations if they are to stay in balance with the rest of the ecosystem, which for better or worse now contains Man as a main predator on fish (Bonner, 1982).

One wonders to what extent public opinion, already excited by the harp seal hunt, was manipulated by the media. It is clear to me that the decision to abandon the cull was made by the Secretary of State in response to relatively uninformed public opinion; this is not necessarily inappropriate, for the decision to cull is a political, not a scientific, one.

Scientists can provide data and informed opinion on what the situation is, and on what the likely results of proposed activities will be. Politicians (or administrators) have to decide whether to take action to secure a desired end. In this case the scientific opinion was almost unanimous that the grey seal population had a significant effect on fisheries and that if it were desired to return to the status quo of the 1960s a certain management plan should be instituted. The decision of the Secretary of State to put the interests of the seals, supported by general public opinion, before those of the fishermen, supported by very few others, was one he was certainly entitled to make. However, it will be unfortunate for the cause of conservation as a whole if as Charles Summers vividly put it, 'trial of wildlife management by public opinion' (Summers, 1978b) becomes standard practice.

8 Interactions with man: 3. Indirect effects

SEALS AS BY-CATCH

Not only are seals sought out by hunters to be killed, they may also be vulnerable to losses inflicted on them inadvertently. Fishing nets set to catch fish may also catch seals, with fatal results. Seals may be caught in trawl nets, or in drift nets in which they become entangled. The drowning of seals on long-lines and in salmon bag nets has already been referred to (Chapter 7). It is difficult to quantify such mortality, though some studies have been carried out. Off the Californian coast, for example, observations were made on the activities of gill- and trammel-netters working in the near-shore waters. It was found that marine mammals were frequently caught in the nets, with an average of one marine mammal for every 534 m of nets hauled. Harbour seals were the species most commonly caught, with one harbour seal for every 712 m of nets hauled, though sea lions, sea otters, elephant seals and porpoises were also caught (Henry, 1986).

Most accounts of seals dying in nets as a result of fishing activities refer to northern fur seals, Steller sea lions or other otariids. As far as phocid seals are concerned, deaths from by-catch do not seem to be a major cause of mortality anywhere; however, one should view this conclusion with caution, since fishermen may be unaware of such incidental kills, or be reluctant to report them. A more serious cause of mortality occurs when nets have ended their useful life as far as the fishermen are concerned.

ENTANGLEMENT WITH NETS AND MARINE DEBRIS

Every year, thousands of fishing nets, or parts of such nets, are lost by the fishing industry, the result of warps parting, anchors coming away or buoys becoming detached. Furthermore, many other nets are damaged. If the net is damaged beyond repair, it is discarded; if the damage is less extensive, the affected panel may be cut out and replaced. In either case, the traditional way of disposal of the unwanted netting has been to throw it over the ship's side. All rubbish on board ships has been dumped in this way until recently, when awareness of the problems caused by marine debris has caused goverments to enter into agreements to ban (or limit) such practices.

Much of the debris discarded in this way is made of plastic, and this has two highly undesirable qualities from the environmental point of view. Firstly, it is not biodegradable, and hence stays in the sea for a very long time; and secondly, it floats and thus has the potential to entrap animals swimming in the sea. The range of animals that may succumb to such floating debris is very wide, and includes whales, from large rorquals to small porpoises; fur seals, sea lions and seals; birds; marine turtles; and fish. Such floating debris tends to attract fish, which in turn may attract seals. These may then become entangled by trying to pluck out already entangled fish, or by attempting to haul out and rest on the debris, or by playing with the debris itself (Laist, 1987).

Hawaiian monk seals seem especially prone to suffer in this way. Karl Kenyon (1980) has drawn attention to the habit of these seals of playing with trawl netting scraps and apparently deliberately entangling themselves in it. The seals Kenyon watched were all able to free themselves subsequently from the netting but it is likely that others do not always escape. In 1983, eleven of the 26 pups of Hawaiian monk seals born on one of their few remaining breeding islands were seen to be either entangled in netting or playing among netting and debris in the water. Four pups were caught in netting snagged on coral, and would have drowned with the next tide, had they not been cut free by their discoverers (Tinney, 1984, quoted in Wallace, 1984).

Entanglement in large pieces of netting can cause a seal to drown directly. Smaller pieces may severely restrict normal swimming, and hence food-gathering ability. Phocid seals are not often seen entangled in netting fragments that look as though they have been there for a long time, otariids frequently are, and some experimental work has been done to determine their effect. Steven Feldcamp at the Scripps Institute of Oceanography in California trained a female sea lion to bite onto a neoprene mouthpiece and be towed through the water behind a moving cart on which was fixed a tensiometer and recorder. In this way the extra drag caused to the swimming seal by netting could be measured directly. Feldcamp found that a piece of trawl netting 1.4 m × 5 m and weighing 580 g increased the drag by a factor of 4.7 times when the seal was swimming at 2 m/sec (Feldcamp, 1985). The increased power output needed to overcome this extra drag must have a significant deleterious effect on the energy balance of a sea lion encumbered in this way in the wild.

Other forms of floating debris, such as plastic packing bands, plastic sacks, or smaller fragments which may be swallowed, can also pose threats to marine mammals including seals. In general, marine debris seems to be one of the most serious threats facing marine mammals today, though phocid seals are probably less affected than others. Steps have been taken by international agreement to reduce the dumping of such rubbish in the sea, and fishermen have been warned of the dangers caused to animals by the discard of netting fragments. This latter approach may be counterproductive, however, for many fishermen strongly disapprove of seals and may discard netting deliberately once the danger has been publicised. In fact, it is not in the fishermen's interests to do so, for nets which can entangle a seal can also entangle a propeller. It is believed that human lives have been lost during storms in the Bering Sea as a result of loss of power or manoeuvring ability from fouled propellers, shafts and engine intakes (Wallace, 1984). Self-interest may prove a more effective inducement in reducing net discards than legislation or exhortation.

Plastic debris at sea has a long life. Eventually, floating plastic will wash up on a beach, where it may become embedded in sand and become no more than aesthetically offensive. The action of ultraviolet light renders most plastics more brittle and they break up. This may happen while the plastic is floating in the surface waters, but is more likely to happen once the debris has beached. Whatever its fate, the removal of plastic debris from the sea is a slow process and the present burden will certainly go on causing mortality amongst marine mammals for some time.

COMPETITION FOR FOOD

If one can argue that large numbers of seals will have an impact on the fishing industry, then it would seem logically to follow that a large fishing industry must have an impact on seals. The scale of the fishing industry has grown enormously in the last century, both through an increase in the tonnage of fishing vessels employed and by the adoption of new techniques of fish finding and capturing. Furthermore, the range taken by the fishing industry has extended to cover all the abundant and accessible species in temperate waters.

Despite this, there is no firm evidence that the removal of vast quantities of fish has directly affected seal numbers. There is, however, some inferential evidence. A study of the energy reserves of nursing north-west Atlantic harp seals showed that these were lower in 1978 than they had been in 1976 (Innes et al., 1978). In 1976 the catch of capelin in the North Atlantic was nearly 400,000 tonnes; by 1978 it had fallen to less than 100,000 (Beddington and Williams, 1979). It is tempting to put these two observations together and suggest that the destruction of the capelin stocks by heavy industrial fishing had led to the seals going short of food (for this would have been the effect on the young of reduced reserves in their mothers).

More recently, in 1987, the western seaboard of Norway was invaded by huge numbers of harp seals. Estimates of the number of seals reported from the fjords and around the offshore islands, particularly the Lofotens, varied between 100,000 and 250,000. Most of these seals were young ones, of two years or less, and all showed signs of depleted blubber reserves. It is easy to suggest that the increasingly heavy pressure on capelin stocks had resulted in the harp seals going short and having to extend their range southwards to find sufficient food. A contrary argument produced promptly by Norwegian fishermen was, of course, that the reduction in hunting pressure on the seals had resulted in an explosive population increase, of which the effects were being observed. It is impossible to refute either claim absolutely. Capelin stocks are heavily fished. They also fluctuate erratically. Iceland landed 640,000 tonnes in 1981 but only 13,000 tonnes in 1983. Balancing such fluctuations against fishery effort and quotas is a difficult task. The collapse of the north-west Atlantic harp seal hunt in 1983 should certainly have allowed many more seals to survive and added to competition. But it is possible that neither of these factors was the decisive one. The winter of 1986–7 was an extremely hard one, with temperatures in January throughout northern Scandinavia falling to below −30°C for weeks at a time. This itself may have had an effect on the food of the seals or their movements.

At the other end of the world a decline has been observed in southern elephant seals at the Kerguelen Archipelago in the Indian Ocean since 1970. Although complete surveys are not available, representative surveys of parts of the coastline indicate that the population fell by about 33 per cent between 1970 and 1979 (Pascal, 1985). Fishing by Soviet trawlers around Kerguelen began in 1970–1, with the first heavy catch the following season. Fishing has continued at a high, but fluctuating, level, which has led to suggestions that the decline of the seals has been caused by depletion of the fish stocks. This is an uncertain argument, however. We really have very little idea of what part fish plays in the diet of elephant seals. The evidence obtained from stomach contents of animals taken ashore may not reflect actual feeding during the seals' pelagic episodes. Indeed, if we rely on the available data, it would seem that the Kerguelen elephant seals yearly consume more than the total stock of fish around the archipelago! In fact it seems likely that elephant seals may rely more on squid as a component of their diet than the existing stomach-contents data indicate, and that they may feed oceanically, away from the continental shelf area where the fishery is concentrated.

The general situation may be complicated further. Selective fisheries for predator fish may actually increase the availability of prey species for seals. When the effects of fisheries on the marine ecosystem in the North Pacific were modelled, the model indicated that the intensive fishery for pollack was actually beneficial to the production of fish biomass. Adult pollack are cannibalistic on smaller fish and by removing the older pollack, the fishery reduces the predation pressure on the juveniles, whose growth rate is higher than that of the adults. The net result was calculated to be an enhancement of the pollack biomass overall (North Pacific Fishery Management Council, 1979). The same effect can work between species. The selective removal of cod by the fishery may increase the stock of sand eels, on which both cod and seals may feed. However, sand eels are now also subject to a fishery, and the possible competition between the fishery and the seals has moved to a new level.

There must, of course, be a limit to any compensatory processes. As fishermen become more efficient in cropping fish stocks, and as they diversify their catches, the situation is likely to deteriorate for seals and other marine predators (Bonner, 1982). Seals might be left with few alternative prey species to switch to and the fish population level at which a fishing area is abandoned by fishermen might be too low to support a viable population of seals.

POLLUTION AND SEALS

In our modern civilisation, the oceans seem to be the ultimate dumping ground. In general, by virtue of their vast extent and mostly energetic mixing, the oceans have great buffering capacity. This is definitely not the case with many enclosed sea areas and estuaries. Here those components of wastes which cannot be biologically recycled or degraded in a reasonably short time accumulate. Those which have adverse effects on living organisms are regarded as pollutants. Some of these, like mercury, may be natural products but which can occur at elevated concentrations as a result of Man's activities. Some, like the polychlorinated biphenyls (PCBs), are new, man-made substances, for which no biological systems have evolved adequately to degrade them to less biologically active compounds.

Many of these substances are concentrated biologically as they pass through the food chain, and seals, as 'top predators' are likely to accumulate high concentrations in their tissues. The hazards of pollution in seals were highlighted in the late 1960s when Koeman and van Genderen (1966) reported residues of chlorinated hydrocarbon insecticides in the blubber of seals from the Netherlands and Helminen and his colleagues (1968) found mercury in the liver and kidneys of ringed seals from Lake Saimaa in Finland.

Chlorinated hydrocarbons, both aromatic and aliphatic, are an important group of synthetic compounds for which a wide variety of uses has been found in our industrial society. The first to attract attention as a contaminant of wildlife was DDT. This was very widely used as an insecticide from the closing years of the Second World War onwards. It was cheap and effective and possible adverse effects on wildlife were either unforeseen or ignored. DDT and its degradation products, DDE and TDE, are now almost universally spread throughout the world. Another important class of organochlorine contaminants are the PCBs. These are very stable compounds used for a variety of industrial applications, such as plasticisers in paints and varnishes, or as heat-absorbent filling fluids in electrical transformers and capacitors. Unfortunately they are highly active biologically.

Organochlorines are soluble in lipids and hence accumulate in fatty tissues, in particular in the blubber of seals from areas associated with high levels of industrial or agricultural effluent, such as the southern North Sea, the Gulf of St Lawrence or the Baltic. Sensitive methods of analysis, such as gas chromatography allow the accurate identification of very small traces of contaminant, but in many cases such precision is unnecessary, as concentrations in blubber may reach levels of several hundred parts per million wet weight.

Although most organochlorine contaminant is found in the blubber, it is also found elsewhere in the body. Holden (1975, 1978) showed that dieldrin (another insecticide), DDT and PCBs could be found throughout the body of grey seals, though in lower concentrations than in the blubber. In particular, concentrations in the brain were lower than those from other tissues (Frank et al., 1973; Holden, 1978). This is because the fatty tissue in the brain is present in the form of phospholipids.

At first it was difficult to demonstrate any pathological effects of these sometimes massive levels of contaminants. Groups of seals appeared to continue to live in a comparatively healthy state in such contaminated waters as Liverpool Bay, the Wadden Sea and the Baltic. It was in the Baltic that the first convincing evidence of a link between pollution and pathological effects in seals was found. In the Bothnian Bay (the most northerly arm of the Baltic in the wide sense) the population of ringed seals has declined alarmingly in recent years. Some of this decline could be accounted for by shooting, or by entanglement in fishing nets, but it was noticed that the surviving seals showed a very low incidence of pregnancy — less than 28 per cent. A group of Finnish and Swedish biologists working together examined a sample of ringed seals which had been caught in fish nets. They found that about 40 per cent of the females in the sample showed pathological changes in the uterine horns. The lumen of the uterus was greatly reduced, a condition known as stenosis, or closed altogether by an occlusion. When concentrations of DDT and PCBs from the blubber of the seals were compared, it was found that those females with stenosis or occlusions had significantly higher concentrations of the contaminants than non-pregnant females without stenosis or occlusion, or pregnant females (Helle, 1976a, 1976b).

Helle and his colleagues concluded from this that the high levels of PCBs were the causative factor, since equally high levels of DDT had been found in Californian sea lions which were breeding normally (DeLong et al., 1973). They noted also that captive mink fed doses of PCBs produced fewer young than those fed equivalent doses of DDT. The amount of PCBs associated with resorbtion of the mink embryos was about the same as that observed in the ringed seals from the Bothnian Bay.

Although the conclusion seemed well-founded, the situation was not as simple as it first seemed. The observations were difficult to interpret because species specific sensitivity had been observed and moreover no properly controlled experiment had been carried out. This was to await work from the Dutch Research Institute for Nature Management on the island of Texel by the Dutch Wadden Sea. Peter Reijnders had been alarmed at the rapid decline of the population of harbour seals in the Dutch Wadden Sea. In the ten years from 1964 to 1974 numbers fell from about 1,500 to around 500 (Reijnders and Wolff, 1981) and it seemed doubtful if sufficient pups were being produced to maintain the population even at the lower level. Reijnders set up a long-term experiment to test the effect of continuous doses at environmental levels of pollutants. He acquired two groups, each of twelve female harbour seals and three males which were allowed access to both female groups. Each female group consisted of seven seals collected from the Wash in East Anglia and five which had been rescued as pups by the Museum of Natural History at Texel. The seals were housed in considerable comfort in some modified disused shellfish rearing enclosures adjacent to his laboratory. One group was fed on a diet of fish, predominantly plaice, flounder and dab, with some eelpout and hooknose, which had been caught in the western part of the Wadden Sea. The other group received fish, mainly mackerel, from the north-east Atlantic. The two diets were nutritionally comparable but showed statistically significant differences in their content of PCBs and DDE. The daily intake over two years for the seals fed on the highly polluted Wadden Sea fish was about 1.5 mg PCBs and 0.4 mg DDE, while those receiving the relatively clean Atlantic mackerel took in only 0.22 mg PCBs and 0.13 mg DDE per day.

Three males, fed on Atlantic fish, were alternated between the two groups during the mating period, and the groups' reproductive success compared. In each group all the females ovulated, but while the twelve females fed on Atlantic fish produced ten healthy pups, the twelve seals chronically poisoned with the Wadden Sea fish produced only four pups (Reijnders, 1986).

This was the first demonstration of a causal relationshipo between naturally occurring levels of pollutants and a physiological response in any marine mammal. Earlier studies (Reijnders and Wolff, 1981; Reijnders, 1980) had shown that it was only in the western, Dutch, part of the Wadden Sea that pup production by harbour seals declined sharply, and it was only the levels of PCBs that differed significantly, a high level of PCBs originating from the Rhine and spreading throughout the western part of the Wadden Sea. From this it followed that it was the PCBs (or their break-down products) that were causing the loss of reproductive potential, rather than the DDE or any other pollutant present in the Wadden Sea fish.

It was significant that female harbour seals from the Wadden Sea did not show occlusions in their uteri like the Bothnian Bay ringed seals, though the level of PCBs in their tissues was higher. This caused Reijnders to doubt whether the PCBs had directly caused the occlusions. In the Wadden Sea seals the loss of the developing embryo occurred mostly around the time of implantation of the blastocyst, though the actual mechanism which caused the loss could not be determined. It was probably interference by PCBs with the steroid hormone balance, causing implantation failure or early resorption of the embryo. Reijnders suggested that there might be two stages in the development of occlusions: first a resorption caused by the pollutant, followed by the development of the pathological changes in the uterus (Reijnders, 1984). He suggested that it was the latter process that had caused the occlusions in the Bothnian Bay seals.

PCBs and DDT and its degradation products are not the only organochlorine pollutants to be found in seals. From Lake Saimaa ringed seals have been reported containing besides PCBs and DDT, chlordane and chlorophenol compounds (Helle et al., 1983). We do not know of any specific damage to seals that can be attributed to these compounds, but it is naive to suppose that they are harmless. Chlordane is a powerful biocide (it may be familiar to some as a compound sold to gardeners to kill harmless earthworms in their lawns) and chlorophenols have been used as antiseptics (trichlorophenol may be better known as TCP). As insecticides like DDT are banned by governments because of the environmental damage they cause, the chemical industry responds by developing other novel compounds, in many cases just as undesirable environmentally but not yet prohibited for public use. No doubt there are other compounds equally likely to be toxic, waiting to be found in the tissues of seals and other marine mammals.

A sinister feature of these lipid-soluble pollutants is that their concentrations continue to accumulate in male seals as they grow older, whereas in females the increase slows down at maturity (Addison and Brodie, 1977; Addison and Smith, 1974; Addison et al., 1973). This is because the females pass on part of their burden of lipid-soluble pollutants to their pups in their milk. It is a chilling thought that even at its first feed, the seal pup may be introduced to the less desirable products of industrialisation.

'Heavy metals' is a collective term used to describe elements such as mercury, lead, cadmium, zinc or chromium (together with many others) that are known to have harmful biological effects. Interest in heavy metals in marine life was excited when high levels of mercury were found in tuna and swordfish in the 1970s. These are now believed for the most part to represent natural levels though mercury can occur at artificially elevated and toxic levels in marine mammals. Mercury in the metallic form is not very poisonous (many of us have some hundreds of milligrams of mercury in the form of silver amalgam, stopping cavities in our teeth) but when it is combined with organic compounds as alkyl mercury it is highly toxic. The proportion of methyl mercury (the commonest alkyl form) in mature seals is usually small (10–20 per cent), though nearly 100 per cent of the mercury in the fish they prey upon is present as methyl mercury.

This suggests that seals possess a method for de-methlyating organic mercury. Koeman and his colleagues (1973) found that there was a one-to-one relationship on a molecular basis between mercury and selenium in Wadden Sea seals, dolphins and porpoises. Selenium is known to have a protective effect against the toxicity of mercury in rats and quails and it may operate the same way in seals. Mercury concentrations of 387 parts per million wet weight have been found in the liver of harp seals in eastern Canada (Sergeant and Armstrong, 1973) and of 106 parts per million in the liver of harbour seals from East Anglia (Roberts *et al.*, 1976). Unlike organochlorines, mercury compounds are not particularly soluble in lipids, so blubber values are lower. The liver seems able to accumulate mercury up to a value of about 200 ppm, after which there are rapid increases in concentration in the brain (Koeman *et al.*, 1972). Clinical mercury poisoning in seals seems very rare. Only one case has been reported where deaths of some harbour seals might be related to mercury poisoning (Reijnders, 1988).

Besides mercury, several other heavy metals, such as cadmium, lead, selenium, zinc and chromium (Roberts *et al.*, 1976; Helle, 1981) have been found in seals, but firm evidence of pathological consequences is lacking.

Heavy metals in seals accumulate with age in both sexes. Unlike the lipid-soluble hydrocarbon pollutants they are not excreted to the same extent by being passed on in the mother's milk.

Seals and Oil

Petroleum residues form conspicuous and unsightly pollution on our beaches. It is probably the form of pollution that people are most familiar with and the pitiful sight of oiled birds struggling weakly or lying dead on the beaches has done much to stimulate international action to prohibit tank-washing at sea and control oil losses from drilling installations and terminals. However oil, though very conspicuous, may be less of a biological threat than is often supposed, and this is particularly true in the case of seals.

Petroleum is, of course, a naturally occurring substance and much of the oil in the oceans has originated from natural seeps. At San Miguel Island off California on the Santa Barbara Channel side the rocks are covered with crude oil. This is not pollution; the oil has seeped out of cracks and fissures in the rock. The same area is frequented by a healthy colony of harbour seals; indeed, San Miguel has one of the highest densities of pinnipeds anywhere, and the other side of the island supports over 10,000 California sea lions, as well as hundreds of elephant seals and the occasional northern fur seal and Steller sea lion.

The first case of oil pollution that attracted attention on a worldwide scale was when the supertanker *Torrey Canyon* ran aground on the Seven Stones Reef off the Scilly Isles in March 1967. Her cargo of 119,000 tonnes of crude oil was spilt into the sea and caused massive contamination of beaches in south-west England and Brittany. About 250 grey seals inhabited the area in which the *Torrey Canyon* went ashore, but only three grey seals were found oiled on the beaches, two of which were alive when found but died later (Gill *et al.*, 1967). No attempts were made to find out whether the seals had died from the effects of the oil or from other causes, and in retrospect it seems likely that if their deaths resulted from the incident, the more probable immediate cause was the highly toxic detergent that was recklessly used in an attempt to wash the rocks clean of oil for aesthetic reasons. My own view is that the three seals were most probably natural casualties which were reported because of the increased vigilance on the shore as a result of the interest in the disaster.

A blow-out in the Santa Barbara Channel in California in 1969 caused contamination of an elephant seal rookery at San Miguel Island and over 100 pups were coated with oil, to which sand and debris adhered (Le Boeuf, 1971). Burney Le Boeuf tagged 58 pups and five yearlings that were at least 75 per cent covered with the crude oil, and then monitored sightings and tag returns over the following 15 months. At the time the tags were read the coats of all the experimental animals (except for one) showed no traces of oil. On comparing the progress of the oiled animals with a control group, he was unable to find any evidence of significant or long-term deleterious effects on their health. However, Le Boeuf thought that if the blow-out had occurred at the time the females were feeding their pups, then the latter might have ingested the oil and the results could have been more serious.

An oil spill of unknown origin off the Pembrokeshire coast in South Wales in September 1974 caused extensive, though light, fouling of beaches. John Davis and Sheila Anderson (1976) followed the effects of this on grey seal pups which were born in the area. They thought that most pups had not been polluted directly, but had become coated with oil through contact with their mothers who had swum through oil patches floating on the sea. Some pups, however, had acquired their oil by swimming in oil-covered shallow pools. Cows were able to contact and feed their pups successfully, even those that were oiled, but oiled pups had lower weaning weights. This would probably have affected survival but it was not certain that this was a result of the oil contamination, since oiled pups were subject to disturbance from visiting observers and from attempts to clean them. There was a high mortality of both oiled (40 per cent) and unoiled (46 per cent) pups, but subsequent examination of dead pups showed that none of them had ingested oil. The only deaths that could be directly attributed to the oil were those of two pups, so encased with thick, tarry oil that they were unable to swim and drowned when they were washed off the beach.

Five of the oiled pups were successfully cleaned by using detergents. However, one of these subsequently became recontaminated, and Davis and Anderson concluded that it was probably not worth trying to clean the pups unless recontamination could be ruled out. This is a common-sense conclusion, though I would extend it to any case, whether recontamination could be ruled out or not. The disturbance to both mother and offspring involved in cleaning is very great and the benefits are unproven.

These are somewhat encouraging reports, but there are others which are less so. When the supertanker *Arrow* broke up off Nova Scotia in 1969 there were reports that some seals experienced considerable pain and suffering from contact of oil with their eyes, ears, noses, mouths and throats, and that the prime cause of death from oil was physical suffocation (Canada Ministry of Transport, 1970). After an oil spill on the Alaskan coast seals were reported to be 'acting in an unusual way and had a white glazed look in their eyes' (Anon. 1971, quoted in Geraci and St. Aubin, 1980).

Such vague and unspecific reports are not very helpful in determining the effect of oil on seals. Even the more careful field observations made by Le Boeuf, or by Davis and Anderson, need to be interpreted by experimental studies. Joe Geraci, at the University of Guelph in Canada, in conjunction with Tom Smith of the Arctic Biological Station, undertook such studies.

Their experiments (Smith and Geraci, 1975; Geraci and Smith, 1976) involved exposing ringed seals and harp seals to oil. The seals were either placed in outdoor sea pens with a 1 cm layer of light crude oil floating on the top of the water, or had oil painted on them with a brush, or had oil given to them by mouth. They found that after 24-hour exposure to crude oil the eyes of healthy ringed seals were affected, with signs of severe conjunctivitis and corneal ulceration; there were also minor kidney and possibly liver lesions. However, the seals recovered rapidly when placed in clean water and there was no sign of permanent damage. On the other hand, when the experiment was repeated at a higher temperature (12–14°C) an enclosed room at Guelph University the three seals (which had been in captivity for some time previously) all died, within 21, 60 and 71 minutes of exposure to the oil. Geraci and Smith thought that the stress of captivity was central to the deaths of these seals, but it has since been suggested (Griffiths *et al.*, 1987) that the seals might have been suffering from the directs effects of hydrocarbon intoxication. The symptoms described — trembling, thrashing and loss of co-ordination — are all signs of acute cerebral intoxication, which inhalation of the lighter components of oil is known to produce.

When 3–4 week old harp seal pups were coated with oil no significant differences in core body temperature were noted and no other deleterious effects were observed. No significant lesions or behavioural changes were noticed in ringed or harp seals fed oil with their food or given as much as 75 ml of crude oil in a single dose.

These results are moderately encouraging. (The death of the oil-immersed seals in the enclosed room probably does not reflect realistic conditions.) We have to accept that major industrial reliance on oil involves the transport of huge quantities by sea and that accidents will occur, releasing oil into the environment of marine mammals. Phocid seals, in the short term at least, seem to tolerate exposure to petroleum fairly well, though we do not yet know enough about the effects of long-term chronic exposure. An important factor is likely to be the chemical composition of the oil. The more volatile components will pose a greater threat if seals inhale the fumes; chronic exposure to the heavier, persistent fractions is likely to be less serious.

The worst oil spill in North American history occurred on 24 March 1989 when the supertanker Exxon Valdez struck the Bligh Reef in Alaska's Prince William Sound, releasing 11 million gallons of Prudhoe Bay Crude. The impact on the local ecology was devastating. Worst affected of the higher vertebrates were birds and sea otters; some 4,000 or 40 per cent of the population of the latter are believed to have perished. At the time of writing, the number of seals which have died as a result of this spill is not known, but the oil is unlikely to have had such severe effects on these animals for the reasons noted earlier. Inevitably, there will be local effects but, fortunately, none of the seals in this region are from endangered populations and there is every reason to hope that, as far as seals are concerned, the Exxon Valdez spill will have temporary effects only.

Pollution and Disease: Is There a Link?

In the spring of 1988 reports began to come in about dead seals being washed up around the coasts of north-west Europe. The first signs were the premature births of nearly 100 harbour seal pups at Anholt in the Kattegat. Soon after, sick adults were noticed on both the Danish and the Swedish sides. The seals were lethargic, they had a nasal discharge and obviously had difficulty in breathing. The course of the disease was rapid. In one hour, it was said, a seal could go from being lively to being dead. When dead seals were autopsied it was found that their lungs were grossly congested, and there were signs of interstitial emphysema. The immediate cause of death was pulmonary oedema.

The disease spread rapidly. By mid-May some hundreds of seals had died in the Kattegat and bodies began to wash ashore on the adjoining coasts (Figure 8.1). By the end of June 3,800 dead seals had been found in the Skagerrak/Kattegat area and another 2,700 in the Wadden Sea. These deaths coincided with a major algal bloom that moved westwards from the Baltic along the Kattegat, and an almost complete failure of some seabird colonies in the Shetlands to breed (Harwood and Reijnders, 1988).

By the end of July there were reports of unusually large numbers of dead harbour seal pups at Blakeney Point in North Norfolk. By mid-August ten dead adults, some with pups, had been found there. By the end of August 133 dead seals had been collected at Blakeney and the local warden reported that the numbers frequenting the point were considerably lower than usual. By the end of September only 234 seals hauled out at Blakeney; there had been 720 in May.

Over a thousand seals died in East Anglia between the beginning of August and the end of September and there were other reports which with the East Anglian deaths totalled 1,996 around the British Isles (Figure 8.2).

The nature of the seal disease was not clearly understood. Early reports claimed it was caused by canine distemper, perhaps as a result of distempered sledge-dog carcasses being thrown into the sea in Greenland, or owed its origin to an infection from Lake Baikal, where seals were also dying. Concern was expressed that the already endangered

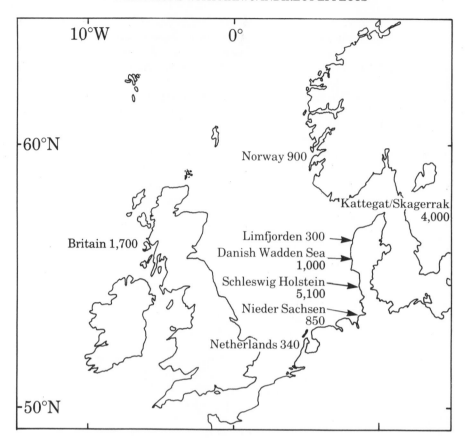

Figure 8.1 Distribution of mortality from 'seal plague' around the North Sea to the end of September, 1988.

European otter population might be at risk. Meanwhile, virologists had been at work trying to identify the causative agent. It was soon shown to be a morbillivirus of the virus family Paramyxoviridae (Osterhaus and Vedder, 1988). Four morbilliviruses were known. One was canine distemper virus, CDV, another (MV) caused measles in Man, and the other two (PPRV — *peste des petits ruminants*, and RPV — rinderpest virus) affected grazing animals. The seal virus did not exactly fit any of these, though it appears to be closely related to CDV (Mahy *et al.*, 1988). It has since tentatively been named as phocine distemper virus, PDV (Cosby *et al.*, 1988)

While the scientific research was being carried out, the press was full of suggestions that the seal deaths were caused by pollution of the North Sea and Baltic. The evidence of the algal bloom and the reproductive failure of the seabirds in Shetland was adduced to support this claim. Once a causative organism, the morbillivirus, had been identified, it was not of course possible to support the claim that the seals' death had been directly caused by pollution. John Harwood and Peter Reijnders (1988), in a carefully reasoned review of the situation, pointed out that seals accumulate pollutants in their blubber which are released when the seals mobilise their reserves at times of stress. At the breeding season, when the seals call on their reserves, contaminants such as PCB or pesticide residues, which are known to suppress the immune system of mammals under laboratory conditions, might have been released into the seals' bodies, thus rendering them more susceptible to infection. In this way, it is possible that pollution had contributed to the severity of the outbreak, though it could not be held to be directly responsible.

This is certainly a possible explanation, but it needs some qualification. The severity of the outbreak does not correlate well with the areas of

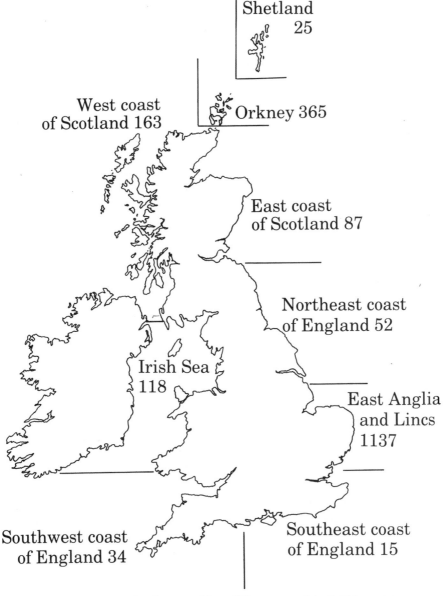

Figure 8.2 Numbers of dead seals reported from different parts of the British coast, to October 1988.

highest pollution. The occurrence of seal deaths off north-west Scotland, an area of low contamination, would be hard to explain if pollution is behind it all. Perhaps it was simply a very virulent outbreak of a virus which acted independently of pollution, but whose effect was exacerbated where the immune systems of the seals had been debilitated by the effects of pollutants. There have been other accounts of seal plagues in the past, before pollution could have played any part. Flemming, writing in 1828 (quoted in Scheffer, 1958) said: 'About fifty years ago, multitudes of carcasses [of seals] were cast ashore in every bay in the north of Scotland, Orkney and Zetland, and numbers were found at sea in a sickly state.' During the 1920s there was an epizootic among harbour seals in Shetland. Old sealers who remembered the event said that the dead or dying seals had a swelling, usually on the back (Bonner, 1972). This last characteristic would not fit the PDV epizootic very well and this event may have been caused by a different organism.

An interesting outbreak of disease in a wild seal population that could not have been exposed to any form of pollution was recorded in the Antarctic. In 1955 some 3,000 crabeater seals wintered on the ice in Prince Gustav Channel in the Antarctic Peninsula. This was an unusual phenomenon, but the seals had access to the sea through pools and tide cracks. One group, of about a thousand seals, was 80 km from the open sea and early in September it was noticed that some of the seals were dying. By the third week of October 97 per cent were dead, and deaths were still occurring in the remainder when the sea ice broke up in mid-November (Laws and Taylor, 1957). The outbreak coincided with the breeding season, and there were numerous abortions. The overall mortality for the whole group was in the region of 68 per cent; no live pups at all were born. Pathological changes affecting the lungs, spleen and kidneys were noticed and it was concluded that death was caused by a disease, probably a viral infection. How interesting it would be if it were possible to compare tissue from those crabeaters, thirty years ago, with samples from the more recent epizootic!

Initially, the PDV disease was confined to harbour seals, though Kennedy *et al.* (1988) reported finding the virus in a harbour porpoise found dead on the coast of Northern Ireland. However, later investigations showed the presence of antibodies to PDV in the blood of British grey seals sampled in 1988, though not in earlier years (Harwood, 1989). Fortunately, the grey seal, a much rarer species than the harbour seal, appears to show much greater resistance to the virus. It has been suggested that the virus may have originated in harp seals, which invaded the North Sea in large numbers in 1987, when more than 60,000 drowned in fishing nets in southern Norway and stragglers were found as far south as northern Spain. In 1988 a smaller invasion occurred and adult harp seals appeared on the east coast of England and in the Netherlands (Harwood, 1989). C.B. Goodhart (1988) suggested that the disease may long have been endemic in harp seals, allowing them to build up immunity to it, but had the chance to jump to harbour seals when the harps penetrated south.

The sight of dead and dying seals on the beaches in the summer of 1988, and the extensive coverage of these events in the press and on television, attracted much public attention. Rescue centres were set up where sick seals were treated. Many, probably most, succumbed, but some survived and after being restrained until they had again built up their blubber reserves, were released back into the wild. These animals should have a good chance of survival as they can now be expected to be resistant to PDV. There were many calls for vaccination to protect the seals, but these ignored the fact that it was uncertain what immunity would be conferred by using vaccines prepared against canine distemper on seals suffering from PDV. Furthermore, there were no vaccines available that required only one injection and in any case the catching of animals to administer the vaccine might create so much disturbance as to cause more harm than good.

It is too soon to say what the final outcome of this episode will be. Over 17,000 harbour seals had died in Europe by the beginning of 1989. This is a heavy toll, though a large stock of seals remain, particularly in the United Kingdom. If immunity has been established in the survivors, one can expect the stocks to rebuild rapidly, though those which have impaired reproductive potential because of PCB burdens, such as the seals of the Dutch Wadden Sea, will be unable to do so. However, harbour seals disperse widely (Bonner and Witthames, 1974) and recolonisation should eventually occur in suitable sites.

As I write this the breeding season for harbour seals around the North Sea is about to begin. Sadly, reports are already arriving of sick seals showing the typical symptoms of PDV in the Wash and around north Norfolk. The epizootic is not yet over, and more deaths must be anticipated. However, resistance will build up in the surviving population and while thousands of harbour seals and hundreds of grey seals have already died from the infection, neither species is threatened by extinction from this cause. But as John Harwood has pointed out (1989), there is a potential threat to a seal that is already hovering on the brink of extinction. The largest surviving colony of Mediterranean monk seals is on the Atlantic coast of northern Mauretania, and some animals probably move between Mauretania and the Desertas Islands of Madeira. Recently (July, 1986) the first sighting of a harbour seal was reported from Madeira; the animal was later found dead. Should a North Sea seal infected with PDV transmit the disease to one of the monk seals, the population of the latter, small as it already is, would be very vulnerable to extinction.

As always, it is impossible to predict the future with certainty. The seal epizootic is one of the best-documented case studies of disease in a wild animal population. It has encouraged widespread public interest and focused attention on problems of the marine environment in general. Let us hope that out of all the gloom there is a ray of hope that this sad event will lead to a renewed commitment to prevent further deterioration of the North Sea environment.

OTHER INDIRECT EFFECTS ON SEALS

By-catch, entanglement, fisheries competition, and pollution in its various forms are not the only impacts on seals arising from Man's activities. Habitat destruction is perhaps the most severe threat facing wildlife today. Fortunately, seals and other marine mammals are little affected by this. Man has relatively little use for the sea that changes its status as an environment. There are exceptions, of course, and land reclamation schemes have converted areas of shallow sea into dry land. These areas would have been productive breeding grounds for the sorts of fish that seals feed on, but the extent of such activities is small in relation to the habitat as a whole. Probably only the harbour seal is affected by reclamation, and probably only in the Netherlands has polderisation proceeded far enough to destroy significant amounts of the Wadden Sea harbour seals' habitat.

A more serious threat has been disturbance by Man. Increased mobility and the development of tourism has meant that many once isolated localities where seals occur are now regularly invaded by humans. The plight of the monk seals in the Mediterranean has already been referred to. The Hawaiian species is another example. These seals evolved without any threat from terrestrial predators and are, as Karl Kenyon (1980) puts it, 'genetically tame'. Nevertheless, they are greatly disturbed by human intrusion. Nursing mothers will break off suckling their pups to bellow and charge at intruders. Kenyon found that some 39 per cent of the monk seals born at Midway Island during his late 1950s study died before weaning, most likely owing to the malnutrition that resulted from disrupted nursing periods.

Tourists can now afford to travel in considerable luxury even to the world of the Antarctic seals. These are also 'genetically tame' but seem far more resistant to disturbance than monk seals. In any case, few tourists can arrive during the critical suckling period of the ice-breeding seals.

Seals are undoubtedly an attraction to tourists who for the most part mean them no harm. However, the effects of scaring seals into the water may be more serious than at first appear. Eberhardt Drescher (1978) noticed that many of the harbour seals that he observed in the Schleswig-Holstein part of the Wadden Sea had large open ulcers on the skin of their bellies. He considered that these ulcers arose from umbilical infections in pups a few days old. Healing, followed by fresh infection, could occur, and the lesions could persist for many years. An undisturbed group of harbour seals hauled out on a sandbank will stay without moving until the tide rises and they are floated off again. But should the seals be scared into the water a pup with an unhealed navel, following in the track of an adult with an open ulcer, might pick up the infection. In this way Drescher believed that protection of hauling-out sites from disturbance would lessen the risk of infection as well as giving the pups a greater opportunity to obtain milk from their mothers. These lesions are found in grey seals as well as harbour seals (Anderson et al., 1974), and are not confined to seals that haul out on sandbanks. Protection of breeding sites is unquestionably a good thing for seals, but I am not certain it will reduce the incidence of this condition.

Seals can rapidly become habituated to the presence of humans. Lobster fishermen (who have no reason to dislike seals) commonly note that their boats, making their regular rounds of the creels, do not disturb basking seals, but the sound of an unfamiliar engine will send them into the water very promptly. Advantage is taken of this by some fishermen in the summer who take out parties of tourists to view the seals. Grey seals on the Carricks just west of St Ives in Cornwall, or harbour seals at Lismore Island, outside Oban on the west coast of Scotland, permit regular tourist boats to approach very closely, but slide off into the water should an unfamilar boat come within twice the distance.

A form of disturbance which has been little studied in seals is the sound produced by human activities. The ocean is in general a noisy environment. Waves break or crash on rocks, ice floes grind together or crepitate as they melt in the sea, and there is much biological sound also, from snapping shrimps to humpback whales. Whether the addition to all this of mechanical noises from ships has significantly affected seals is not certain. Jack Terhune set out to examine this at the harp seal breeding grounds in the Gulf of St Lawrence (Terhune *et al.*, 1979). Recordings were made of the underwater vocalisations of the seals throughout the day and night. Following the arrival of a vessel in the vicinity there was a marked decrease in seal vocalisations. The underwater motor noises of a sealing vessel completely masked the seal calls within at least a 2 km radius. It was not certain whether the decrease in vocalisations recorded was the result of a change in the seals' vocal behaviour or whether the seals simply moved away from the vicinity.

I do not believe that underwater sounds would do any direct harm to seals, though unusual or unfamiliar sounds might disturb them. Of course, if the sounds reached levels that could cause physical damage, this would not be true. Very intense sounds in this category are produced during marine seismic surveys, carried out by geophysicists to investigate the structure of the earth's crust under the sea. Shock waves are generated, either using explosive charges or by releasing compressed air from an air gun, which are differentially reflected back from sediment interfaces in the underlying strata. It is difficult to separate the effects of the sound from the effects of the explosions. In general, air guns are reckoned to do less damage to living organisms than explosives, but both at short range can be harmful. The effects depend not only on the quantity of explosive (or compressed air) used, but also on the depth at which it is set off and the underlying depth of water. Seals, like other marine mammals, have very sensitive ears (p.18) and, because of the effectiveness of water in transmitting pressure waves, severe damage to essential sense organs is likely to occur if seals are in the vicinity of seismic surveys.

My final example of indirect effects of human activity on seals is a very indirect one indeed. Between December 1977 and July 1978 a number of the monk seals on Laysan Island were seen to be comatose or paralysed for several days or weeks before they died. By the end of the outbreak 22 of these rare animals had died. On autopsy, the heart and lungs were found to be congested (which might have suggested PDV infection, had the condition been known then!) but the livers of two of the dead seals were found to be positive for ciguatoxin, the active principle which produces ciguatera, a form of fish poisoning (Kenyon, 1980). Ciguatoxin is produced by a dinoflagellate, *Gambierdiscus toxicus*, in the plankton. This is passed through the food chain until following a bloom of *Gambierdiscus*, some fish become poisonous (Hokama and Miyahara, 1986). The Laysan monk seals must have consumed poisonous fish, to which they had no immunity, and died. Kenyon speculated that the real cause of the poisoning might have been human meddling with the environment. Ciguatera outbreaks in other areas have occurred after coral reefs have been disturbed, and during the years preceding the outbreak at Laysan there had been much dredging of coral to enlarge the harbour at Midway Island. Fish at Midway became toxic to Man and a drastic decline in monk seals at Pearl and Hermes Reef took place prior to the observed deaths at Laysan.

This is a depressing catalogue of the effects of the interactions between seals and Man. In the next chapter I shall consider some of the ways in which attempts have been made to redress the balance.

9 Conservation and seals

CHANGING ATTITUDES

Attitudes to seals have changed greatly within the last half-century. Rather than regarding them as potential prey to be exploited for subsistence or commercial reward, or as competitors for a fish resource, many people now see seals as an attractive component of marine wildlife, a common-property amenity which should be conserved so that future generations can share in their enjoyment. This is a rather sophisticated view and it is largely confined to the more developed countries. It is not universal even there, of course, for seals are not popular among Newfoundland sealers or Scottish salmon fishermen, yet it does represent the opinion of a large and influential lobby.

To what can we attribute this dramatic change? In part it has been the steady enlightenment of the general public on the importance of the world environment to the continued existence of the human race. Works like Rachael Carson's *Silent Spring* (1962) drew attention to the dangers of ignoring the environment. More directly, conservation interests came to the fore. Often these originated with groups of people who enjoyed nature, and in particular watching birds, and did not want to see further species disappear. Bird watchers came from a wide spectrum of society and from many countries and had great influence in setting up reserves and in sponsoring protective legislation. But perhaps the most potent force was the advent of television, with its power of bringing the beauties and realities of nature into people's homes. Nature programmes, which tended to concentrate on the rare and spectacular, became exceedingly popular and their presenters, led by Sir Peter Scott, rarely failed to to preach the cause of conservation. This message was readily accepted by the viewers, who for the most part were not directly involved with the issues concerned but felt that the preservation of the attractive animals and environments they saw on their screen would be a good thing.

In this way a far greater segment of the population became involved with wildlife. From being for the most part ignorant of the status of wildlife around the world, people began to be aware and concerned. Television was not the sole factor in causing this change, of course, but it was, and is, a very potent one. Nowhere has it been more important than in changing attitudes to seals.

THE CONSERVATION MOVEMENT AND HARP SEALING

In March 1964, a television film made by Artek Film Productions of Montreal was screened by the Canadian Broadcasting Corporation. It showed the sublime serenity of the Arctic pack ice around the Magdalen Islands in the Gulf of St Lawrence and the appealing beauty of the dark-eyed white-coated harp seal pups. It also showed their blood flowing over the ice and the brutalities of slaughter and pelting. Not everyone believed the excesses shown in the Artek film were genuine. As Dave Lavigne and Kit Kovacs (1988) put it: 'The debate continues today on the legitimacy of the footage, on whether it accurately portrayed the Canadian seal hunt, or whether some scenes were actually staged using a few young and inexperienced sealers, possibly under the influence of alcohol.' But the authenticity of the scenes depicted in the film was irrelevant. They had enormous dramatic impact and brought an overwhelming surge of public opinion against the seal hunt.

The protests after the Artek film were not the first. From the 1950s onward, observers from various animal protection societies had gone out to the ice with the sealers and witnessed the hunt. Few of them had failed to comment adversely on the clubbing of the pups. In 1955 a meeting was held in Halifax, Nova Scotia, in response to public concern over inhumane practices in sealing. It was chaired by the president of the Nova Scotia Society for the Prevention of Cruelty to Animals and both government and sealing industry representatives were present. One of the government biologists said he was not satisfied with the methods then used to kill seals though in the opinion of another 'inhumane killing was not the rule'. He did agree, however, that cruelty did occur as a result of haste and rivalry.

There was little follow-up to this meeting, but after the screening of the Artek film and the public outrage it produced the Canadian government responded by introducing new regulations for the seal hunt. These included banning the killing of seals from an airborne vehicle, the requirement that clubs used to kill seals should be at least 24 inches (61 cm) long and weigh at least 0.78 kg, and that no one should attempt to skin a seal until it was completely dead. These new regulations came into force for the 1965 season and it was in that year that Brian Davies of the New Brunswick Society for the Prevention of Cruelty to Animals made his first attempt to visit the seal hunt. Davies became deeply involved in moves to abolish the commercial exploitation of seals and in 1969 set up the International Fund for Animal Welfare (IFAW) with this as its main aim.

Attention continued to be focused on killing methods. For many people, and particularly those who had no practical experience of slaughter, clubbing seemed self-evidently a brutal and inhumane method of killing, and especially so when applied to pups. Further regulations were introduced in Canada concerning clubs, whose weight was increased to at least 2½ pounds (1.13 kg) (1966) and which had to be constructed of hardwood, at least 2 inches (5 cm) in diameter for half of their length (1967). Gaffs, which had been used for killing seals before 1966, were also affected by controls. New killing devices were introduced. Mr T.I. Hughes of the Ontario Humane Society introduced a shot pistol which was found to be effective and humane. No explanation was given as to why shooting was considered more humane than clubbing, but it certainly seemed so to the public. In contrast to the pistol, the Canadian National Research Council developed a device which consisted of a metal bell which fitted over a seal pup's head and from which a spring-loaded spike could be driven into its skull. This was heavy, clumsy and ineffective, its only advantage seeming to be that it was not a club.

In 1969 the Canadian Parliamentary Standing Committee on Fisheries held public meetings in Ottawa. After hearing evidence from the fisheries departments, humane societies, and media representatives, the committee recognised that there had been inhumane killing of seals in the past and that federal supervision was required. It further accepted that the club was the most humane killing method then available.

Meanwhile, the Norwegian government had introduced controls on killing methods for its ships at the Front. The use of a Canadian-type club was strictly forbidden and specifications for the construction of the *hakapik* ensured that the iron pick end weighed at least 400 g and had a spike of between 12 and 15 cm length. If a *slagkrok* was used this had to be at least 50 cm long and weigh at least 800 g. Seals were to be struck on the head at least twice and then turned over and bled by cutting the arteries to the fore flippers. Skinning was not allowed to commence until the animal had been completely bled out. When a rifle was used to kill older seals it had to be of at least 6.5 mm calibre, using ammunition with an expanding point and developing an impact energy of at least 200 kg at 100 m.

Great emphasis had been put on killing methods by both the Canadian and the Norwegian authorities and there seems little doubt that the killing of seal pups on the ice compared very well in terms of humaneness with slaughter methods for cattle in general abbatoir practice. Tales of seals being skinned alive abounded and had been reinforced by the Artek film. It is, of course, possible that the sealing crews included some sadistic or indifferent people, though it is more likely that a good many of the most gruesome yarns were deliberately exaggerated accounts, told to shock the listener or viewer. Sealers, like all slaughtermen, became hardened to killing, but in their own interests the job needed to be done efficiently, and it was more efficient to make sure the seal was dead than to attempt skinning while it was still alive, with the risk of the knife slipping from a writhing animal and inflicting wounds on its wielder.

Some genuine misconceptions about 'skinning alive' may have resulted from untrained observers noting that the seals' hearts continued to beat strongly even after skinning was complete. Experiments performed by Arnoldus Blix and Nils Øritsland (1970) showed that although a blow to the head with a *slagkrok* brought an instantaneous end to all electrical activity in the brain, respiratory activity was observed up to 15 minutes later and heart activity lasted between 30 and 56 minutes. It is easy to see how some people, observing the skinned carcass of a seal showing signs of breathing and with its heart beating, might conclude that the animal was alive.

But by now public opinion was concentrating not on ensuring that sealing was conducted humanely (and for most of the public it was a common belief that clubbing could never be humane), but of stopping commercial sealing altogether. In 1976 Greenpeace adopted the anti-sealing campaign. Greenpeace's very professional organisation, its ability to generate media coverage and its general appeal to the public, ensured that the campaign remained in the public eye. The Canadian government responded by organising its own publicity to justify the continuation of the hunt, but this was coolly received both within much of Canada and elsewhere. The Committee on Seals and Sealing (Chapter 6), reviewed not only the scientific background to the exploitation of the seals but also the humanitarian aspects involved. Some members of COSS joined a Canadian government delegation touring major centres in the United States and Europe to give the pro-sealing side of the story. But, as Lavigne and Kovacs (1988) pointed out, this pro-sealing publicity campaign only served to escalate the controversy further, since every appearance of pro-sealing spokesmen on the television was accompanied by vivid footage of the seal hunt in progress, with whitecoats being bloodily clubbed to death.

In the late 1970s and early 1980s the anti-sealing campaign concentrated on Europe, the main market for the products of the seal hunt. IFAW lobbied politicians with very successful results. In 1980, a Euro-MP Mr Stanley Johnson proposed a motion in the European Parliament calling on the European Commission to ban the import of products from pups of harp and hooded seals into the European Economic Community. After consideration by the Committee on the Environment, Public Health and Consumer Protection, which produced a report calling for a ban on trade in products derived from young harps and hoods, and receiving petitions signed by several million constituents (the organising of these petitions was an important IFAW and Greenpeace activity), the European Parliament adopted the resolution by 160 votes to 10 in March 1982.

The European Parliament has no legislative power itself, but makes recommendations to the European Commission, which if it approves them, passes them to the Council of Ministers. This was what happened with the sealing resolution. In October 1983, the importation of pelts taken from whitecoat harp seals and blueback hooded seals was banned for a trial period of two years. In 1985 this ban was extended to October 1989, with dire results for the sealers. As mentioned in Chapter 6, harp sealing has not ended, but it is greatly reduced. Its total abolition is still an objective of bodies such as Greenpeace, IFAW and the World Society for the Protection of Animals as well as various other bodies.

It is possible, but I think unlikely, that the anti-sealing campaign would have taken the same course in the absence of television. The pictures of blood on the ice, the appeal of the melting black eyes of the whitecoats, and the instinctive reaction to the sight and sound of the club crushing the soft tissues of the pup's skull had a profound effect on viewers. Because of the drama of the images, harp seal pictures were screened when almost any topic concerning seals came into the news. Coverage reached saturation point and there were few families in Europe or North America who did not at once associate the term 'sealing' with a dead whitecoat on the ice. The conservationists had won a notable victory.

But the campaign was not really based on conservation at all. The harp seals represented a depleted, but not an endangered, species. Conservation, in the sense in which it is used in IUCN's *World Conservation Strategy* (1980), has as one of its objectives ensuring the sustainable utilisation of species and ecosystems. Although opinions differ on what might constitute sustainable harvesting of the north-west Atlantic harp seals, there is no doubt at all that the stock could provide a substantial crop. For most people the argument simply did not turn on this. Their views were based on a gut-feeling that it was wrong to bash in the heads of baby seals. Victor Scheffer, who spent a lifetime studying seals, agreed with this view. He admitted that his real argument for conserving marine mammals was emotional and he believed that sentiment was a good reason for saving marine mammals (Scheffer, 1978).

Whatever views one may take on the anti-sealing campaign there is no doubt that it did much to advance the cause of wildlife conservation generally with a large body of people. Its results have caused hardship to seal hunters in Labrador and Greenland, eking out their existance in a way of life that is perhaps an anomaly in the present century. The market for their harbour seal or ringed seal skins is just as poor as it is for harp seals and, with few other cash crops to turn to, their way of life will necessarily cease. They must join the groups of urbanised Eskimos to make their way as best they can in an imported alien culture. But if the saga of the harp seals has persuaded others that there is something intrinsically worthwhile in the concept of conservation (however interpreted), then it has had wider relevance than the seals themselves, which may prove of greater value to mankind.

SEALS IN THE UNITED KINGDOM

The heightened public awareness generated by the harp seal hunt and its antagonists was to affect attitudes to seals in the United Kingdom. The history of conservation legislation for grey seals in the United Kingdom goes back to 1914. These seals were, in fact, the first British mammals (apart from game animals such as deer) to be given legal protection. The inspiration for the Grey Seals Protection Act 1914 came from a sportsman and hunter, H. Hesketh Prichard. He published an article in the *Cornhill Magazine* (1913) which described the clubbing of grey seals at Haskeir in the Hebrides. Prichard had not actually observed this himself — he obtained his information by questioning local people and from Martin Martin's *Description of the Western Islands of Scotland* (1703) — but his vivid description of the slaughter, which he claimed was 'slowly but surely advancing [the grey seals] along the road to extinction' inspired a Member of Parliament, Mr Charles Lyell, to promote a bill.

Bennet Rae (1960) has cast scorn on Prichard's article and the processes leading up to this bill. He pointed out that Prichard was aware that the yearly toll of seals at that time was an order of magnitude less than in Martin's time and that the habits of the seals and the inaccessibility of Haskeir ensured that opportunities for such killings were comparatively rare and did not occur each year. He went further: 'Prichard's article . . . set a standard in emotional appeal, in scientific inaccuracy and in illogical reasoning which appears to have been followed, doubtless under misapprehension, in subsequent press articles and statements on the grey seal.'

Be that as it may, it was generally accepted that the grey seal was nearing extinction in Britain, with a population perhaps as low as 500. How this figure was arrived at was not clear; some grey seals may have been believed to have been harbour seals, and some populations may simply simply been ignored. Concern was general and without much debate (or even interest) Lyall's Bill became law. The Grey Seal Protection Act established a close season of 1 October to 15 December each year, in which it was unlawful to kill or take grey seals, and prohibited altogether the killing of grey seals at Haskeir. It was to provide protection initially for five years, but was extended from year to year thereafter by the Expiring Laws Continuance Act.

By the 1920s, complaints of damage to salmon fisheries in Scotland were beginning to be heard from the fishermen (Chapter 7) while the protectionists were concerned that many grey seal pups were at risk at both ends of the close season. In 1932 a new act was passed which extended the close season from 1 September to 31 December. It also contained the important provision that orders could be made suspending or altering the close season in specified areas. In this way the new act satisfied the demands of both fishermen and protectionists. Haskeir was still afforded special treatment, in that in its case the only order that could be made was one to extend the close season.

During the period of the Grey Seal Protection Acts (but not necessarily because of them) the grey seal population increased rapidly, undoubtedly assisted by the progressive human depopulation of many small islands near the seals' breeding areas. Seals had ceased to have much significance as a resource to the crofters and there was little incentive to kill, either within or outside the close season.

Meanwhile, protests from fishermen became more stringent, and ultimately resulted in the control measures described earlier (Chapter 7). Control was hampered by the fact that there were no powers in the 1932 Act to enter land to kill seals in order to protect fisheries. Because of this the National Trust, for example, was able to prevent further seal killing at the Farne Islands (page 141). The Act was thus less than satisfactory to the fishermen. The conservationists also had problems with it. While it provided adequate protection for grey seals it did nothing at all to protect harbour seals. By the end of the 1960s, about 800 harbour seal pups were being taken each year in the Shetland Isles, between 400 and 600 in the rest of Scotland, and about 600 in the Wash (Bonner 1972). As described in Chapter 7, much of this industry had been generated by the grey seal pup culls that had taken place in Orkney, inspired by the apparent need to protect fisheries. The Shetland hunt, however, had a much longer history. Before 1960 about 300–400 harbour seal pups were killed each year in Shetland, but with increasing interest in sealing this rose dramatically, reaching a peak of about 900 pups in 1968 (Tickell, 1970). In places this kill was estimated to amount to 24 per cent of all pups born and the population was believed to be declining (Bonner *et al.*, 1973).

There was real concern amongst conservationists at the situation then developing in Shetland, while the more widely publicised hunting in the Wash, coming at a time when emotions had already been aroused by the harp seal hunt, created a demand for wider legislation.

The Earl of Cranbrook, who was at that time President of the Mammal Society, introduced a bill which would have provided protection for common seals (as harbour seals were more generally known in the British Isles) into the House of Lords in 1968. Owing to a shortage of parliamentary time this bill lapsed but another similar bill was introduced in the House of Commons by Mr John Temple in 1969 (Bonner, 1971).

The Conservation of Seals Act received Royal Assent in August 1970. It covers both grey and harbour seals (called common seals throughout the Act) in its provisions. It maintains the 1 September to 31 December close season for grey seals and set up a close season for harbour seals from 1 June to 31 August, during which periods it is unlawful to kill, injure or take a seal. When it appears necessary for proper conservation an order can be made prohibiting the killing of seals at any time for specified places (an early order prohibited the hunting of harbour seals in Shetland). Neither the prohibition on killing seals in the close season nor any orders on conservation grounds applies to seals killed to prevent them causing damage to a fishing net or fishing tackle, provided the seals were in the vicinity of the gear at the time.

The Act further allows the killing of seals in the close season or in prohibited areas under licence. Such licences can be issued for scientific purposes, or for the prevention of damage to fisheries, or for the reduction of a population surplus of seals for management purposes, or for the use of a population surplus of seals as a resource.

The Act also regulates killing methods. If a firearm is used it must be a rifle firing a bullet weighing not less than 45 grains (2.9 g) and with a muzzle energy of not less than 600 foot pounds (813 J). This provision excludes the use of shot guns or conventional .22 rim-fire rifles. The use of poisonous substances for killing seals is also prohibited. These regulations can be relaxed by licence, except that strychnine, a very cruel poison, can in no circumstances be used for killing seals. This exception reflects the personal wishes of Lord Cranbrook, but unfortunately for fishermen no effective substitute has been found for strychnine in poison baits for seals in salmon nets.

A very impoprtant provision of the Act was a clause that enabled the Secretary of State to authorise entry to private land for the purpose of obtaining information about seals, or to kill seals for the purpose of preventing damage to fisheries. This was in line with legislation affecting agricultural pests and had been included as a result of the purchase of an important seal breeding island in Orkney by an animal protection group, with the purpose of preventing seal killlling there.

The Conservation of Seals Act was a model piece of wildlife legislation. It put the emphasis on conservation by providing protection where it was needed. It provided potential relief to fishermen and catered for the commercial harvesting of seals where the stocks could withstand it. It further ensured that if seals were to be killed, adequate weapons were used to do so. In fact, however, it has failed to operate in the way its sponsors intended.

Licences were granted to kill grey seals for the protection of fisheries (Chapter 7), but this would have been possible anyway under the old Grey Seals Protection Acts, and as we have seen, the proposed management plan was never brought to a conclusion. For three years (1971–3) seal hunters in the Wash were licensed to take up to 380 pups a year (about 63 per cent of the average take over the previous nine years), but thereafter no further licences were issued (Vaughan, 1978). The rational approach to seals, typified by Lord Cranbrook, who took the trouble to acquaint himself with seals, fishermen, hunters and conservationists in the field, was replaced by the emotional response of people who were moved by television pictures of the killing of baby harp seals, but who were not themselves associated directly with any of the issues. The Secretary of State in these circumstances was unwilling to follow the scientific advice of the fisheries departments or to respond to the requests of the seal hunters.

The provision under the act for issuing licences to kill seals for the reduction of a population surplus for management purposes was used at the Farne Islands, off the Nothumbrian coast (Figure 7.4). The Farne Islands colony of grey seals is by far the largest in England and fortunately accurate records of it have been kept since 1956. Nearly all the seals breed on four of the islands in the group — Staple, Brownsman and North and South Wames. In 1956, 751 pups were born on these islands but by 1970 this had increased to 1956, a rate of increase of about 9 per cent a year (Bonner and Hickling, 1971). The increasing density of seals on these small islands resulted in increased pup mortality. This is related to the disturbance created at access points along the shore when seals come and go. Disturbance, as noted in Chapter 4, can lead to the rupture of the bond between mother and pup, or to the bond never becoming established. If pup mortality is plotted against the number of pups per 100 m of accessible shore there is a clear correlation (Figure 9.1). The level of agressive behaviour in the seals at the Farne Islands is high when compared with seals in less crowded localities, such as Orkney. This aggressiveness is associated with high site-tenacity by the lactating cows. Since the major cause of mortality of the young is starvation consequent on separation from their mothers, site-tenacity, which keeps the pairs together, has high survival value in the absence of terrestrial predators. By contrast, the aggressiveness that accompanies site-tenacity tends to increase the mortality of the offspring of less aggressive parents (Bonner, 1975).

Another result of the increased density of the seals at the Farne Islands was the effect on the soil and vegetation there. In the mid-1950s when the population was less than a thousand breeding cows, the seals seemed to have little effect on the vegetation. With increasing numbers of seals, however, there was progressive destruction of the fragile soil cap that covered these rocky islands. For centuries or longer, the summer vegetation on the Farnes has suffered from the burrowing activities of puffins and the tugging up of vegetation by nesting gulls, but the presence of large numbers of seals ashore in the autumn prevented or destroyed regrowth, and left the soil exposed to erosion. Perennial plants, such as sea-campion, *Silene maritima*, or scurvy grass, *Cochlearia officinalis*, and various grasses, tended to be replaced by annual species, notably common orache, *Atriplex hastata*. These annuals die in autumn

170

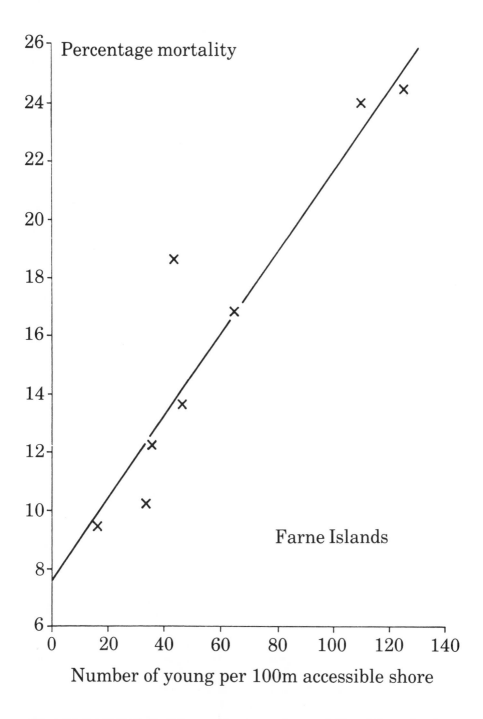

Figure 9.1 Correlation between the percentage grey seal pup mortality and the number of pups per 100 m of accessible shore at the Farne Islands.

and so offer no protection to the soil, which is blown or washed away by wind or rain in winter. In some parts of the islands soil losses in the early 1970s amounted to as much as 2.5 cm per year.

These conditions at the Farne Islands were causing concern to their owners, the National Trust. The islands were operated as a nature reserve, and attracted thousands of tourists who came to see the birds and seals. The sight of hundreds of dead or dying seal pups did not present a pleasing picture and it was feared that the destruction of vegetation and soil erosion would degrade the habitat for the birds. It was therefore decided to attempt to reduce the breeding population of seals to 1000 cows, at which level mortality had been less and vegetation damage negligible. For this purpose a licence was obtained under the Conservation of Seals Act for reducing a population surplus of seals for management purposes.

In 1972 a Norwegian sealer was chartered and started work at the Farnes on 6 November. The crew were used to working in the calm conditions of the pack ice taking the much more docile harp seals. The dangerous rocks and currents of the Farnes, the strong winds of a North Sea winter, and the greater size and ferocity of the grey seals surprised the sealers. By the time work was called off on 22 November 132 bulls, only 603 cows and 573 pups had been shot and their carcasses taken on board the sealer (Bonner and Hickling, 1971), a result well below the level that had been planned.

In 1975 the control operation was repeated and 158 bulls, 486 cows and 804 pups were killed. However, despite the considerable effort involved, the breeding stock was reduced only to about 70 per cent of its 1971 level. Since 1975 management culls at the Farne Islands have been on a smaller scale and have been confined to the removal of animals from sensitive areas. Starting in 1977, wardens have been stationed on Brownsman to scare seals off this island and its neighbour, Staple. This has resulted in a wider distribution of breeding seals, with other, non-vegetated, islands being used. Part of the Farnes colony has migrated to the Isle of May, in the Firth of Forth, some 90 km away. Three hundred and seventy-three grey seal pups were found at the Isle of May in December, 1980 (Prime, 1981). They were extremely healthy and well fed, in contrast to conditions at the original breeding islands in the Farnes.

The management operation at the Farnes aroused considerable public opposition. It constituted seal killing and the man (or particularly, the woman) in the street, influenced by the publicity of the anti-sealing campaign, regarded this as always wrong. However, in general the National Trust was able to convince its membership of the need for the action it had taken. Seals no longer breed on the vegetated islands of Brownsman and Staple; any cows that try to come ashore are scared off by the wardens or deterred during the night by propane gas operated bird scarers. Adult seals are now killed only if other, non-lethal, measures prove ineffective. Exposed areas of bare soil are being replanted with seedlings of various grasses and sea campion, and the islands are beginning to resume their previous appearance. The lost soil, however, can never be replaced in human time scales.

As far as the environmental issues at the Farne Islands are concerned, the management scheme may be judged to be a success. The population that now breeds there is around the number projected in the plan, but fluctuates rather stongly (Hickling and Hawkey, 1986). The migration of part of the Farnes colony to the Isle of May, and its dispersion to other islands in the Farnes group, may have increased its resilience to minor catastrophes (though some of the skerries in the group now used for breeding by the seals are liable to be inundated in severe storms). It seems likely, however, that the increase in grey seals will continue and that management measures will have to be accepted indefinitely at the Farne Islands if they are to continue to fulfil their role as a diverse habitat for plants, birds and seals.

THE PROBLEM OF THE MONK SEALS

We have already seen (Chapter 5) that the monk seals costitute the most threatened group of seals. With one species already extinct and the other two reduced to a remnant of their previous abundance, they seem likely candidates for early extinction. Charles Repenning, commenting on the inability of monk seals to adapt to changing conditions, describes them as living fossils 'comparable to the last of the dinosaurs surviving in the remains of a forgotten environment' (Repenning, 1980).

Monk seals, existing in such tiny numbers, can play little part in the ecology of the Mediterranean or the Hawaiian Pacific and their disappearance would have a negligible effect on the environment. However, as the most primitive group of extant seals, they have much to teach us scientifically, and perhaps more importantly, many people feel a responsibility not to let more species (particularly birds and mammals) become extinct.

There is a United States Federal Government responsibility to conserve the remaining Hawaiian monk seals, for in 1976 it was officially declared to be an endangered species. All but two of the Leeward Islands are within the Hawaiian Islands National Wildlife Refuge and the public has been barred from some breeding areas. Fines as high as $20,000 can be imposed for violation of the laws protecting the seals. Scientists working in the Monk Seal Recovery Team appointed by the National Marine Fishery Service in 1980 are studying as well as they are able all aspects of monk seal life that may affect their survival and rehabilitation. The task is not an easy one. Twelve hundred seals were counted at the Leeward Islands in 1958, fewer than 700 in 1976; there may now be as few as 500 in Hawaii.

While disturbance of seals hauled out on the beaches may be controlled, their low reproductive rate, the peculiar 'mobbing' habit of the males, in which they kill adult females and immatures during mass mating attempts, shark attacks, the risks of entanglement with marine debris, and the general disturbance caused by commercial fisheries, make the monk seal's survival in the wild problematic.

It is difficult to see what can be done further to help the Hawaiian monk seal, more particularly because the cause of its 50 per cent decline since the late 1950s is not understood. With so few seals left any sort of experimental studies are viewed with suspicion and even observational work is hampered by lack of subjects.

The situation is no better, and perhaps worse, with the Mediterranean monk seal. Once abundant enough to have a Greek city, Phocaea, named after it, and to support a commercial fishery in the fifteenth century, it is now reduced to a few groups scattered throughout the Mediterranean (the greatest number occurring in its classical haunt of the eastern Aegean Sea), with some very few at the Desertas Islands, and on the African Atlantic coast just north of Cape Etienne in the western Sahara (Cabo Blanco, Rio de Oro). The total population is really unknown but in 1978 David Sergeant and his colleagues concluded that it was between 500 and 1,000, and declining (Sergeant *et al.*, 1978). The Mediterranean seals are perhaps more tolerant of human disturbance than those from Hawaii. They have, after all, had many millennia of co-evolution with Man. Nevertheless, it is the opinion of many biologists who have studied them that the greatest threat to the Mediterranean monk seals is industrial and tourist expansion around the sea shores (Marchessaux, 1977; Sergeant *et al.*, 1978), though conflicts with fishermen are also clearly of importance.

An extra difficulty in the Meditearranean is that several countries are involved so that there is no single authority which can make decisions for conservation measures. Most, if not all, countries having monk seals within their territorial waters have enacted protective legislation, but there are generally problems of enforcement. Political instability in areas like the Mauritanian coast or the Lebanon may result in more people carrying guns and fewer controls than usual, with unfortunate consequences for the seals.

There is an active body of scientists from several countries working towards the conservation of the monk seal. The League for the Conservation of the Monk Seal publishes a newsletter which reviews and records recent work and observations. This is clearly an active field, but as in the case of the Hawaiian monk seal, it is not immediately obvious what can be done. A meeting convened by IUCN and the United Nations Environment Programme (UNEP) in January 1988, put forward, amongst other things, the following urgent recommendations:

* Caves or other breeding and resting sites used by monk seals should be identified and given strict protection.
* Waters surrounding breeding or resting sites that are used for feeding by seals should be designated as buffer zones. Large-scale commercial fishing should be prohibited and small-scale inshore fishermen should be given exclusive rights within these zones.
* Regional co-ordination should be instigated for activities such as regional data collection, an information exchange network set up for the co-ordination of research projects, distribution of information materials, and to provide assistance to governments on subjects such as the establishment of protected areas for seals, etc.
* A fund should be set aside to pay for the transport of wounded or orphaned seals to an existing rehabilitation centre, as well as for the husbandry and nursing of the animals, until another centre in the Mediteranean Basin can be established.

These are laudable aims, but there may be some doubt as to whether they are really practicable for monk seals. Identifying and providing legal protection for breeding and resting caves is relatively easy; ensuring that the protection is effective is less so in an area like the Mediterranean which teems with small boats, many carrying tourists who would like to see a seal. Setting up buffer zones for the seals' feeding areas is much more difficult. For any species of seal it is very difficult to determine its feeding range. If for monk seals this should turn out to be extensive it is highly unlikely that fisheries interests would agree to give up commercial fishing in those areas, in view of the general competitive state of fisheries in the Mediterranean. Furthermore, setting up such zones would in many cases involve bilateral or multilateral agreements between states, which are always difficult to negotiate. The third recommendation is perhaps the easiest to put into effect, but will do the least for the seals in the short term (and have we a long term?). The fourth recommendation concerns rescue operations. The existence of wounded or orphaned seals does not bode well for the remainder of the stock, but clearly it is necessary to do what we can to help such animals. A facility at Pieterburen in the Netherlands has had some considerable success in rearing abandoned monk seal pups. The mention in the recommendation of the establishment of another rehabilitation centre in the Mediterranean Basin perhaps reflects some regional jealousies, but a much weightier problem is what to do with animals once rehabilitated. There are currently no areas in the Mediterranean where monk seals can be said to be thriving and to add healthy animals to a declining stock may not be in their best interests.

An issue that has arisen with regard to the Mediterranean monk seal is that of captive breeding. For some endangered species, the Arabian oryx, for example, captive breeding and subsequent release to the wild has proved notably successful, but there is controversy over the application of this technique to monk seals. Some people hold the view that their survival in the wild is now highly uncertain and that to collect a founding group of 10–15 animals from which healthy juveniles could be released into a protected marine area, such as the marine Parc National de Port-Cros at Hyères, would play an important role in ensuring the survival of the species. Others feel that a captive breeding programme is a precarious proposal which may further endanger the wild population. It would certainly be very difficult to know where a healthy founding stock of monk seals could be found, and probably even more difficult to get permission to take them from the wild. Nor is it at all clear that the laws protecting monk seals are sufficiently well enforced in any area of the Mediterranean to make the release of new stock a sensible action.

My own views lie with Charles Repenning. I regard the extinction of monk seals as inevitable though I will not go so far with him as to agree that Mankind need not feel responsible for this, since it is a process that began 8 million years ago (Repenning, 1980). On the contrary, I feel we should do all we reasonably can to preserve the last poor remnants of the monk seals. If we succeed we shall have a conservation triumph; if we fail, at least we will have tried and perhaps the rest of the world will learn something from the endeavours.

CONSERVATION OF ANTARCTIC SEALS

The lobodontine seals of the Antarctic, and particularly the vast stock of crabeater seals, offer a resource of huge potential. In view of Mankind's record it may seem surprising that this has not already been tapped, as other seal stocks throughout the world have been tapped. The reason for this lies not only in the remoteness of the Antarctic, but also in the behaviour patterns of the seals concerned. The first seal hunters to visit the Antarctic, the nineteenth century fur and elephant sealers, had little interest in the lobodontine seals, which for the most part they would have encountered only in small numbers. Some specimens were taken, the 'sea leopards' that James Weddell found at the South Orkney Islands, and which were subsequently named after him as Weddell seals, for example, but the first commercial catches we know about were taken by whalers, not sealers. In the Antarctic summer season of 1893–4 a Norwegian expedition led by Carl Anton Larsen (the man who was eventually to found the Antarctic whaling industry) and consisting of the vessels *Jason, Castor* and *Hertha*, visited the South Shetland Islands, the South Orkney Islands and the Antarctic Peninsula. The expedition returned without any whales but with 13,223 seal skins and 6,600 barrels of seal oil. Unfortunately, we do not know what species of seals were taken, or where. Because of the large number involved it is generally supposed that the seals were crabeaters, though a good number of them were probably young elephant seals and Weddells which would have provided better skins.

Although subsequently many seals were shot to provide food for the men and sledge dogs of the exploring teams that worked in the Antarctic in the twentieth century, the commercial operators concentrated on the abundant stocks of whales. It was not until the whaling industry was in its death throes that another expedition was organised to take Antarctic seals. This was a Norwegian sealer, the *MV Polarhav*, which from 25 August to 31 September 1964, hunted in the pack-ice of the northern Weddell Sea and around the South Orkney and South Shetland Islands. *Polarhav's* catch amounted to only 852 seals, so the expedition was not a commercial success. The sealers had hoped to find in the Southern Ocean an analogue of the harp seal breeding grounds in the north-west Atlantic. But conditions were very different in the south. Crabeater seals do not congregate for breeding as do harp seals. Triads of male, female and pup are widely spaced out over the ice and it is impracticable to moor the ship against the ice and send hunting parties out on foot to kill seals and drag the skins back, as in the harp seal hunt. The larger size of the crabeaters made them more difficult to handle and the ice conditions were worse. In consequence, catch rates were very low and the Norwegians did not repeat the experiment.

However, the *Polarhav* expedition alerted concerned nations to the fact that there were no international regulations controlling the harvesting of seals at sea in the Southern Ocean. In 1959 the twelve nations that were then active in the Antarctic — Argentina, Australia, Belgium, Chile, France, Japan, New Zealand, Norway, South Africa, the USSR, the UK and the USA — had signed the Antarctic Treaty in Washington. The main purpose of this treaty was to freeze the situation with respect to the recognition or non-recognition of territorial claims, so that scientific research could continue unhampered, but it also recognised the 'preservation and conservation of living resources in the Antarctic' as one of the matters that the Treaty parties should consult about. An early product of such consultations was the Agreed Measures for the Conservation of

Antarctic Fauna and Flora (1964). These provided protection for all native mammals and birds in the Antarctic, though it was possible to grant permits to take, *inter alia*, seals for scientific or educational purposes or for the provision of essential food for men or dogs. The Agreed Measures, like the Treaty itself, applied to all land and ice shelves south of 60° South latitude. Within this area seals (and other wildlife) were very adequately protected. Few seals were taken for human food, though several nations maintained sledge dogs in the Antarctic which were fed on seal meat. Other seals were taken for research or educational purposes (zoos, museums, etc.). The average number taken each year between 1964 and 1974 was 695; for the period 1974 to 1985 this had declined to 290, reflecting a smaller number taken for feeding dogs. There was no reason to believe that this level of killing was having a significantly harmful effect on the total stocks of seals, or on the ecology of any locality.

This might not have been the case had a commercial sealing industry developed in the Southern Ocean. In the 1960s, concern for the north-west Atlantic harp seal stocks led one Canadian seal biologist to make the suggestion that sealing vessels should be diverted from the north to hunt the abundant pack-ice seals in the south. This suggestion, though well meant, was ill advised. Had sealing efforts been diverted in this way and the southern sealing been successful, it would probably have resulted in continued hunting of harp seals at a level which would otherwise have been uneconomic without the support of the southern enterprise (Bonner, 1982). There was thus a perceived need among the Antarctic Treaty nations for a further international agreement to control southern sealing.

A conference was held in London in 1972 at which the states which had signed the Antarctic Treaty were present and the Convention for the Conservation of Antarctic Seals was drawn up and signed. This recognises that Antarctic seals are an important living resource which is vulnerable to commercial exploitation and that consequently any harvests should be regulated so as not to exceed the optimum sustainable yield. The Convention sets a close season of from 1 March to 31 August, during which sealing is banned, has provision for special reserves where killing seals is prohibited, and divides the rest of the sea area south of latitude 60° into six zones, to be worked in rotation, one being closed to sealing each year (an analogous system to what was then operated under the International Whaling Convention regulations). Licences to take seals can be issued by member states to take limited numbers of seals commercially, or for special purposes (such as to provide scientific specimens, educational purposes or essential food for men or dogs). An annexe to the Treaty, which is capable of amendment in the light of further knowledge, lays down catch limits for permitted species. These are:

Crabeater seals	175,000
Leopard seals	12,000
Weddell seals	5,000

The killing of Ross, southern elephant seals or fur seals is prohibited absolutely for commercial purposes.

If an industry should begin, reports on the numbers of seals taken and relevant biological information and specimens would be provided to the

Group of Specialists on Seals of the Scientific Committee for Antarctic Research (SCAR), a component body of the International Council of Scientific Unions. SCAR would be invited to report on any harmful effects the harvest of seals might have, or to suggest ammendents to the Annexe of the Convention.

Dick Laws, convenor of the SCAR Group of Specialists on Seals, has written:

'This Convention is probably unique in that it makes detailed provisions for conserving species on the high seas before a potential industry has developed. There is provision for the adoption of further measures, when an industry starts, such as a scheme of international inspection. Because of the low level of Permissable Catches, the provision for reporting the catches and stopping sealing, and for further meetings to consider action, there is no doubt that it will provide protection for the Antarctic seals which has previously been lacking.' (Laws, 1973).

The Convention for the Conservation of Antarctic Seals remained untested until in 1987, when reports were received of seal hunting by two Soviet vessels in the Antarctic. The *MV Zubarevo* and the *MV Zakharovo*, both vessels of 2,600 tonnes and with crews of 72 people, carried out sealing operations between 9 December 1986 and 2 February 1987 near the Balleney Islands and the Ninnis and Mertz Glaciers (between approximately 145° E and 165° E and 66° S). In all, 4,802 seals were taken, made up of 4,014 crabeaters, 649 leopards, 107 Weddells, 30 Ross seals and two elephant seals.

The motives behind this expedition were not entirely clear. According to the report provided by the Soviet authorities to SCAR (which arrived somewhat later than might have been expected), the crabeaters and leopards were taken as part of a commercial harvest, while the Weddells, Ross and elephants had been taken on a permit issued under 'Article 4, para 1 b, c' of the Convention, i.e. for scientific research (b), and to provide specimens for museums, educational or cultural institutions (c). Some observers suspected that the expedition might have represented local enterprise by the department that runs the sealing in the Soviet eastern Arctic, without much prior reference to the department responsible for Soviet obligations under the Convention for the Conservation of Antarctic Seals. There were suggestions that the scientific permits might even have been issued *post hoc*. There is no evidence to support these suspicions and the Soviet authorities have entered into collaborative research with the United States to analyse the scientific results of the expedition, in particular the age structure of the pack ice seals, as determined from a study of teeth collected during the expedition.

I do not see the Soviet 1986–7 sealing expedition as presaging the start of major commercial sealing in the Antarctic. A catch of fewer than 5,000 seals by two 2,600 tonne vessels operating some 14,000 km from their base cannot be economically attractive. On the other hand, demographic data from crabeaters (and possibly other ice seals) derived from large scientific samples (say over 1,000 animals) can be of considerable potential value in studying ecological changes in the Southern Ocean resulting from fisheries operations there. If expeditions such as the Soviet ones were to be repeated at five-yearly intervals, a valuable body of information could be amassed. It is unlikely that equivalent data could be obtained from purely research cruises, because of the cost and logistic difficulties. The Soviet method of employing sealers with the capacity to offset the costs of research by a commercial catch seems, therefore, justifiable.

PROSPECTS FOR THE FUTURE

The world today is not a good place for wildlife. The relentless increase in human population is jostling many species, particularly large mammals, along the road to extinction. Demands for resources, notably fuel wood, are degrading habitats over a large part of the world's surface. Sadly, much of this degradation consists of loss of soil and tropical forests, which can never be made good in the time scales that apply to most human aspirations. Pollution of the atmosphere threatens changes in climate which in the short term, at any rate, are likely to be adverse to agriculture as we know it; the thinning of the ozone layer is likely to cause changes of more profound significance than an increase in skin cancers in the white races.

No sensible person can be optimistic about the future for the human race or for many of the higher animals with which we share this planet. But things are perhaps a little brighter for seals than for some other mammals. Seals live and feed in the sea and the sea has been far less affected by the expansion of the human population than the land. Except locally, the sea remains unrestricted by Man's activities. Chemical pollution seems to be a problem to seals only in enclosed sea areas, though we must be cautious in our optimism here, for the long-term population effects of low levels of contamination are unknown. Entanglement in fishing gear and marine debris generally does not seem to be as grave a menace to phocid seals as to other marine mammals. A possibly serious threat might be the penetration of biologically damaging ultraviolet B radiation, passing to the earth's surface through a thinned ozone layer, into the surface layers of the oceans, thus affecting phytoplankton growth on which the rest of the marine food-web depends. This is another field where we do not yet know sufficient to be able to forecast the likely consequences. We can be sure, however, that whatever we do now, the destruction of the protective ozone layer will continue to increase before ameliorative measures like banning CFCs lead to any improvement. Seals themselves, incidentally, are very unlikely to suffer any direct effects from increased UV radiation, for they all have very densely pigmented skins which would absorb such radiation before it penetrated deep enough to cause damage.

Competition from an increasingly efficient fishing industry may make it more difficult for seals to find their food. This is more likely to lead to changes in population levels than to the extinction of stocks. With few exceptions (indeed, perhaps only the crabeater seal) seals are versatile predators and well able to turn from one food resource to another. And I do not believe that the world fishing industry will continue its recent rate of expansion for very much longer. Fish are costly to harvest in terms of capital investment and energy input in comparison with conventional agricultural produce. When the crunch comes in human population in the next century the starving billions will have to be fed with grains and pulses rather than with fish.

Environmentally, then, seals are perhaps rather better off than many other mammals. Earlier in this chapter I have suggested that there has been a change in attitudes to seals which has led to a lessening of direct pressures on them. Subsistence hunting of seals by native peoples will almost certainly continue to decline. Organised commercial hunting, as of harp seals by the Russians in the White Sea, will continue in some places but will probably be conducted more rationally than in the past, leading to harvesting on a sustainable basis. I do not think it is likely that an Antarctic sealing industry will develop, because of the very high energy costs involved.

Public interest in seals will lead to active conservation measures in some places. Where these are directed to species that are already threatened, like the monk seals, they may have little chance of success. Where abundant, resilient species are concerned, such as harp seals or harbour seals, they are more likely to be successful.

Within the last couple of decades a new leisure industry has developed — whale watching. In certain areas, around Cape Cod or Hawaii for example, this has significant effects on the local economy. Seal watching is less easy to organise. Outside the Antarctic most seals are (with very good reasons) much less approachable than whales. Nevertheless, for many years tripper boats have been taking holidaymakers out to 'see the seals' at the Farne Islands, or around the Western Isles of Scotland, for example. More recently, fully organised tours have been taking people out to see the harp seals on the ice off Newfoundland. Dave Lavigne and Kit Kovacs's charming book *Harps and Hoods* (1988) was originally conceived as a field guide for these fortunate few. The more people that can be interested in seals in this way, and in other ways also — I have already stressed the importance of television — the better it will be for the future of seals and probably for other wildlife as well.

References

Addison, R.F. and Brodie, P.F. (1977) 'Organochlorine residues in maternal blubber, milk and pup blubber from grey seals (*Halichoerus grypus*) from Sable Island, Nova Scotia', *Journal of the Fisheries Research Board of Canada* **34**, 937–42.

Addison, R.F., Kerr, S.R. and Dale, J. (1973) 'Variation of organochlorine residue levels with age in Gulf of St Lawrence harp seals (*Pagophilus groenlandicus*)', *Journal of the Fisheries Research Board of Canada* **30**, 595–600.

Addison, R.F. and Smith, T.G. (1974) 'Organochlorine residue levels in Arctic ringed seals: variation with age and sex', *Oikos* **25**, 335–7.

Alderdice, D.F., Brett, J.R., Idler, D.R. and Fagerlund, U. (1954) 'Further observations on the olfactory perception in migrating adult coho and spring salmon', *Fisheries Research Board of Canada, Pacific Coast Station, Progress Reports* **98**, 10–12.

Allen, S.G. (1985) 'Mating behaviour in the harbour seal', *Marine Mammal Science* **1**, 84–7.

Amoroso, E.C., Bourne, G.H., Harrison, R.J., Matthews, L.H., Rowlands, I.W. and Sloper, J.C. (1965) 'Reproductive and endocrine organs of foetal, newborn and adult seals', *Journal of Zoology, London* **147**, 430–86.

Anderson, S.S., Burton, R.W. and Summers, C.F. (1975) 'Behaviour of grey seals (*Halichoerus grypus*) during the breeding season at North Rona', *Journal of Zoology, London* **177**, 179–95.

Anderson, S.S., Bonner, W.N., Baker, J.R. and Richards, R. (1974) 'Grey seals, *Halichoerus grypus*, of the Dee Estuary and observations on a characteristic skin lesion in British seals', *Journal of Zoology, London* **174**, 429–40.

Anderson, S.S. and Curry, M.G. (1976) Grey seals at the Monach Isles, Outer Hebrides, 1975. International Council for the Exploration of the Sea. CM 1976/N:9.

Anderson, S.S. and Fedak, M.A. (1982) 'Grey seal males: energetic and behavioural links between male size and sexual success', *Animal Behaviour* **33**, 829–38.

Anderson, S.S. and Hawkins, A.D. (1978) 'Scaring seals by sound', *Mammal Review* **8**, 19–24.

Anderson, S.S. and Harwood, J. (1985) 'Time budgets and topography: how energy reserves and terrain determine the breeding behaviour of grey seals', *Animal Behaviour* **33**, 1343–8.

Anon. (1971) Alaska Peninsula oil spill. Event No. 36–70. In Smithsonian Institute Center for Short-Lived Phenomena. Annual Report 1970, pp. 154–7.

Anon. (1986) 'Impact of seals on fisheries, Part 5b', In: *Report of the Royal*

Commission on Seals and the Sealing Industry in Canada, Vol. 3, pp 273–453. Canadian Government Publishing Centre, Ottawa.

Árnason, U. (1972) 'The role of chromosomal rearrangement in mammalian speciation with special reference to Cetacea and Pinnipedia', *Hereditas* **70**, 113–18.

Bartholomew, G.A. (1970) 'A model for the evolution of pinniped polygyny', *Evolution* **24**, 546–59.

Beddington, J.R. and Williams, H.A. (1979) The structure and management of the NW Atlantic harp seal herd. Draft Report to the US Marine Mammal Commission. Washington.

Bengtson, J.L. and Siniff, D.B. (1981) 'Reproductive aspects of female crabeater seals (*Lobodon carcinophagus*) along the Antarctic Peninsula', *Canadian Journal of Zoology* **59**, 92–102.

Benjaminsen, T. (1973) 'Age determination and the growth and age distribution from cementum growth layers of bearded seals at Svalbard', *Fiskeridirecktoratets Skrifter, Havforsknings Undersøkelse* **16**, 159–70.

Berland, B. (1966) 'The hood and its extrusible balloon in the hooded seal *Cystophora cristata* Erxl.', *Report of the Norwegian Polar Institute*, 1965, 95–102.

Berta, A., Ray, C.E. and Wyss, A.R. (1989) 'Skeleton of oldest known pinniped, *Enaliarctos mealsi*'. *Science, N.Y.* **244**, pp. 60–62.

Bertram, G.C.L. (1940) 'The biology of the Weddell and crabeater seals', *Scientific Reports of the British Grahamland Expedition* **1**, 1–139.

Beverton, R.J. (1985) 'Analysis of marine mammal-fisheries interaction'. In: *Marine Mammals and Fisheries*, eds. Beddington, J.R., Beverton, R.J. and Lavigne, D.M., pp 3–33. George Allen and & Unwin, London.

Bigg, M.A. (1969) The harbor seal in British Columbia. Bulletin of the Fisheries Research Board of Canada, No. 172.

Bjorge, A.J. (1985) The relationship between seal abundance and codworm (*Phoconema decipiens*) infestation in cod in Norwegian waters. International Council for the Exploration of the Sea. CM 1985/N:4.

Blix, A.S., Grav, H.J. and Ronald, K. (1975) 'Brown adipose tissue and the significance of the venous plexuses in seals', *Acta Physiologica Scandinavica* **94**, 133–5.

Blix, A.S. and Øritsland, N.A. (1970) 'Current regulations for killing of seals evaluated by electrographic recordings of brain and heart activity', *Acta Veterinaria Scandinavia* **11**, 335–7.

Boas, F. (1888) *The Central Eskimo*. Sixth Annual Report, Bureau of Ethnology, Smithsonian Institution, Washington.

Boness, D.J., Anderson, S.S. and Cox, C.R. (1982) 'Functions of female aggression during the pupping and mating season of grey seals, *Halichoerus grypus* (Fabricius)', *Canadian Journal of Zoology* 2270–8.

Boness, D.J. and James, H. (1979) 'Reproductive behaviour of the grey seal, *Halichoerus grypus* (Fab.), on Sable Island, Nova Scotia', *Journal of Zoology* **188**, 477–500.

Bonner, W.N. (1955) 'Reproductive organs of foetal and juvenile elephant seals', *Nature, London* **176**, 982–3.

—— (1971) 'Legislation on seals in the British Isles', *The Salmon Net* **7**, 30–3.

—— (1972) 'The grey seal and common seal in European waters', *Oceanography and Marine Biology Annual Review* **10**, 461–507.

—— (1975) 'Population increase of grey seals at the Farne Islands', *Rapports et Procès-Verbaux des Réunions de Conseil pour l'Exploration de la Mer* **169**, 366–70.

—— (1979) 'Grey seal'. In: *Mammals in the Seas, 2*, pp 90–4. FAO Fisheries Series, No. 5.

—— (1982) *Seals and Man: A study of interactions*. University of Washington Press, Seattle.

—— (1984) 'Lactation strategies in pinnipeds: problems for a marine mammalian group', *Symposia of the Zoological Society of London*, No. 51, 253–72.

Bonner, W.N. and Hickling, G. (1971) 'The grey seals of the Farne Islands', *Transactions of the Natural History Society of Northumberland, Durham and Newcastle upon Tyne* **17**(4) (NS), 141–82.

Bonner, W.N., Vaughan, R.W. and Johnston, L. (1973) 'The status of the common seal in Shetland', *Biological Conservation* **5**, 185–90.

Bonner, W.N. and Witthames, S.R. (1974) 'Dispersal of common seals (*Phoca vitulina*) tagged in the Wash, East Anglia', *Journal of Zoology, London* **174**, 528–31.

Bowen, W.D., Oftedal, O.T. and Boness, D.J. (1985) 'Birth to weaning in 4 days: remarkable growth in the hooded seal, *Cystophora cristata*', *Canadian Journal of Zoology* **63**, 2841–6.

Boyd, I.L. (1984) 'The relationship between body condition and the timing of implantation in pregnant grey seals (*Halichoerus grypus*)', *Journal of Zoology, London* **203**, 113–23.

Bryden, M.M. (1964) 'Insulating capacity of the subcutaneous fat of the southern elephant seal', *Nature, London* **203**, 1299–1300.

—— (1969) 'Relative growth of the major body components of the southern elephant seal', *Australian Journal of Zoology* **17**, 153–77.

Bryden, M.M. and Stokes, G.B. (1969) 'Metabolism of fatty acids in the southern elephant seal, *Mirounga leonina* (L.), *Canadian Journal of Biochemistry* **47**, 757–60.

Burns, J.J. (1981) 'Ribbon seal *Phoca fasciata* Zimmerman, 1783'. In: *Handbook of Marine Mammals, Vol. 1*, eds. Ridgway, S.H. and Harrison, R.J., pp 89–109. Academic Press, London.

Burns, J.J. and Fay, F.H. (1970) 'Comparative morphology of the skull of the ribbon seal, *Histriophoca fasciata*, with remarks on systematics of Phocidae', *Journal of Zoology, London* **161**, 363–94.

Burton, R.W., Anderson, S.S. and Summers, C.F. (1975) 'Perinatal activities in the grey seal (*Halichoerus grypus*)', *Journal of Zoology, London* **177**, 197–201.

Busch, B.C. (1985) *The War Against the Seals: a history of the North American seal fishery*. McGill-Queen's University Press, Kingston and Montreal.

Canada Ministry of Transport (1970). *Seals*. In: Report of the task force — operation oil (Clean-up of the Arrow oil spill in Chedabucto Bay) to the Minister of Transport, Vol. 1, pp. 46–47. Information Canada, Ottawa.

Capitan, L., Breuil, H., Burrinet, D. and Peyrony, C. (1906) 'L'Abri Mège. Une station magdalérienne a Teyat (Dordogne)', *Revue d'école d'anthropologie de Paris* **6**, 196–212

Capstick, C.K., Lavigne, D.M. and Ronald, K. (1976) Population forecasts for northwest Atlantic harp seals, *Pagophilus groenlandicus*. International Commission for Northwest Atlantic Fisheries, Research Document 76/X/132.

Carson, Rachel (1962) *Silent Spring*. Houghton Mifflin, Boston.

Clark, A.H. (1877) 'The Antarctic fur seal and sea-elephant industry'. In: *The Fisheries and Fishery Industries of the United States, Section 5, Volume 2*, ed. Goode, G.B., pp 400–67. Government Printing Office, Washington.

Clark, J.G.D. (1946) 'Seal-hunting in the Stone Age of north-western Europe: a study in economic prehistory', *Proceedings of the Prehistorical Society* **12**(2), 12–48.

Clarke, M.R. and McLeod, N. (1982) 'Cephalopod remains in the stomachs of eight Weddell seals', *British Antarctic Survey Bulletin* No. 57, 33–40.

Cline, D.R., Sinoff, D.B. and Erickson, A.W. (1971) 'Underwater copulation of the Weddell seal', *Journal of Mammology* **51**, 204.

Colman, J.S. (1937) 'The present state of the Newfoundland seal fishery', *Journal of Animal Ecology* **6**, 145-59.

—— (1949) 'The Newfoundland seal fishery and the Second World War', *Journal of Animal Ecology* **18**, 40–6.

Cosby, S.L. and eleven other authors (1988) *Nature, London* **336**, 115–16.

Council for Nature (1979) *A Report to the Secretary of State for Scotland from the Council for Nature Seal Group*. Council for Nature, London.

Davis, J.E. and Anderson, S.S. (1976) 'Effects of oil pollution on breeding grey seals', *Marine Pollution Bulletin* **7**, 115–18.

DeLong, R.L., Gilmartin, W.G. and Simpson, J.G. (1973) 'Premature births in California sea lions: association with high organochlorine pollutant residue levels', *Science, New York* **181**, 1168–9.

DeLong, R.L., Kooyman, G.L., Gilmartin, W.G. and Loughlin, T.R. (1984) 'Hawaiian monk seal diving behavior', *Acta Zoologica Fennica* **172**, 129–31.

Doutt, J.K. (1942) 'A review of the genus *Phoca*', *Annals of the Carnegie Museum* **29**, 61–125.

Drescher, H.E. (1978) 'Hautkrankenheiten beim Seehund, *Phoca vitulina* Linne, 1758, in der Nordsee', *Saugetierkunde Mittelungen* **26**(1), 50–9.

Essapian, F.S. (1955) 'Speed-induced skin folds in the bottle-nosed porpoise, *Tursiops truncatus*', *Breviora Museum of Comparative Zoology* No. 43, 1–4.

Fanning, E. (1832) *Voyages and Discoveries in the South Seas, 1792–1832*. Marine Research Society of Salem Publications No. 6.

Fisher, H.D. (1952) Harp seals of the northwest Atlantic. Fisheries Research Board of Canada, Arctic Biological Station, Circular 20.

Fogden, S.C.L. (1986) 'Suckling behaviour in the grey seal (*Halichoerus grypus*) and the northern elephant seal (*Mirounga angustirostris*)', *Journal of Zoology, London* **164**, 61–92.

—— (1971) 'Mother–young behaviour at grey seal breeding beaches', *Journal of Zoology* **164**, 61–92.

Frank, R., Ronald, K. and Braun, H.E. (1973) 'Organochlorine residues in harp seals (*Pagophilus groenlandicus*) caught in eastern Canadian waters', *Journal of the Fisheries Research Board of Canada* **30**, 1053–63.

Geraci, J.R. and Smith, T.G. (1976) 'Direct and indirect effects of oil on ringed seals (*Phoca hispida*) of the Beaufort Sea', *Journal of the Fisheries Research Board of Canada* **33**, 1976–84.

Geraci, J.R. and St. Aubin, D.J. (1980). Offshore petroleum resource development and marine animals: a review and research recommendations. *Marine Fisheries Review* **42** (11) pp. 1–12.

Gill, C., Booker, S. and Soper, A. (1967) *The Wreck of the 'Torrey Canyon'*. David & Charles, Newton Abbot.

Gjessing, G. (1936) *Nordenfjelsker Ristninger og malinger av den Artiske Gruppe*. Institutet for Sammenlignde Kulturforskning. No. 30. 208pp. Oslo.

Goodhart, C.B. (1988) 'Did virus transfer from harp seals to common seals?', *Nature, London* **336**, 21.

Griffiths, D.J., Øritsland, N.A. and Øritsland, T. (1987) Marine mammals and petroleum activities in Norwegian waters. Rapporter og Meldinger fra Fiskeridirektoratets Havsforskningsinstitutt, Bergen, Serie B, No. 1.

Gulland, J.A. (1987) 'The impact of seals on fisheries', *Marine Policy*, July, 1987, 196–204.

Harrison, R.J. and King, J.E. (1980) *Marine Mammals*, 2nd Edition. Hutchinson, London.

Harwood, J. (1978) 'The effect of management policies on the stability and resilience of British grey seal populations', *Journal of Applied Ecology* **15**, 413–21.

—— (1989) 'Lessons from the seal epidemic'. *New Scientist*, 18 February 1989, 38–42.

Harwood, J. and Greenwood, J.J.D. (1985) 'Competition between British grey seals and fisheries'. In: *Marine Mammals and Fisheries*, eds. Beddington, J.R., Beverton, R.J.H. and Lavigne, D.M. pp 153–69. George Allen and Unwin, London.

Harwood, J. and Prime, J.H. (1978) 'Some factors affecting the size of British grey seal populations', *Journal of Applied Ecology* **15**, 40–11.

Harwood, J. and Reijnders, P. (1988) 'Seals, sense and sensibility', *New Scientist*, 15 October 1988, 28–9.

Helle, E., Olsson, M. and Jensen, S. (1976a) 'DDT and PCB levels and reproduction in Ringed Seal from the Bothnian Bay', *Ambio* **5**, 188–9.

—— (1976b) 'PCB levels correlated with pathological changes in seal uteri', *Ambio* **5**, 261–3.

Helminen, M., Karppanen, E. and Kovisto, J.I. (1968) [Mercury content of the Lake Saimaa ringed seal], *Finsk Veterinske Tidskrifter* **74**, 87–9.

Hendey, Q. and Repenning, C.A. (1972) 'A Pliocene phocid from South Africa', *Annals of the South African Museum* **59**(4), 71–98.

Henry, M.E. (1986) Observations of gill and trammel net fishing activity between Pt Buchar and Pt Sur, California, June–October 1985. Marine Mammal Commission, Washington.

Hewer, H.R. (1957) 'A Hebridean breeding colony of grey seals, *Halichoerus grypus* (Fab.) with comparative notes on the grey seals of Ramsey Island, Pembrokeshire', *Proceedings of the Zoological Society of London* **128**, 23–66.

—— (1964) 'The determination of age, sexual maturity and a life-table in the grey seal (*Halichoerus grypus*)', *Proceedings of the Zoological Society of London* **142**, 539–624.

Hewer, H.R. and Backhouse, K. (1968) 'Embryology and foetal growth rate in the grey seal (*Halichoerus grypus*)', *Journal of Zoology, London* **155**, 507–33.

Hickling, G. (1962) *Grey Seals and the Farne Islands*. Routledge & Kegan Paul, London.

Hickling, G. and Hawkey, P. (1986) 'The grey seal *Halichoerus grypus* (Fabr.) at the Farne Islands: 1983–1985', *Transactions of the Natural History Society of Northumbria* **53**, 3–12.

Hobson, B.M. and Boyd, I.L. (1984) 'Gonadotrophin and progesterone concentrations in placentae of grey seals (*Halichoerus grypus*)', *Journal of Reproduction and Fertility* **72**, 521–8.

Hokama, Y. and Miyahsara, J.T. (1986) 'Ciguatera poisoning: clinical and immunological aspects', *Journal of Toxicology, Toxin Reviews* **5**(1), 25–53.

Holden, A.V. (1975) 'The accumulation of oceanic contaminants in marine animals', *Rapports et Procès-Verbaux des Réunions Conseil International pour l'Exploration de la Mer* **169**, 353–61.

—— (1978) 'Pollutants and seals — a review', *Mammal Review* **8**, 53–66.

Howell, A. Brazier (1930) *Aquatic Mammals: their adaptations to life in water*. Charles C. Thomas, Baltimore, (1970 reprint by Dover Publications, New York.)

Innes, S.R., Stewart, E.A. and Lavigne, D.M. (1978) Growth in north-west Atlantic harp seals, *Pagophilus groenlandicus*: density-dependence and recent changes in energy availability. Canadian Atlantic Fisheries Scientific Advisory Committee, Working Paper 78/46.

Irving, L., Fisher, K.C. and McIntosh, F.C. (1935) 'The water balance of a marine mammal, the seal', *Journal of Cellular and Comparative Physiology* **6**, 387–91.

IUCN (1980) *World Conservation Strategy*. International Union for the Conservation of Nature and Natural Resources, Gland.

IUCN (1981) *Report of the IUCN Workshop on Marine Mammal/Fishery Interactions, La Jolla, California, 30 March–2 April 1981*. International Union for the Conservation of Nature and Natural Resources, Gland.

Jamieson, G.S. (1971) 'The functional significance of corneal distortion in marine mammals', *Canadian Journal of Zoology* **49**, 19–23.

Jamieson, G.S. and Fisher, H.D. (1973) 'The pinniped eye: a review'. In: *Functional Anatomy of Marine Mammals, Vol. 1*, ed. Harrison, R.J., pp 245–61. Academic Press, London and New York.

Kennedy, S. and five other authors. (1988) 'Viral distemper now found in porpoises', *Nature, London* **336**, 21.

Kenyon, K.W. (1980) 'No man is benign: the endangered monk seal', *Oceans* 13, 48–54.

—— (1981) 'Monk seals: *Monachus* Flemming, 1822'. In: *Handbook of Marine Mammals, Vol. 2*, eds. Ridgway, S.H. and Harrison, R.J., pp 195–220. Academic Press, London.

King, J.E. (1961) 'The feeding mechanism and jaws of the crabeater seal (*Lobodon carcinophagus*)', *Mammalia* 25, 462–6.

—— (1983) *Seals of the World*. British Museum (Natural History) and Oxford University Press, London and Oxford.

Koeman, J.H. and Van Genderen, H. (1966) 'Some preliminary notes on residues of chlorinated hydrocarbon insecticides in birds and mammals in the Netherlands', *Journal of Applied Ecology* 3 (Supplement), 99–106.

Koeman, J.H., Peeters, W.H.M., Smit, C.J., Tjioe, P.S. and de Goeij, J.J.M. (1972) 'Persistent chemicals in marine mammals', *TNO-Nieuws* 27, 570–8.

Koeman, J.H., Peeters, W.H.M., Koudstaal-Hol, C.H.M., Tjioe, P.S. and De Goeij, J.J.M. (1973) 'Mercury–selenium correlation in marine mammals', *Nature, London* 245, 385–6.

Kooyman, G.L. (1966) 'Maximum diving capacity of the Weddell seal (*Leptonychotes weddelli*)', *Science, New York* 151, 1553–4.

——(1981a) 'Weddell seal — *Leptonychotes weddelli*'. In: *Handbook of Marine Mammals 2*, eds. Ridgway, S.H. and Harrison, R.J., pp 275–96. Academic Press, London.

—— (1981b) *Weddell seal: consummate diver*. Cambridge University Press, Cambridge.

Kooyman, G.L., Castellini, M.A. and Davis, R.W. (1981) 'Physiology of diving in marine mammals', *Annual Review of Physiology* 43, 343–56.

Kooyman, G.L., Schroeder, J.P., Denison, D.M., Hammond, D.D., Wright, J.J. and Bergman, W.P. (1972) 'Blood N_2 tensions of seals during simulated deep diving', *American Journal of Physiology* 223, 1016–20.

Laist, D.W. (1987) 'Overview of the biological effects of lost and discarded plastic debris in the marine environment', *Marine Pollution Bulletin* 18(6b), 319–26.

Lavigne, D.M. (1979) 'Management of seals in the northwest Atlantic Ocean', *Transactions of the 44th North American Wildlife Conference*, 488–97.

Lavigne, D.M., Bernholz, C.D. and Ronald, K. (1977) 'Functional aspects of pinniped vision'. In: *Functional Anatomy of Marine Mammals, Vol. 3*, ed. Harrison, R.J., pp 135–73. Academic Press, London and New York.

Lavigne, D.M., Innes, S., Stewart, R.E.A. and Worthy, G.A.J. (1985) 'An annual energy budget for North-west Atlantic harp seals'. In: *Marine Mammals and Fisheries*, eds. Beddington, J.R., Beverton, R.J. and Lavigne, D.M., pp 319–36. George Allen & Unwin, London.

Lavigne, D.M., Innes, S., Worthy, G.A.J., Kovacs, K.M., Schmitz, O.J. and Hickie, J.P. (1986) 'Metabolic rates of seals and whales', *Canadian Journal of Zoology* 64, 279–84.

Lavigne, D.M. and Kovacs, K.M. (1988) *Harps and Hoods: ice-breeding seals of the Northwest Atlantic*. University of Waterloo Press, Waterloo, Ontario.

Lavigne, D.M., Stewart, R.E.A. and Fletcher, F. (1982) 'Changes in composition and energy content of harp seal milk during lactation', *Physiological Zoology* 55, 1–9.

Laws, R.M. (1952) 'A new method of age determination for mammals', *Nature, London* 169, 972.

—— (1953a) A new method of age determination in mammals, with special reference to the elephant seal (*Mirounga leonina* Linn.). Falkland Islands Dependencies Survey Scientific Reports, No. 2.

—— (1953b) The elephant seal (*Mirounga leonina* Linn.) 1. Growth and age. Falkland Islands Dependencies Survey Scientific Reports, No. 8.

—— (1953c) 'The elephant seal at South Georgia', *Polar Record* 6, 1–62.

—— (1956a) The elephant seal (*Mirounga leonina* Linn.) 2. General, social and reproductive behaviour. Falkland Islands Dependencies Survey Scientific Reports, No. 13.

—— (1956b) The elephant seal (*Mirounga leonina* Linn.) 3. The physiology of reproduction. Falkland Islands Dependencies Survey Scientific Reports, No. 15.

—— (1959) 'Accelerated growth in seals, with special reference to the Phocidae', *Norsk Hvalfangsttidende* **48**, 425–52.

—— (1960) 'The southern elephant seal (*Mirounga leonina* Linn.) at South Georgia', *Norsk Hvalfangsttidende* **10 & 11**, 466–76 & 520–42.

—— (1973) 'The current status of seals in the Southern Hemisphere'. In: *Seals, Proceedings of a Working Meeting of Seal Specialists on Threatened and Depleted Seals of the World, Guelph, Ontario, 18–19 August 1972*, pp 144–61. International Union for the Conservation of Nature and Natural Resources, Morges, Switzerland.

—— (1984) 'Seals'. In: *Antarctic Ecology, Vol. 2*, ed. Laws, R.M., pp 612–715. Academic Press, London.

Laws, R.M. and Taylor, R.J.F. (1957) 'A mass dying of crabeater seals, *Lobodon carcinophagus* (Gray)', *Proceedings of the Zoological Society of London* **129**, 315–24.

Le Boeuf, B.J. (1971) 'Oil contamination and elephant seal mortality: a "negative" finding'. In: *Biological and Oceanographic Survey of the Santa Barbara Channel Oil Spill, 1969–1970*, ed. Straughan, D., p 277–85. Special Publication of the Alan Hancock Foundation, University of Southern California.

—— (1974) 'Male-male competition and reproductive success in elephant seals', *American Zoologist* **14**, 163–76.

—— (1978) 'Sex and evolution'. In: *Sex and Behaviour*, eds. McGill, T.E., Dewsbury, D.A. and Sachs, B.D., pp 3–33. Plenum Publishing Corp., London and New York.

Le Boeuf, B.J. Costa, D.P., Huntley, A.C., Kooyman, G.L. and Davis, R.W. (1986) 'Pattern and depth of dives in northern elephant seals, *Mirounga angustirostris*', *Journal of Zoology, London* **208**, 1–7.

Linnaeus, C. (1745) 'Ölandska och Gothlandska Resa 1741 (Öland and Gothland Journey 1741)', trs Åsberg, M. and Stearn, W.T., *Biological Journal of the Linnean Society* **5**(2), 109–220.

Lister-Kaye, J. (1979) *Seal Cull*. Penguin Books, Harmondsworth, Middlesex.

Lockley, R.M. (1966) *Grey Seal, Common Seal*. André Deutsch, London.

Lythgoe, J.N. and Dartnall, H.J.A. (1970) 'A "deep sea rhodopsin" in a mammal', *Nature, London* **227**, 955–6.

McCann, T.S. (1980) 'Population structure and social organization of southern elephant seals, *Mirounga leonina* (L.)', *Biological Journal of the Linnean Society* **14**, 133–50.

—— (1981a) The social organization and behaviour of the southern elephant seal, *Mirounga leonina* L.). PhD thesis, University of London.

—— (1981b) 'Aggression and sexual activity of male southern elephant seals, *Mirounga leonina*', *Journal of Zoology, London* **195**, 295–310.

McClelland, G., Misra, R.K. and Marcogliese, D.J. (1983) Variations in abundance of larval anisakines, sealworm (*Phoconema decipiens*) and related species in Scotian Shelf (4VS and 4W) cod and flatfish. Canadian Technical Reports of Fisheries and Aquatic Sciences, No. 1202.

McLaren, I.A. (1958) The biology of the ringed seal (*Phoca hispida* Schreber) in the eastern Canadian Arctic. Bulletin of the Fisheries Research Board of Canada, No. 118.

—— (1960) 'Are the Pinnipedia diphyletic?', *Systematic Zoology* **9**(1), 18–28.

—— (1967) 'Seals and group selection', *Ecology* **48**, 104–10.

—— (1977) 'The status of seals in Canada'. In: *Canada's Threatened Species and Habitats*, eds. Mosquin, T. and Suchal, C., pp 71–8. Canadian Nature Federation, Ottawa.

—— (1984) 'The 19 species of true seals'. In: *The Encyclopaedia of Mammals, Vol 2*, ed. McDonald, David, pp 276–8. George Allen & Unwin, London.

Mahy, B.W.J., Barrett, T., Evans, S., Anderson, E.C. and Bostock, C.J. (1988) 'Characterisation of a seal morbillivirus', *Nature, London* **336**, 115.

Mansfield, A.W. and Beck, B. (1977) The grey seal in eastern Canada. Fisheries and Marine Services Technical Report No. 704.

Marchessaux, D. (1977) 'Will the Mediterranean monk seal survive', *Aquatic Mammals* **5**, 87.

Margolis, L. (1977) 'Public health aspects of "codworm" infection: a review', *Journal of the Fisheries Research Board of Canada* **34**, 887–98.

Martin, M. (1703) *A Description of the Western Isles of Scotland*. Bell, London. (Facsimile edition reprinted 1976, James Thin, Edinburgh.)

Matthews, L.H. (1929) 'The natural history of the elephant seal', *'Discovery' Reports* 1, 233–56.

—— (1952) *Sea Elephant: the life and death of the elephant seal*. MacGibbon and Kee, London.

Møhl, B. (1964) 'Preliminary studies on hearing in seals', *Videnskabelige Meddelse fra Dansk Naturhistorik Forening* **127**, 283–94.

Møhl, U. (1970) 'Fangstdyrene av den Danske strand: den zoologiske baggrund for harpunerne', *KUML (Årbog for Tyske Arkaeologiske Selskab)* 1970, 297–239.

Molyneux, G.S. and Bryden, M.M. (1975) 'Arteriovenous anastomoses in the skin of the Weddell seal, *Leptonychotes weddelli*', *Science, New York* **189**, 100–2.

—— (1978) 'Arteriovenous anastomoses in the skin of seals. 1. The Weddell seal *Leptonychotes weddelli* and the elephant seal *Mirounga leonina* (Pinnipedia: Phocidae), *Anatomical Record* **191**, 239–52.

Muizon, C. de (1981) Les vértebrés fossiles de la formation Pisco (Perou). Institute d'études Andines. Récherche sur les grandes civilisations. Memoire No. 6. Paris.

Muizon, C. de and Hendey, Q. (1980) 'Late Tertiary seals of the South Atlantic Ocean', *Annals of the South African Museum* **82**(3), 91–128.

Nature Conservancy (1963) *Grey Seals and Fisheries: Report of the Consultative Committee on Grey Seals and Fisheries*. Her Majesty's Stationery Office, London.

Nelson, R.K. (1969) *Hunters of the Northern Ice*. University of Chicago Press, Chicago.

Newby, T.C. (1973) 'Observations on the breeding behavior of the harbor seal in the State of Washington', *Journal of Mammology* **54**, 540–3.

North Pacific Fishery Management Council (1979) Fishery Management Plan for the Groundfish Fishery in the Bering Sea–Aleutian Islands area. Anchorage, Alaska, November 1979.

O'Gorman, F. (1963) 'Observations on terrestrial locomotion in Antarctic seals', *Proceedings of the Zoological Society of London* **141**, 837–50.

Øritsland, T. (1977) 'Food consumption of seals in the Antarctic pack ice'. In: *Adaptations Within Antarctic Ecosystems*, ed. Llano, G.A., pp 749–68. Smithsonian Institution, Washington.

Ortiz, C.L., Costa, D. and Le Boeuf, B.J. (1978) 'Water and energy flux in elephant seal pups fasting under natural conditions', *Physiological Zoology* **51**, 166–78.

Osterhaus, A.D.M.E. and Vedder, E.J. (1988) *Nature, London*. **335**, p. 20.

Parrish, B.B. and Shearer, W.M. (1977) Effects of seals on fisheries. International Council for the Exploration of the Seas, CM/M: 14.

Pascal, M. (1985) 'Numerical changes in the population of elephant seals (*Mirounga leonina* L.) in the Kerguelen Archipelago during the past 30 years'. In: *Marine Mammals and Fisheries*, eds. Beddington, J.R., Beverton, R.J.H. and Lavigne, D.M., pp 170–86. George Allen & Unwin, London.

Platt, N.E., Prime, J.H. and Witthames, S.R. (1975) 'The age of the grey seal at the Farne Islands', *Transactions of the Natural History Society of Northumbria*

42, 99–106.

Potter, E.C.E. and Swain, A. (1979) Seal predation in the North East England coastal salmon fishery. International Council for the Exploration of the Seas, CM 1979/N:9.

Power, G. and Gregoire, J. (1978) 'Predation by freshwater seals on the fish community of Lower Seal Lake, Quebec', *Journal of the Fisheries Research Board of Canada* **35**, 844–50.

Prichard, H.H. (1913) 'The grey seals of Haskeir', *Cornhill Magazine* **35**.

Prime, J.H. 'Breeding grey seals on the Isle of May, 1980', *Transactions of the Natural History Society of Northumbria* **47**, 13–16.

Racovitza, E.G. (1900) 'La vie des animaux et des plantes dans L'Antarctique', *Bulletin de la Societé Belge Géographique* **24**, 177–230.

Rae, B.B. (1960) Seals and Scottish Fisheries. Marine Research, 1960, No. 2.

—— (1972) A review of the codworm problem in the North Sea and in Western Scottish waters. Marine Research, 1972, No. 2.

Rae, B.B. and Shearer, W.M. (1965) Seal damage to salmon fisheries. Marine Research, 1965, No. 2.

Reidman, M. and Ortiz, C.L. (1979) 'Changes in milk composition during lactation in the northern elephant seal', *Physiological Zoology* **52**, 240–9.

Reijnders, P.J.H. (1980) 'Organochlorine and heavy-metal residues in harbour seals from the Wadden Sea and their possible effects on reproduction', *Netherlands Journal of Sea Research* **14**, 30–65.

—— (1986) 'Reproductive failure in common seals feeding on fish from polluted coastal waters', *Nature, London* **324**, 456–7.

—— (1988) 'Accumulation and body distribution of xenobiotics in marine mammals'. In: *Pollution of the North Sea: an assessment*, eds Salomons, W., Bayne, B.L., Duursma, E.K. and Förstner, U. Springer Verlag, Heidelberg.

Reijnders, P.J.H. and Wolff, W.J. (eds) *Marine Mammals of the Wadden Sea*. Stichting Veth tot Steun aan Waddenonderzoek, Leiden.

Reiter, J.R., Panken, K.J. and Le Boeuf, B.J. (1981) 'Female competition and reproductive success in northern elephant seals', *Animal Behaviour* **29**, 670–89.

Reiter, J.R., Stinson, N.L. and Le Boeuf, B.J. (1978) 'Northern elephant seal development: the transition from weaning to nutritional independence', *Behavioural Ecology and Sociobiology* **3**, 337–67.

Renouf, D. (1979) 'Preliminary measurements of the sensitivity of the vibrissae of harbour seals (*Phoca vitulina*) to low frequency vibrations', *Journal of Zoology, London* **188**, 443–50.

—— (1980) 'Fishing in captive harbour seals (*Phoca vitulina concolor*): a possible role for vibrissae', *Netherlands Journal of Zoology* **30**(3), 504–9.

—— (1984) 'Seal echolocation?', *Nature, London* **308**, 753.

Renouf, D. and Davis, M.B. (1982) 'Evidence that seals may use echolocation', *Nature, London* **300**, 635–7.

Repenning, C.A. (1972) 'Underwater hearing in seals: functional morphology'. In: *Functional Anatomy of Marine Mammals, Vol. 1*. ed. Harrison, R.J., 307–31. Academic Press, London.

—— (1980) 'Warm-blooded life in cold ocean currents', *Oceans* **13**(3), 18–24.

Roberts, T.M., Hepplestone, P.B. and Roberts, R.D. (1976) 'Distribution of heavy metals in tissues of the common seal', *Marine Pollution Bulletin* **7**, 194–6.

Ross, G.J.B., Ryan, F., Saaman, G.S. and Skinner, J. (1976) 'Observations on two captive crabeater seals at the Port Elizabeth Oceanarium', *International Zoo Yearbook* **16**, 160–4.

Scheffer, V.B. (1950) 'Growth layers on the teeth of Pinnipedia as an indication of age', *Science, New York* **112**, 309–11.

—— (1962) *Seals, Sea Lions and Walruses: A review of the Pinnipedia*. Stanford University Press and Oxford University Press, Stanford and Oxford.

—— (1978) 'Conservation of Marine Mammals'. In: *Marine Mammals of Eastern North Pacific and Arctic Waters*, ed. Delphine Haley, pp. 234–44. Pacific Search

Press, Washington.

Schusterman, R.J. (1981) 'Behavioural capabilities of seals and sea lions: a review of their hearing, visual, learning and diving skills', *The Psychological Record* **31**, 125–43.

Scott, D.M. and Fisher, H.D. (1958) 'Incidence of the ascarid *Porrocaecum decipiens* in the stomachs of three species of seals along the southern Canadian Atlantic seaboard', *Journal of the Fisheries Research Board of Canada* **15**, 495–561.

Sergeant, D.E. (1973) 'History and present status of populations of harp and hooded seals', *Biological Conservation* **10**, 95–117.

Sergeant, D.E. and Armstrong, F.A.J. (1973) 'Mercury in seals from eastern Canada', *Journal of the Fisheries Research Board of Canada* **30**, 843–6.

Sergeant, D.E., Ronald, K., Boulva, J. and Berkes, F. (1978) 'The recent status of *Monachus monachus*, the Mediterranean monk seal', *Biological Conservation* **14**, 259–87.

Siniff, D.B., Stirling, I., Bengtson, J.L. and Reichle, R.A. (1979) 'Social and reproductive behaviour of crabeater seals (*Lobodon carcinophagus*) during the austral spring', *Canadian Journal of Zoology* **57**, 2243–55.

Smith, E.A. (1968) 'Adoptive suckling in the grey seal', *Nature, London* **217**, 762–3.

Smith, T.G. and Geraci, J.R. (1975) The effect of contact and ingestion of crude oil on ringed seals in the Beaufort Sea. Beaufort Sea Technical Report No. 5. Beaufort Sea Project, Institute of Ocean Sciences, Patricia Bay, Sidney, B.C.

Söderberg, S. (1972) Gears and methods used for seal hunting in Sweden. International Council for the Exploration of the Sea, CM 1972/N:8.

—— (1975) 'Sealhunting in Sweden'. In: *Proceedings of the Symposium on the Seal in the Baltic*, pp 104–16. Swedish Environmental Protection Board SNV PM 591, Stockholm.

Spotte, S. (1982) 'The incidence of twins in pinnipeds', *Canadian Journal of Zoology* **60**, 2226–33.

Stewart, R.E.A. and Lavigne, D.M. (1980) 'Neonatal growth of northwest Atlantic harp seals, *Pagophilus groenlandicus*', *Journal of Mammalogy* **61**, 670–80.

Stirling, I. (1975) 'Factors affecting the evolution of social behaviour in the Pinnipedia', *Rapports et Procès-Verbaux des Réunions de Conseil International pour l'Exploration de la Mer* **169**, 205–12.

Stirling, I. and Calvert, W. (1979) 'Ringed seal'. In: *Mammals in the Seas, 2*, pp 83–5. FAO Fisheries Series, No. 5.

Summers, C.F. (1978a) 'Trends in the size of the British grey seal populations', *Journal of Applied Ecology* **15**, 395–400.

—— (1978b) 'Grey seals: the "Con" in conservation', *New Scientist*. 30 November 1978, 694–5.

Summers, C.F., Burton, R.W. and Anderson, S.S. (1975) 'Grey seal (*Halichoerus grypus*) pup production at North Rona: a study of birth and survival statistics collected in 1972', *Journal of Zoology, London* **175**, 439–51.

Tarasoff, F.O. (1972) 'Comparative aspects of the hind limbs of the river otter, sea otter and seals'. In: *Functional Anatomy of Marine Mammals, Vol. 2*, ed. Harrison, R.J., pp 333–59. Academic Press, London.

—— (1974) 'Anatomical adaptations in the river otter, sea otter and harp seal with reference to thermal regulation'. In: *Functional Anatomy of Marine Mammals, Vol. 2*, ed. Harrison, R.J. pp 111–41. Academic Press, London.

Tedford, R.H. (1976) 'Relationship of pinnipeds to other carnivores', *Systematic Zoology* **25**(4), 363–74.

Terhune, J.M. and Ronald, K. (1974) Underwater Hearing of Phocid Seals. International Council for the Exploration of the Sea. CM 1974/N:5.

Terhune, J.M., Stewart, R.E.A. and Ronald, K. (1978) 'Influence of vessel noises on underwater vocal activity of harp seals'. *Canadian Journal of Zoology* **57**(6), 1337–1338.

Thompson, P.M. (1987) The effects of seasonal changes in behaviour on the distribution and abundance of common seals, *Phoca vitulina*, in Orkney. PhD thesis, University of Aberdeen.

—— (1988) 'Timing of mating in the common seal (*Phoca vitulina*)', *Mammal Review* **18**, 105–12.

Tickell, W.L.N. (1970) 'The exploitation and status of the common seal (*Phoca vitulina*) in Shetland', *Biological Conservation* **2**, 179–84.

Tinney, R.T. (1984) Testimony before the Senate Commerce Committee, Marine Mammal Protection Act Reauthorisation, 26 April 1984. (Quoted in Wallace, 1984).

Van Weiren, S.E. (1981) *Broedbiologie van de gewone zeehond* Phoca vitulina *in het Nederlandse Wadden-gebied*. Rijksinstituut vor Natuurbeheer, Texel.

Vaughan, R.W. (1978) 'A study of common seals in the Wash', *Mammal Review* **8**, 25–34.

Venables, U.M. and Venables, L.S.V. (1955) 'Observation on a breeding colony of the seal *Phoca vitulina* in Shetland', *Proceedings of the Zoological Society of London* **125**, 521–32.

Wallace, N. (1984) Debris entanglement in the marine environment: a review. Proceedings of a Workshop on the Fate and Impact of Marine Debris, Honolulu, Hawaii, 26–29 November 1984.

Ward, A.J., Thompson, D. and Hiby, A.R. (1987) 'Census techniques for grey seal populations', *Symposia of the Zoological Society of London*, No. 58, 181–91.

Wartzok, D. and McCormick, M.G. (1978) 'Color discrimination by a Bering Sea spotted seal *Phoca largha*', *Vision Research* **18**(7), 781–4.

Watkins, W.A. and Schevill, W.E. (1968) 'Underwater playback of their own sounds to *Leptonychotes* (Weddell seals)', *Journal of Mammalogy* **49**, 287–96.

Williams, H.A. (1981) The grey seal and British fisheries. Background paper IUCN/CMM/WG3/10, pp 31–54. IUCN Committee on Marine Mammals, Working Group on Marine Mammals/Fishery Interactions. International Union for the Conservation of Nature and Natural Resources, Gland.

Williams, T.M. and Kooyman, G.L. (1985) 'Swimming performance and hydrodynamic characteristics of harbor seals *Phoca vitulina*', *Physiological Zoology* **58**(5), 576–89.

Wyss, A.R. (1988) 'Evidence from flipper structure for a single origin of pinnipeds'. *Nature, London* **334**, 427–9.

Young, P.C. (1972) 'The relationship between the presence of larval anisakine nematodes in cod and marine mammals in British home waters', *Journal of Applied Ecology* **9**, 459–85.

Zapol, W.M., Liggins, G.C., Schneider, R.C., Qvist, J., Snider, M.T., Creasy, R.K. and Hochachka, P.W. (1979) 'Regional blood flow during diving in the conscious Weddell seal', *Journal of Applied Physiology* **47**, 968–73.

Index

Acrophoca 103
adaptation to aquatic
    environment 2–5, 10,
    15–18, 42
Addison, R F 151
adoptive feeding 64
age determination 49, 123
Alderdice, D F 128
Allen, S G 63
Amoroso, E C 45
Anderson, S S 47, 64, 65,
    136, 140, 153, 154, 160
Anholt 107, 113, 137, 155
Año Nuevo Island 71
Árnason U 97, 99
arteriovenous anastomoses,
    AVA 14

Baikal seal 80:
    classification 97–8;
    evolution 103;
    longevity 51
Bartholomew's model 72–6
bearded seal 86–7:
    classification 97, 98;
    evolution 103;
    flipper 7;
    longevity 51;
    mammary gland 42;
    teeth 26, 27
Beck, B 128, 129, 134, 136
Beddington, J R 147
Bengtson, J 58
Benjaminsen, T 51
Berland, B 57
Beverton 129, model
    130–133
Bigg, M A 50
birth 43–4, 57,
—— dates 77–92 *passim*

—— weights 48, 49–50, 54,
    57, 58, 59, 61, 64–5, 69
Bjorge, A J 135
Blix, A S 14, 40, 165
blood 33–4:
    oxygen carrying capacity
    36;
    volume 34
blubber 12–4, 28, 30, 75,
    112, 119–20, 122 (*see
    also* oil)
Boas, F 109
Boness, D J 64, 65
Bonner, W N 10, 45, 62, 63,
    104, 120, 121, 125, 143,
    148, 158, 159, 168, 169,
    170, 172, 177
bounties 136–7
Bowen, W D 48
Boyd, I L 44, 45
breathing hole 59, 61, 110
breeding: on ice 53–61, 62,
    63; on land 61–72; *see
    also* reproduction
Brodie, P 151
brown fat 14, 54
Bryden, M M 12, 14, 50
Burns, F 9, 92
Burton, R W 19, 64
Busch, B C 115, 120
Bynch, A 113

Calvert, W 59
capelin 31, 32
Capitan, L 106
Capstick, C K 116
Carson, Rachel 163
Caspian seal 80:
    classification 97–8;
    evolution 103

cephalopods 23–4, 27
chlordane 151
chlorophenyl 151
ciguatera 161
Clark, A H 119
Clark, J G D 105, 108, 112
Clarke, M R 21
classification 96–103
claws 7, 25, 59, 97
Cline, D R 61
codworm 134–5
Coman J S 116
Committee on Seals and
    Sealing (COSS) 117,
    166
common seal *see* harbour
    seal
conservation 118, 163–80
    (*see also* protection)
Conservation of Seals Act
    169
Convention for the
    Conservation of
    Antarctic Seals 177–8
copulation *see* mating
corpus albicans 44, 46
corpus luteum 44, 46
crabeater seal 89–90:
    birth weight 58;
    breeding 58;
    classification 98;
    disease 158;
    feeding 25–6;
    fighting 58;
    food 23, 89;
    locomotion 10;
    as prey 23;
    teeth 25, 26
Cranbrook, Earl of, 169–70
Curry, M 140

Cystophora cristata
   see hooded seal

Dartnall, H J A 16
Davies, Brian 164
Davis, John 153–4
Davis, M B 18
DDE 149, 150–1
DDT 149–50
debris, marine 145–7
delayed implantation 45, 75
DeLong R L 35, 150
depth histogram recorder
   (DHR) 35
development:
   embryonic 44–5
   foetal 44, 49, 50
digestive system 27–8
disease 155–59
distribution 77–96
disturbance, effect of 160–1,
   170
diving 32–9
   dive duration 34; dive,
      exploratory 35; dive,
      hunting 35;
   physiology 36–7
Drescher, E 160

ear 3, 18:
   in diving 38
elephant seal:
   birth weight 49;
   breeding 67–76;
   blubber 12;
   classification 98, 99;
   diving 34, 35–6;
   eye 15, 16;
   fasting 28–9, 50;
   fighting 69–70;
   intestine 28;
   longevity 51;
   maturity, sexual 50;
   teeth 26, 27;
   vocalisation 18
elephant seal, northern
   95–6:
   breeding 68, 71–2
   diving 34, 35–6
   fasting 28
   fighting 70
   oil pollution and 153
   water balance in 28
elephant seal, southern
   94–5:
   birth weight and growth
     48;
   breeding 50, 67, 68–71;
   fighting 69–70;
   food 24, 95

protection 177;
   sealing 119–25
Enaliarctos mealsi 101
energetics 29–32, 47–8
entanglement 145–7
Erignathus barbatus see
   bearded seal
Essapian, F S 12
European Commission 166
evolution 99–103
eye 15–7

Fanning, E 119
Farne Islands 170–73
fasting 28–9, 47, 50, 65,
   74–5
Fay, F H 97
Fedak, M 47
feeding 24–7, 32
fighting 58, 59, 61, 64
Fisher, H D 16, 117, 134
fisheries:
   interactions with 126–44;
   control of seals 135–44,
     169;
   damaged nets 127–9;
   depletion of stocks
     129–33;
   effect on food of seals
     147–8;
   grey seals and 137–44;
   parasites and 133–5
flippers 5–10, 13, 101
Fogden, S C R 19, 64
food 21–4, 26–7, 77–96
   passim
Frank, R 149
fur *see* hair, lanugo, pelage,
   skins

Geraci, J R 154
Gill, T 153
Gjessing, G 108
Greenpeace 118, 142, 166
Greenwood, J R 22, 141, 143
grey seal 84–5:
   adoptive feeding in 64
   birth weight and growth
     48;
   bounties 136–7;
   breeding 63–5, 66;
   classification 97, 98, 99;
   damage to fish 129;
   evolution 103;
   fasting 74–5;
   feeding 25;
   fighting 64;
   food 22, 85;
   gestation 45;
   host to codworm 134–5;

hunting 113;
   Stone Age 106–8;
   lactation 47;
   longevity 51;
   mother/young bond 19;
   multiple births 46–47;
   reproduction 44
Griffiths, D J 154
growth 48–51 *see also*
   development
Gulland, J A 135, 137

haemoglobin 34
hair 11–12, 14 *see also*
   whiskers
Halichoerus grypus
   see grey seal
harbour seal 83–84:
   birth weight and growth
     48, 49;
   bounties 136, 137;
   breeding 62–3;
   classification 97, 98, 99
   damage to fish 129;
   disease 155–9, 160;
   diving 34;
   entanglement 145;
   evolution 103;
   feeding 25;
   fighting 63;
   habitat destruction of
     160;
   hunting 114;
   maturity, sexual 50;
   pollution, effects of
     150–1;
     mercury poisoning 152;
     oil 152;
   reproduction 44;
   sealing 140;
   swimming 9;
   teeth 26
harp seal 80–1:
   birth weight and growth
     48, 50;
   breeding 53–6;
   classification 97, 98, 99
   conservation 164–7;
   disease 158;
   diving 34;
   energetics 31–2;
   entanglement 158
   hair 11;
   hunting, Stone Age
     105–6;
   lactation 48, 81;
   mercury accumulation
     152;
   oil pollution 154;
   reproduction 44;

sealing 115–8;
control 164
harpoons: Stone Age 108;
Eskimo 109–112
Harrison, R J 45
Harwood, J 22, 64, 140, 141,
143, 156, 158, 159
Hawkey, P 173
Hawkins, A D 136
heat *see* oestrus
heat balance *see*
thermoregulation
heat exchanger 13, 40
heavy metals 151–2
Helle, O 150, 151
Hendey, Q 99, 103
Henry, M E 145
Hesselø 107, 108, 113
Hewer, H R 64, 138
Hickling, G 114, 170, 172,
173
Histriphoca 97, 98 *see also*
ribbon seal
Hobson, E S 45
Holden, A V 150
Homiphoca 103
hooded seal 85–6:
birth weight and growth
48;
breeding 56–8, 61;
classification 98, 99;
evolution 103;
fighting 58;
hood 57–8;
lactation 48;
sealing 117, 118
Howell, A B 6
Hughes, T I 165
hunting: *see also* sealing
early European 113–4;
Eskimo 109–112
Stone Age 104–9
Hydrurga leptonyx
see leopard seal

International Commission
on North-west Atlantic
Fisheries (ICNAF)
117–8
International Fund for
Animal Welfare
(IFAW) 164, 166
International Union for the
Conservation of Nature
and Natural Resources
(IUCN) 142, 167, 174
Irving, L 28

James, H 64
Jamieson, G S 17

Johnson, Stanley 166

Kennedy, S 158
Kenyon, K W 66, 146, 160,
161
King, Judith E 6, 15, 18, 25,
28, 36, 45, 103
Koeman, J H 149, 152
Kooyman, G L 9, 14, 22,
34–9
Kovacs, K 34, 54, 57, 115,
116, 118, 164, 166, 180
krill 22, 23, 26
Kuril seal 84

lactation 42, 47–8, 54, 63,
64, 77–96 *passim*
lairs 59, 60, 78
Laist, D W 146
landsmen 115, 117
lanugo 14, 54, 59, 62, 64,
77–96 *passim*, 97, 99
largha seal *see* spotted seal
Larsen, C A 176
Lavigne, D M 15, 29–32, 34,
48, 50, 54, 57, 115–8,
164,
166, 180
Laws, R M 23, 28, 49, 50, 70,
123–4
Le Boeuf, Burney J 35, 36,
70–1, 153–4
leopard seal 90–1:
classification 98;
flipper 7;
food 23, 91;
swimming 9;
teeth 26
Leptophoca 102
Leptonychotes weddellii
see Weddell seal
limbs 4–10
Linnaeus, C 97, 114
Lister-Kays, J 141–2
Lockley, R M 136
Lobodon carcinophagus
see crabeater seal
locomotion 4–10
Lythgoe, J N 16
longevity 51

McCann, T S 69, 70, 125
McClelland, G 135
McCormick, M G 15
McLaren I A 51, 59, 75, 101,
136
McLeod, N 21
Mahy, B W J 156
Mansfield A W 128, 129,
134, 136

marginal haematoma 45
Marchessaux, D 174
Margolis, L 135
Martin, Martin 112–4, 167
maternal care 62–3
mating 44, 55, 59, 61, 65, 70,
71–2, 75
Matthews, L H 121, 122
meat, seal 104, 114
metabolic rate 30, 31
migration 55–6
milk 42, 47–8, 54
Mirounga angustirostris
see elephant seal,
northern
—— *leonina see* elephant
seal, southern
Møhl, B 18
Møhl, U 108, 113
Molyneux, 14
Monachus monachus
see monk seal,
Mediterranean
—— *schauinslandi see*
monk seal, Hawaiian
—— *tropicalis see* monk
seal, Caribbean
Monk seals 173–5
classification 98, 99
mammary gland 42
—— Caribbean 88;
—— Hawaiian 89, 173;
birth weight 65;
breeding 65;
disease 161;
disturbance 160;
diving 35;
lactation 47, 90;
skeleton 7;
—— Mediterranean 88,
174–5;
breeding 65;
caught in nets 127;
disease 159;
lactation 47, 88;
Monotherium 102
Montgaudier baton 106
mother/pup bond 19, 53–4,
64
moulting 70–1
Muizon, C 103
multiple births *see* twins
muscles 7–9, 32
myoglobin 34, 36

Nelson, R K 112
nets:
for catching seals 108,
114, 115;
damaged by seals 127–29;

salmon 127–8;
  entanglements in 145–6
North-west Atlantic
  Fisheries Organization
  (NAFO) 118
nose 19, 57, 69
nostrils 32

oestrus 45, 64
Oftedal, O 48
O'Gorman, F 9
oil (petroleum) 152–5
oil (seal) 114, 115, 116, 117,
  119–20, 123 see also
  blubber
olfactory epithelium 19
Ommatophoca rossii
  see Ross seal
Øritsland, T 26
Øritsland, N 165
Ortiz, C L 28, 48
Osterhaus, A D M E 156
oxygen 33–4, 3637

Pagophilus 97, 98 see also
  harp seal
parasites 133–5
Parrish, B B 135, 141
Pascal, M 148
pelage 57, 77–96 passim
Phoca caspica
  see Caspian seal
—— fasciata see ribbon seal
—— groenlandica see harp
  seal
—— hispida see ringed seal
—— largha see spotted seal
—— sibirica see Baikal seal
—— vitulina see harbour
  seal
phocine distemper virus
  (PDV) 155–59
Piscophoca 103
plankton 21, 22, 27
Platt, N E 51
Potter, E C E 129
pollution 148–55, 156–8
polychlorinated biphenyls
  (PCBs) 149–51
polygamy, serial 58, 63
polygyny 65, 66, 70, 72–6,
  125
population 77–96 passim
Potamotherium 101
predators 23, 52–3, 59, 63
Prichard, Hesketh 167
Prime, J H 140–1, 172
proboscis 69
properties of air and water
  3, 10, 15, 17

proprioceptive sense 20
protection 113, 120–1,
  175–79 see also
  conservation
Pusa 97, 98, 103 see also
  ringed seal

Racovitza, E G 25
Rae, B B 127, 129, 135, 136,
  167
Reidmann, C 48
Reijnders, P R 150–2, 156
Reiter, J 72, 76
Renouf, D 18–9
Repenning, C A 18, 99, 102,
  173, 175
reproduction 40–8, 49–50
  see also breeding
respiratory system 33,
  37–8, 39
ribbon seal 77
  classification 97, 98
  evolution 104
  locomotion 9
ringed seal 8
  birth weight 59
  breeding 59–60
  classification 97, 98
  evolution 103
  fighting 59
  hunting
    Eskimo 109–12
    Stone Age 108
  lanugo 59, 78
  maturity, sexual 50
  pollution, effects 150
    oil 154
  teeth 26
Ronald, K 18
Ross, G J B 25
Ross seal 93
  classification 98
  eye 15
  flipper 7
  food 24, 93
  intestine 28
  protection 177
  teeth 26, 27
  vocalisation 18

salmon 127–29
Scheffer, Victor 11, 49, 158,
  167
Schevill, W E 18
Schusterman, R J 15, 18
Scott, D M 134
Sea Mammal Research Unit
  (SMRU) 140
sealing see also hunting
  crabeater seal 176

control 177
elephant seal
  nineteenth century
  119–20
  twentieth century
  120–5
    control 120–1, 123–5,
    177
  Eskimo 112, 167
  grey seal 140, 169
    control 168–9
  harp seal 115–8
    control 117–8, 164–5
  for scientific specimens
    178–9
senses
  hearing 17–8
  proprioceptive 20
  sight 15–7
  smell 19
  touch 19
Sergeant, D E 117, 152, 174
sex organs
  female 41–2
  male 40–1, 42
sexual dimorphism 75, 84
sexual cycle 43–6
  maturity 50–1
Shearer, W M 129, 135, 141
Siniff, D B 58
size 77–96 passim
skins 114, 117, 140 see also
  pelage and hair
skeleton 5–7
sleep 36
Smith, E A 64
Smith, T G 151, 154
Söderberg, S 114, 137
South Georgia 67, 69, 120–5
Soviet sealing in 1987 178
Spotte, S 46–7
spotted seal 82
  breeding 62
  classification 97, 98
  evolution 103
squid see cephalopods
streamlining 3–4
Stewart, R E A 48, 50
Stirling, I 53, 59
Summers, C F 140–1,
  143–4
surface/volume
  relationship 10–1, 25
Swain, A 129
swimming 7–9, 25
  speed 9

Tarasoff, F J 11
Taylor, R J F 158
Tedford, R H 101

teeth 25–7
  use of in age
    determination 49, 123
Temple, John 169
Terhune, J 18, 161
thermoregulation 10–4
Thompson, P M 63
Tickell, W L N 168
time-depth recorders
    (TDRs) 34–5
Tinney, R T 146
tourism 160
traps for seals 108, 114
twins 46–7

United Nations
  Environment
  Programme (UNEP)
  174

Van Genderen, H 149

Van Weiren, S E 63
vascular system 14, 36–7,
    40
Vaughan, R W 170
Vedder, E J 156
Venables, L S V and U M 62
vibrissae see whiskers
vocalisation 18–9, 54, 55, 69

Wadden Sea 150–1, 156,
    159
Wallace, N 147
water balance 28, 48
Watkins, W A 18
Wartzok, D 15
Weddell seal 91–2
  birth weight and growth
    48
  breeding 60–1
  classification 98
  diving 34–5, 36–7

fighting 61
food 21–2, 92
mammary gland 42
protection 177
teeth 61
vocalisation 18–19
weights 77–96 passim
whelping patches 53
whiskers 19–20, 87
Williams, H A 133, 147
Williams, Terrie M 9
Witthames, S R 159
Wolff, W J 150, 151
World Society for the
    Protection of Animals
    (WSPA) 166
Wyss, A R 101

Young, P C 134

Zapol, W M 37